GAME OF EDGES

Also by Bruce Schoenfeld

The Match: Althea Gibson & Angela Buxton

The Last Serious Thing: A Season at the Bullfights

GAME
OF
EDGES

The Analytics Revolution and
the Future of Professional Sports

BRUCE SCHOENFELD

W. W. NORTON & COMPANY
Celebrating a Century of Independent Publishing

For information about permission to reproduce selections from this book, write to
Permissions, W. W. Norton & Company, Inc., 500 Fifth Avenue, New York, NY 10110

For information about special discounts for bulk purchases, please contact
W. W. Norton Special Sales at specialsales@wwnorton.com or 800-233-4830

Manufacturing by LSC Harrisonburg
Book design by Patrice Sheridan
Production manager: Louise Mattarelliano

Library of Congress Cataloging-in-Publication Data

Names: Schoenfeld, Bruce, author.
Title: Game of edges : the analytics revolution and the future of
professional sports / Bruce Schoenfeld.
Description: First edition. | New York, NY : W. W. Norton & Company, Inc.,
[2023] | Includes index.
Identifiers: LCCN 2023009924 | ISBN 9780393531688 (cloth) |
ISBN 9780393531695 (epub)
Subjects: LCSH: Professional sports—Statistical methods. | Professional sports—Data process-
ing. | Professional sports—Technological innovations. | Sports franchises—History.
Classification: LCC GV734 .S36 2023 | DDC 796.04/4—dc23/eng/20230306
LC record available at https://lccn.loc.gov/2023009924

W. W. Norton & Company, Inc., 500 Fifth Avenue, New York, N.Y. 10110
www.wwnorton.com

W. W. Norton & Company Ltd., 15 Carlisle Street, London W1D 3BS

1 2 3 4 5 6 7 8 9 0

People are both emotional and rational. They have passions and they have interests . . . . Although the rationality principle provides excellent guidance to understand human acts, it is sometimes difficult to know when we can expect one type of behavior or the other.

—IGNACIO PALACIOS-HUERTA, BEAUTIFUL GAME THEORY

A third factor . . . was the steady conversion of all norms and values from "qualitative" to "quantitative." It was not the nature of an object but its price that became more and more important. It was not the value of a specific action that counted, not the joy in the activity itself, but how useful it was and what it would yield.

—GEERT MAK, AN ISLAND IN TIME

CONTENTS

INTRODUCTION

THE SPORTS DEPARTMENT at the newspaper in Memphis where I worked in the early 1980s consisted of eight or nine desks tucked into the corner of the newsroom. It didn't get much respect from the other journalists. "How are things going in the toy department?" the business writer liked to say when he wandered past. He was involved in Big Things: special reports on the city's economic prospects, profiles of corporate leaders, exclusives about national companies that might conceivably relocate to Memphis. My colleagues and I were focused on the quarterback controversy at Ole Miss and the vicissitudes of our minor-league baseball team. "Must be nice," he'd chuckle.

But if the stories that ran in our sports section day after day were ephemeral, their reach was wide. When I'd run into one of those business leaders at a party or on an airplane, all they wanted to talk about was sports. What did I hear about the team in the new football league that was coming to Memphis? Who would be the next basketball coach at Memphis State? And how about that quarterback controversy at Ole Miss?

By the start of the 1990s, I'd left daily journalism for magazines.

About that time, it occurred to me that the men—and, infrequently, the women—who owned and ran the clubs I wrote about often had more interesting stories than the athletes who played for them. In part, that was because the profile of the owners that sports leagues were attracting had started to change. When I was growing up, and for the decade or two after that, teams remained cheap enough that successful car dealers and local attorneys could afford them. Ownership was often a risky proposition. Many teams played before half-empty arenas and stadiums. Revenue from television and radio was insubstantial. Franchises relocated, and even folded, with regularity. It's not surprising that sports wasn't perceived as serious commerce.

When a corporate magnate would buy a team, which would happen occasionally, he nearly always ran it as a hobby. I remember watching a New York Giants practice beside Preston Robert Tisch, who told me to call him "Bob." The chief executive of Loews Hotels and Lorillard Tobacco and a member of the Reagan administration, Tisch had bought half of the Giants from Tim Mara, the grandson of their founding owner, for $75 million. That seemed like a lot of money to me, but not to Bob Tisch. "I don't care if I never make a cent on the investment," he said as we stood on the sidelines on a Tuesday afternoon. "I'm just going to pretend I never had that $75 million."

A few years ago, I wrote a story about the investors who own small percentages of sports franchises but have little say in how they're operated. I called Randy Vataha, a former New England Patriots wide receiver. Vataha made his living matching wealthy individuals who wanted to buy franchises with the wealthy individuals who owned them and might be convinced to sell. I was curious to know why anyone would tie up $50 million or $60 million to own a tenth or even a twentieth of a team as a silent partner. He reminded me of all the companies in the Boston area that were perceived as blue-chip at the start of the 1990s, when he started in the business, but had since disappeared. "Wang Laboratories, remember that?" he said. "Gone. They're pretty much all gone."

With hindsight, a wealthy investor in Boston who wanted his capital to appreciate should have figured out a way to put his money into one of four businesses. "You know which four equities turned out to be a sure thing?" he asked. "The Red Sox, the Patriots, the Celtics, and the Bruins." No other companies in the city, he said, had gained nearly as much value over the preceding quarter century.

How did that happen? Slowly, as cable television started to change the entertainment landscape with a few hundred channels— and then very quickly, as more and more Americans gained access to the infinite possibilities of the internet, and consumers were presented with more entertainment than anyone could consume in a lifetime. With every television program floating in the ether, detached from space and time, it's hardly surprising that ratings for even the most popular first-run shows fragmented, then fragmented more. The exception? Live sports events. Because games weren't scripted, nobody knew their outcomes. Ratings stayed strong, which drove rights fees skyward. In 1990, the five networks that broadcast National Football League games paid a combined $900 million a year, which would be about $2 billion in 2022. By 2002, Fox, ABC, and ESPN each had signed long-term deals that paid out a total of $14 billion, or $23 billion in 2022 dollars.

That grew franchise values exponentially. The Simon brothers, who developed shopping malls, bought the National Basketball Association's Indiana Pacers for $4.5 million in 1983. By 1993, it would cost a Caterpillar dealer named Peter Holt $75 million to buy

the San Antonio Spurs. A decade later, the Phoenix Suns sold for
$401 million to real estate developer Robert Sarver. A decade after
that, in 2014, the former Microsoft chief executive Steve Ballmer
paid $2 billion for the Los Angeles Clippers. It should be noted
that the Clippers aren't even the most prestigious basketball team
in their own city.

Ballmer didn't care. Even a second-rate team meant an entrée
to an extremely closed club. There were about 500 billionaires
in America at the time, but fewer than a hundred people owned
majority shares of franchises in one of the four major US leagues.
The expansion boom that had nearly tripled the number of teams
from 43 in 1960 to 120 in 2001 had screeched to a halt. That made
sports franchises the equivalent of oceanfront real estate—there
were only so many of them, and nobody was making more. And
unlike a mutual fund or even a hotel chain, these teams weren't
merely an investment vehicle. You'd get to watch practice on a Tuesday afternoon.

———

THIS BOOK IS the story of how sports teams grew from regional
businesses that sold tickets, hot dogs, and souvenirs into some of
the most important and innovative companies in their markets, and
in some cases around the world. It's also the story of how an information revolution built on data accumulation and analysis, which
started inside hedge funds and Silicon Valley tech companies,
upended the business of sports, and how a new generation of owners and front-office experts applied this new way of thinking to every
aspect of their operations. Driven by data, these franchises grew into
huge businesses, doing everything better on and off the playing field

than they used to do—even as this optimization threatened many of the attributes that made sports so appealing in the first place.

In 2003, a former Salomon Brothers trader named Michael Lewis published a book that demonstrated how one sports franchise was utilizing the investment strategy of arbitrage, finding an imbalance between the perceived and actual value of an asset, to succeed on the field. Before that book, Lewis had been a business writer. In Moneyball, he turned his attention to the business of baseball, in which the financial inequities between the rich clubs and the poor clubs were starker than in any other sport. As chronicled in the book (and the movie that followed), Billy Beane, the general manager of baseball's underfunded Oakland A's, identified major leaguers who weren't valued as highly as they should have been and filled his roster with them. He hired mathematically minded analysts who mined baseball's almost endless storehouse of statistics, seeking inefficiencies in the system. These ranged from what should be considered a successful plate appearance to where infielders positioned themselves on the diamond. Until other teams copied their strategy, Beane's A's finished first or second in their division for eight straight seasons.

Propelled by the success of both the team and the book, data analysis swept through the sport. It spread to basketball, and then to hockey, football, and soccer. It gave teams that were willing to identify and exploit those inherent inefficiencies a competitive edge. It also tweaked the way the games themselves were played—stifling the art of sacrifice bunting in baseball, for example, and doubling the number of three-point shots attempted in the NBA.

All of that was easy enough to see because it was playing out in the public space, on the fields and courts and rinks where the games were unfolding season after season. But the Moneyball revolution was part of a larger shift. As the scale of the franchises grew, the businesses themselves increasingly came to resemble those in which the owners originally made their fortunes. The concept of best practices, as promulgated by management consultants, venture capital firms and investors in public companies, seemed irrelevant when sports teams were glorified hobbies. But when they grew to have values that were significant even in the largest of portfolios, it made sense that they should be run like the other equities in those portfolios. Just as teams were looking for competitive edges on the field, the executives who ran those teams started looking for the same thing off of it.

With the competition for the disposable income of even the most loyal supporters growing increasingly intense, it was no longer enough to market a team by, as someone once said of the Boston Red Sox, unlocking the doors of Fenway Park on Opening Day and announcing to the waiting crowd, "We're ready." In 2003, commodities trader John Henry and his partners paid $700 million for that team and some real estate. That was more than double the price ever paid for a Major League Baseball franchise. At the time, the Red Sox hadn't won a championship since 1918. The new owners set out to build both a World Series winner and a business that would validate their huge investment. Between 2004 and 2017, the Red Sox won the World Series four times. Along the way, the club developed a data-driven methodology that would lead to the construction of a sports empire.

Henry's group, which included television producer Tom Werner, former Fidelity Investments fund managers Jeff Vinik and Mike Gordon, and others, was representative of the new kind of sports owner. Rather than industrialists, the new generation featured internet entrepreneurs such as Mark Cuban, AOL's Ted Leonsis, and Microsoft's Paul Allen; investment bankers and venture capitalists like Wes Edens of the Milwaukee Bucks and David Blitzer of the Philadelphia 76ers; entertainers-turned-moguls and retired superstar athletes such as Jay-Z and David Beckham. To buy their teams, they combined in groups of threes and fours and fives. Franchise prices had grown so high that fewer and fewer individuals could afford to buy one.

One of those who *could* afford to buy a team on his own, a Silicon Valley venture capitalist named Joe Lacob, chose not to. When he acquired the Golden State Warriors from Chris Cohan in 2010, he partnered with several other investors, each of whom had expertise in a particular field. Peter Guber, a movie producer and former owner of minor-league baseball teams, understood video, content, and live entertainment. Chad Hurley had co-founded YouTube. Nick Swinmurn, who had founded Zappos, specialized in fashion and retail marketing. Venture capitalist John Scully had connections that would be invaluable when the time came to finance and build a new arena, which the team did a few years later.

None of them were in for any significant sum in terms of their own holdings—$30 million here and $50 million there. But it was enough to warrant their time and attention. "There's a lot of smart people in the world, you know," Lacob insisted. "I'm not the smartest. I'm just an integrator." The result of that integration, Lacob said, made the Warriors significantly better than any other NBA franchise. And then they started winning championships.

————

SPORTS TEAMS ARE fundamentally different than almost every other kind of business, which are judged principally on their ability to make money. Sports teams are also expected to win games and, occasionally, titles. The two metrics for success are not unrelated, but they aren't completely aligned, either. You can own a losing team for years and still turn a profit, thanks to the institutional socialism of most of the pro leagues. You can also win a title and lose money, as baseball's Florida Marlins managed to do—to the chagrin of the owner at the time, H. Wayne Huizenga, who promptly sold off his most valuable players and, soon enough, the team itself. But in most markets, the surest way to gin up fan enthusiasm, and the lucrative sponsorship and media rights that come with it, is with competitive success.

In most businesses, your success is largely unrelated to anyone else's. Daniel Snyder, who in early 1999 bought the Washington NFL franchise, made his fortune in direct mail, a business in which the growth of his company didn't necessarily erode that of his competitors. Having succeeded in that industry, it was tempting for him to think that he would also succeed in the NFL, especially since he had bought a team he'd enthusiastically followed since childhood. (While other kids were pretending to be ballplayers, he would pretend to be the owner.) Over a dinner with me that summer, Snyder was sanguine about their prospects. Washington had been mismanaged for years, he said. He understood how to make it competitive. When I told him that I hoped my own favorite team, the woebegone Miami Dolphins, would be able to eke out a .500 record, 8–8, Snyder's eyebrows jumped. "If my team ever went 8–8," he said, "I'd kill myself."

But unlike direct mail, the competitive success of football teams is a zero-sum equation. Every time a team wins a game, its opponent loses one. Neophyte owners such as Snyder often found that winning wasn't nearly as easy as they thought it would be. Snyder's 1999 team didn't finish 8–8. It finished 7–9. In 2022, faced with sexual harassment claims against team employees by more than a dozen women, Snyder announced that he was ready to sell the team. In 21 seasons, it had appeared in just five playoff games.

It also turned out that Snyder's previous business experience may not have properly prepared him to optimize the economic potential of an NFL team. As of 2000, Washington, which was then known as the Redskins, was valued by *Forbes* magazine at $741 million. That exceeded *by more than $100 million* the value of every other franchise across all sports, in North America and beyond. (Baseball's New York Yankees were second, at $635 million.) By 2020, Washington's valuation had grown to $3.5 billion, but that hadn't even kept pace with the NFL average. As of that year, the team ranked behind seven others among football teams alone. Worldwide, it no longer made the top 10.

In 1999, Beane's A's also finally managed a winning record after six losing seasons. Nobody realized it at the time, but the *Moneyball* era had dawned. The following year, the A's won their division. The data that Beane's analysts crunched existed in the public domain, right there in the box scores. Anyone could have explored the relationship between a team's on-base percentage and how many runs it scored, or figured out when a sacrifice bunt increases the chances of winning a game and when it doesn't. After the A's regularly started showing up in October, nearly every team began doing exactly that.

Unlike on-base percentage and walks, however, the data fueling the latest revolution in baseball tactics isn't hidden in plain sight. Every major-league ballpark now deploys a network of cameras that can track the movement of the ball and every player on the field during every play. This technology, called Statcast, enables broadcasters to share entertaining detail, such as the distance and trajectory of home runs. It also allows defensive skill and efficiency to be meaningfully assessed for the first time. How many balls does your shortstop reach in a week or a month, compared with the average shortstop, or a shortstop on another team? Which outfielders get to balls because they run fast, which because they get good jumps on the ball—and which merely because they've been positioned in the perfect place by the number crunchers in the bowels of the stadium? Statcast made it possible to know.

The Statcast data is owned by Major League Baseball. It remains unavailable for public consumption, except as doled out in snippets on Twitter feeds and during broadcasts, but each night it gets transmitted in raw form to every team. What the teams choose to do with it after that is their business. A few ignore it. Others have devised mechanisms to download it from the server each night and convert it into what they hope are relevant insights. As a result, a player who is an average hitter but a terrific fielder may be valued more highly by a team that is using the data to measure defensive contribution than one that isn't.

Over the past few years, the same innovation has come to world soccer, though for now the necessary camera systems have only been installed in the biggest leagues. John Henry and his Fenway Sports Group own Liverpool FC, and they have been aggressive in trying to find data-driven arbitrage opportunities in that sport, which traditionally has resisted quantification. They hired Ian Graham, soccer's foremost analyst, and have added a staff that includes a particle physicist to support him. Their tactical insights and advice about which players to pursue helped the club to a Champions League title in 2019. The following season, Liverpool won its first Premier League title.

And the next generation of proprietary data is on the way. The National Hockey League has embedded a transmitter chip in each of its pucks, which will help chart movement patterns. Other leagues, notably the NFL, are experimenting with sensors woven into uniforms that will transmit a steady stream of information about the player who is wearing them. That information can be used to optimize performance. Eventually, it also may be used to give sports gamblers the opportunity to place bets on which player will skate the fastest, run the farthest, or even get his oxygen intake up the highest.

It's no surprise that the owners who are most comfortable with technology are the ones who are best positioned to take advantage of it, both in terms of competitive success and entrepreneurial opportunities. Ted Leonsis, one of AOL's first executives, was among the early advocates of legal sports gambling. The owner of the NHL's Washington Capitals and the NBA's Washington Wizards, he bet on gambling's success with nearly a dozen different investment plays, including a bookmaking website, a company that logs and transmits data about games taking place around the world, a gambling-ready sports bar he put into the arena he owns, and an interactive gambling channel he has proposed for his regional sports network.

The reimagination of sports from a glorified toy department to an engine for creative and economic growth and innovation didn't happen in a straight line, but simultaneously on various fronts. Yet when sports franchises are run with the diligence they have come to deserve, there are often unintended consequences. Today's analytically optimized baseball may follow the same contours as the games that were played throughout our parents' lifetime. Spend even a little time watching, though, and you can't help noticing how infrequently the ball is actually in play. There are more strikeouts and home runs than ever, and fewer extra-base hits and acrobatic fielding plays, though research indicates those are exactly the plays that fans most want to see. As it turns out, the most efficient and productive way to play baseball isn't the most exciting or aesthetically pleasing. Fans have noticed. Television ratings have plummeted.

The problem isn't limited to baseball. Basketball, too, has used analytics to evolve in ways that don't always lead to interesting or enjoyable competition. Like the home run, the three-point shot is valued so highly that it made sense to try to turn the game inside out and feed the ball to a shooter on the perimeter. But while sweeping hook shots and double-pump lay-ups and slam dunks are singular and even occasionally acrobatic, jump shots from the perimeter tend to look indistinguishable. It may be no accident that the NBA's ratings are also down.

Off the field, too, the optimization of franchises as businesses runs the risk of undermining the special relationship between a team and its fans. There's no question that today's stadiums and arenas are more comfortable and cleaner than ever before; the food is better, the replays sharper, the corridors less crowded. Yet many fans complain that they miss the intimacy and informality they experienced when sports teams were run more like corner groceries than multinational corporations.

———————

THE STORIES THAT follow, about owners and players and managers and general managers and analysts, are informed by a series of relationships: between spending money and competitive success, between the use of analytics and that success, and between optimizing the way the sports are played and their aesthetic appeal. None of these relationships are entirely predictive, and all of them continue to evolve. There is clearly a better way to run teams, on and off the field, than the way they were run when I started out in sports journalism. But the ramifications of accumulating all those tiny advantages, those "edges," as analysts like to call them, have led sports to a different place. And what happens from here remains uncertain.

As we enter the next decade, not only do sports teams and leagues constitute big businesses, but they also provide a pathway to the integration of an almost limitless number of other businesses. Considered from a distance, a sports team resembles a mutual fund that includes television and digital content, real estate, retail clothing, hospitality, catering and concessions, and much more. Yet unlike every other consumer category, sports bundles its varied components into a product that generates a fierce passion in those who pay to consume it. It is difficult to imagine someone voluntarily paying $75 to own and wear a Microsoft or Google T-shirt, for example, because they happen to like the company.

That's why those Memphis businessmen wanted to talk about their favorite teams, and why the average pro franchise has quintupled in value over the last two decades. It's why MIT graduates are passing up lucrative offers from corporate America to work in sports, and why many of the smartest and most successful businessmen are buying into the industry, and then using it to generate new revenue streams. It's not just about watching their teams practice—though there's still that, too. Sports, it has become abundantly clear, no longer sits on the margins of the consumer economy, but at the intersection of technology and entertainment, which may well be the best possible position for growth in the coming decades. How that growth will occur, and how it will affect the way we traditionally engage with the sports we follow, is a story unfolding before our eyes.

GAME OF EDGES

1

I DON'T WANT TO OWN
A SOCCER TEAM

JOE JANUSZEWSKI COULDN'T believe the turnstile. This was Anfield? He had been fantasizing about seeing a game at the fabled soccer venue for almost 15 years, ever since he had started following the Liverpool Football Club while attending the University of Texas. Now he had finally made it, and it turned out that getting inside required passing through a gate that resembled a medieval torture device. Who would have guessed that such antiquated equipment was still in use anywhere at the start of the 21st century, let alone at one of the most storied venues in all of sports?

Januszewski didn't see how his broad-shouldered body could fit past the metal spikes. But he had come this far, and there was only one way to find out. He turned his body sideways, ducked his head, and willed himself through. He was in.

It was January 15, 2005. Januszewski knows the date because he kept the ticket on a wall in his office for a decade after that. A salesman serving corporate accounts for baseball's Boston Red Sox, he'd flown to England and spent the night in London. Then he set his alarm for sunrise and caught a train north. In a sense, though, the journey had started years before, when he was a preschooler in Heidelberg, West Germany, kicking a soccer ball with neighbors in front of his apartment. The 1974 World Cup was held in venues around the country, and Januszewski recalls being aware of West Germany winning it, though he wasn't yet three years old. When he moved with his family to Utah, he played soccer in youth leagues. Years later, in Austin, he went to a bar one weekend morning and found a Liverpool game playing on television. He started talking with a table full of Englishmen dressed in red; they indoctrinated him before he knew it. "That became my team," he says.

Januszewski wasn't the first person to remark that Anfield reminded him of Boston's Fenway Park. First constructed in the 1880s, it had been renovated periodically, but it still seemed a structure out of time, more a historic monument than a sports facility. Standing in the crowd, rooting for the home team, it was easy for him to make the connection to the previous generation of spectators who had done the same, and the generation before that, and the one before that. The fans around Januszewski—everyone had seats, but nobody sat in them—watched with a fierce intensity for the first half. Then they hustled down the concrete stairs and drank as many beers as they could during the brief intermission. They spent the second half as involved as they had spent the first. The entire game, all 90 minutes of it, felt to Januszewski like the bottom of the ninth inning.

An instinctive marketer, Januszewski couldn't help sensing an opportunity. Anfield was lovely, majestic, yet somehow intimate. But the bathrooms reeked of urine and the food was terrible, and those turnstiles were a lawsuit waiting to happen. Liverpool's supporters were involved with every detail of their club, but they showed up just moments before kickoff. As soon as a match ended, they headed for the bus stop. They didn't want to spend a minute more at the stadium than they had to. Januszewski couldn't blame them. "What struck me," he says now, "was the lack of sophistication in the game-day presentation. Basically, people were spending top dollar to attend what I would consider a viscerally disgusting experience."

By then, Januszewski had been working in sports for six years, long enough to not take passionate fans for granted. In 1999, he had segued from a brief career in film to a job in corporate development with the San Diego Padres. He soon realized that the locals there had the same detached relationship with the club as they did with most everything else. Life was easy in San Diego—"like living on the Love Boat," as T. J. Simers, a columnist at the local newspaper, once described it to me. The Padres made the World Series in 1998. Then they rapidly returned to their losing ways. They played their games in a charmless, obsolescent stadium that had been designed for football. The team's young sales staff was trying to sell access to what Januszewski characterizes as "a bad team in a bad venue in an apathetic market." Most had little experience in the industry. But they did have ingenuity, and nobody was around to tell them what not to do.

For two years, Januszewski worked under Larry Lucchino, a former Washington lawyer who had arrived in 1994 to be the Padres' chief executive. In 2001, after six successful but contentious seasons, Lucchino quit. He wound up helping Tom Werner—a television producer and, oddly enough, the previous Padres owner—make a bid for the Red Sox. Lucchino and Werner had plenty of baseball connections, but they needed a lot more money. They reached out to John Henry, who at the time owned the Florida Marlins but was in the process of selling them.

Henry, Werner, and Lucchino called their partnership New England Sports Ventures, though none of them actually came from New England. The $700 million it cost them and some other investors to eventually buy the Red Sox was the most anyone had ever paid for a baseball team. At least Fenway Park, with its iconic, 37-foot Green Monster of a left-field wall, was included.

Installed in the same position in Boston that he'd held in San Diego, Lucchino raided the Padres' staff for talent. Theo Epstein, an executive on the baseball side, had played at Brookline High and written about sports for the school paper while at Yale. He still wasn't 30 years old, but Lucchino anointed him as Boston's new general manager. Sam Kennedy, a savvy marketer with irresistible energy, had been a high school teammate of Epstein's. He returned to Boston to work for the new owners. Januszewski, who had worked under Kennedy, rejoined him a few months later. He needed about two days of reading the *Globe* and listening to local sports radio before he appreciated the possibilities inherent in a market where the fans didn't need to be coaxed into caring about their team.

Yet Boston's love affair with the Red Sox was mostly unrequited. Perhaps because of that devoted following, the franchise had made no attempt to cultivate its fan base, or even acknowledge it. Over the years, promoters such as Bill Veeck in St. Louis and Chicago and Charlie Finley in Oakland had, in the long tradition of American hucksterism, used showmanship to sell baseball. Not in Boston. "The attitude was 'We really don't need to do as much as an upstart or small-market franchise because we are the Red Sox, the mighty, mighty Red Sox,'" Lucchino explains. Marketing meant unshuttering the Fenway ticket windows every February and waiting for a line to form.

The new owners were determined to change that. This wasn't

hucksterism, but something more fundamental: treating fans of the club like valued patrons. That happened routinely in most businesses that involved face-to-face contact, but few big-league franchises had made it a priority. So now, when fans slept out in the winter cold the night before tickets went on sale, Charles Steinberg, a young protégé of Lucchino's, delivered them blankets. A former dentist who had worked with Lucchino in Baltimore and then San Diego, Steinberg covered the walls of his tiny office with index cards that represented a fan's journey, from the initial decision to consider buying a ticket to a game to arriving home after it had ended. Then he rated how the team was doing during each step, using a nine-point scale. How do the hot dogs taste? Pretty good. Billboard ads? Could be better. Kennedy and his staff used techniques they'd invented in San Diego to connect with fans, like creating a Kid's Club that sent members free caps and lunch boxes and occasionally even tickets. They also invented new ones. On April 3, 2002, the date of the second game of the new regime, fans arrived at Fenway to find nearly the entire Red Sox roster, in uniform, greeting them at the entrance gates. That June, the Red Sox were on the road for Father's Day, so the club opened Fenway and let families play catch on the field. These were simple but meaningful gestures that let fans know the team's relationship with them would be different going forward.

Watching the game at Anfield in 2005, Januszewski felt like he'd arrived in Boston all over again. It was clear to him that attending a game would be immeasurably more enjoyable if the club made even a minimal effort. He didn't expect to see Peter Crouch, the team's top striker, easing ticket holders through that turnstile. But simply cleaning the bathrooms, or offering something beyond a reheated meat pie at the concession stand, could do wonders for fan morale. He flew home to Boston unable to contain his excitement. "This is such a missed opportunity," he told Kennedy. "It's a great opportunity for someone with some vision."

Kennedy couldn't see it. *Soccer? In England?* "You do realize that's 4,600 miles away from here?" he said.

At the time, Americans still had little international presence in the sport. There were a few players—goalkeepers, mostly—knocking around the Premier League, but no coaches, and certainly nobody who wore a tie to work. Most English clubs were still owned by ruddy-faced businessmen who had kicked a ball around as boys and made their fortunes in parking lots or local real estate. In 1997, Egyptian shipping magnate Mohamed al-Fayed had taken control of a third-tier London club, Fulham. In 2003, Russian oligarch Roman Abramovich, who had become rich from oil and aluminum, bought perennial underachievers Chelsea. But significant American investment wouldn't happen until later in 2005, a few months after Januszewski's trip. That's when the Glazer family, which already owned the NFL's Tampa Bay Buccaneers, acquired Manchester United, which coincidentally was the club that Januszewski had seen beat Liverpool at Anfield.

That deal started a trend. Each year, Januszewski couldn't help noticing, another American with little or no connection to soccer would gain control of a Premier League club. In 2006, Randy Lerner, who owned the NFL's Cleveland Browns, bought Aston Villa. In 2007, Stan Kroenke, who had an NBA team, an NHL team, part of an NFL team, and an insatiable appetite for acquisition, accumulated a majority interest in Arsenal. Each time he heard the news, Januszewski would poke his head into Lucchino's office and make his case again.

"There's just so much opportunity in English soccer," he'd say. "You need to convince John to buy a team."

"Joe, we know you're passionate," Kennedy remembers telling him. "But you have a day job. Why don't you spend more time selling ads on the Green Monster?"

———————

ONE OF THE clubs that ended up with American owners was Liverpool. For half a century, it had been run by the Moores family, which owned retail and catalog shopping businesses and ran legal betting pools. In 2007, unable to compete financially, David Moores sold out to two freewheeling businessmen, Tom Hicks and George Gillett. Based in Dallas, Hicks was a leveraged buyout specialist who had churned his way through the soft drink industry, revitalizing and then selling 7 Up, Dr. Pepper, and A&W root beer. He already owned baseball's Texas Rangers and hockey's Dallas Stars. Gillett, who lived in Vail, Colorado, had somehow parlayed an interest in ski resorts into control of a NASCAR team and the NHL's Montreal Canadiens.

Nearly a generation before, Liverpool had been the dominant club in the world. Between 1975 and 1990, it won 10 titles in England's top division. It won the European Cup, which preceded the Champions League, four times in eight years. Liverpool FC was so successful that, for a time, it figured as one of England's most visible exports. Fan clubs were organized throughout Europe, and in places that hadn't previously followed the sport, such as Australia and across America. But by the time Hicks and Gillett arrived, it hadn't won an English championship in 18 years. It also had fallen behind financially. For all its charm, Liverpool itself was a faded port of half a million inhabitants. Only marginally less dilapidated than the gritty, gray-toned city that had produced the Beatles decades before, it had a far smaller corporate base than London, or even nearby Manchester. Anfield lacked the profit-making amenities of the massive Emirates Stadium that Arsenal had built in 2006, or Manchester United's Old Trafford, which, during a 2005 renovation, had grown its seating capacity to 75,000. And it turned out that, with all their other interests, Gillett and Hicks had little money left over for soccer.

Hicks and Gillett also embodied pretty much every unpleasant stereotype that the British have about Americans. In private, both men can be charming. But they seemed to have little sense of the culture they had invaded, other than a determination that they were going to improve it. That included eventually tearing down Anfield and replacing it with a huge new stadium somewhere else. They bought players according to no apparent plan, fired a popular manager, and alienated much of the fan base. That put the team nearly half a billion dollars into debt remarkably quickly, which in turn derailed their plan to replace Anfield. In 2010, two years into their tenure, some 10,000 Liverpool supporters staged a march through the city's streets, demanding that they sell out. It was clear that an opportunity existed for someone to acquire a distressed asset for well below market value. "Tell John to save my club," Januszewski urged Lucchino.

One evening that August, Januszewski was feeding a bottle to his infant son at his home in Wellesley, outside Boston, when he glanced at his mobile phone and noticed that he had missed a call from Lucchino. Moments later, Januszewski reached him at a suite inside Toronto's Rogers Centre. Shouting to be heard, Lucchino told him he was watching the Red Sox with Henry and Werner and some Blue Jays executives. Someone there had seen news of the protests against Hicks and Gillett, the conversation had turned to soccer, and the subject of Liverpool's availability had been raised. "Tell John what you've been telling me," Lucchino said. He passed the phone to Henry.

At the time, Januszewski hardly knew Henry. With anyone other than his closest associates, Henry could be taciturn, bordering on antisocial. He was the counterweight to both the pugnacious Lucchino and the amiable Werner. And Januszewski was hardly a presence in management's inner circle. If you wanted to find his name in the organizational directory on the club's website, you had to scroll past 129 others. Januszewski began to explain the opportunities inherent in owning Liverpool, but Henry seemed distracted— he was watching his Red Sox, after all. And he and Januszewski could barely hear each other over the din of the game. They'd only been talking for a few minutes when Henry cut him off. "Send it to me in an email," he said. Then he ended the call.

At the time, New England Sports Ventures owned the Red Sox, Fenway Park, and some real estate around it. The company also had most of a local cable sports channel and half a NASCAR team. Henry was open to adding to that portfolio. He and Werner had spent much of 2010 contemplating making an offer for an NBA franchise, either the Golden State Warriors or the Los Angeles Clippers. In the end, they concluded that neither was an ideal fit. Both teams played home games across the continent, three time zones away. And while the Warriors hadn't competed in the NBA finals in 35 years, the Clippers had never even made it that far. Among sports franchises, they were hardly blue-chip equities.

Over eight years in Boston, Henry had found few opportunities worth pursuing. Reading Januszewski's email, he had no reason to believe this one would stand up to critical analysis. Liverpool would cost less than half as much as the Red Sox, but it would still be a significant purchase, one of the more expensive sports transactions ever. And for all that money, what would they get? A losing team in a city hundreds of miles from London that played a sport Henry didn't even understand.

Still, Januszewski had made a strong enough case to warrant at least finding out more about the club, and what buying it might theoretically entail. Late that night, after the Red Sox had closed out a 7–5 victory and moved within five games of first place in the American League East, Henry sent an email to Kennedy, copying Januszewski and the other relevant executives. He asked them to put together a working group and see what it could learn in a week or two. Because until you had all the information, Henry always liked to say, you couldn't know for sure.

────────

GROWING UP, JOHN HENRY would listen to baseball on the radio as he fell asleep at night. Until his asthma forced his family to relocate to California when he was 15, he divided his time between Quincy, Illinois, and Forrest City, Arkansas (his parents were soybean farmers who owned land in both places). The two towns were at opposite ends of the St. Louis Cardinals' Midwestern empire, but both were amply served by a clear-channel radio station, KMOX. The Cardinals became Henry's obsession.

Baseball was the ideal sport for a boy with a predilection for mathematics. Nearly everything a ballplayer could do on the field had a number attached to it, and it turned out that Henry could calculate many of those numbers in his head. One of Henry's passions was APBA baseball, a dice game in which the actual performances of major leaguers are translated into cards representing each player; Stan Musial was as likely to hit a triple on Henry's bedroom floor as he was in Sportsman's Park. Much later, Henry used some of the principles of probability that made APBA realistic to devise an algorithm that predicted fluctuations in the soybean market. Eventually, he opened his own trading firm. By the time he turned 40, in 1989, he had amassed enough money to invest in a baseball team of his own.

The team was the Pacific Coast League's Tucson Toros, the Class AAA affiliate of the Houston Astros. At the time, Henry hadn't yet connected his avocation to his vocation. He wasn't try- ing to use data analysis to determine who should play second base, or even what a bleacher seat should cost. He just liked going to the games. Later that year, he helped create the Senior Professional Baseball Association, in which aging stars played a short season in the Florida sun before a few gawking fans. To manage his own West Palm Beach franchise, he hired Dick Williams, who'd led the 1967 Red Sox team to an improbable American League pennant.

In 1991, he bought a share of around one percent in George Steinbrenner's New York Yankees. He was following Warren Buf- fett's dictum about acquiring the top equities in the category when- ever you invested. But that went out the window, along with his Yankees holdings, when he went after the decidedly non-blue-chip Florida Marlins. He paid Wayne Huizenga $158 million in 1999 for a team that played in a cavernous multi-use stadium in the hinterlands north of Miami and had sold all its best players the year before. Soon after, when Bud Selig, the commissioner of Major League Baseball, advanced the idea of dissolving several money-losing franchises, the Marlins were a prime candidate.

Henry ended up selling the Marlins and partnering with Luc- chino and Werner to buy the Red Sox, who hadn't won a World

Series since 1918, despite playing in four of them and coming close to perhaps half a dozen more. The club was jokingly, or not so jokingly, said to be cursed. In their second season as owners, 2003, the Red Sox won 95 games and again came within a few outs of the American League pennant. The following season, they won the pennant. Then they defeated the Cardinals, Henry's boyhood favorites, to break whatever curse had existed. Three years later, in 2007, the Sox won the World Series again.

The architect of those teams was Epstein, the young general manager. And the strategies he had used to build the team weren't all that different from the types of analyses Henry had done during his financial career.

———————

ON A WARM afternoon some two weeks after Januszewski's phone call with Henry, the members of the working group filed into suite R10 inside Fenway. With them were bankers from a boutique investment firm, Inner Circle Sports, who had flown in from New York. Henry arrived and settled into a chair facing the field. Werner had taken the place two seats over, at the head of the table. The suite had a seductive view of the diamond, but there was no baseball to watch. The Red Sox had left for Tampa after losing at Fenway the previous night. And anyway, this meeting wasn't about baseball. "It was English Football 101, and Liverpool's place in it," says Steve Horowitz, one of the founders of Inner Circle, who had been involved in Hicks and Gillett's purchase of Liverpool three years before.

Horowitz wasn't trying to convince Henry to make a bid. "That's not my job, to convince the people I work with of anything," he says. But it was evident from the start of his presentation that he believed

Liverpool was a worthy target. The club had a famous name, with global reach that included fans throughout North America and in China and Japan. Opportunities could exist for synergy with New England Sports Network, the cable channel the company owned. Liverpool could even play exhibition matches at Fenway. About half an hour into the meeting, the discussion turned to the financial implications of a potential purchase, and whether debt could be used to finance it. But during a brief pause, a voice was heard from the far end of the table. It was Henry. He wasn't responding to Horowitz directly, just making an announcement to nobody in particular. "But I don't *want* to own a soccer team," he said.

In the conference rooms of nearly every other sports franchise, Henry's comment would have ended the discussion. If the majority owner didn't want a soccer team, he wouldn't waste his time talking about buying one. Since the first sports leagues were formed in the late 19th century, the teams that played in them almost always had changed hands on a whim, for purely emotional reasons. That's because there *were* no other reasons. You didn't buy a sports team to make money, you did it because you had money and wanted to do something fun with it.

Throughout the 20th century, most big-league franchises were worth almost nothing compared with the businesses that had made a prospective owner rich in the first place. When Tisch said he pretended he'd never had the $75 million he used to buy half of football's New York Giants, his net worth was maybe 50 times that. He was co-chairman of the Loews Corporation, a conglomerate that owned hotels, Lorillard Tobacco, CNA Financial, and much of Bulova and Diamond Offshore Drilling. Yet, once Tisch bought a share of the Giants, he spent more time thinking about them than he did anything else in his business life. He never missed a game, not at home or on the road. He showed up at those practices twice a week and sometimes more often than that, shuffling along the sideline, taking in the spectacle. "I enjoy it," he said at the time. "I schmooze with the general manager, I schmooze with the coach, I get ready for Sunday. It's a kick."

In 1963, William Clay Ford purchased the NFL's Detroit Lions. He did it in part to make sure that the team wouldn't move somewhere else, and because owning a football team sounded exciting. It cost him $5 million, but what did that matter? His family's actual business was the Ford Motor Company, which had a market capitalization in the billions. Nearly six decades later, his widow still owns the Lions. The team is now valued at more than $2 billion, which is more than the value of the family's equity in the car company.

Once you had purchased a team, you didn't even have to be good at running it, as long as you didn't care about the results of the games. In 1981, Donald Sterling, a personal injury attorney with a growing collection of Los Angeles real estate, spent $12.5 million on the NBA's San Diego Clippers. A high school gymnast who had moved to Southern California from Chicago as a child, Sterling enjoyed basketball. But what he really enjoyed was being important, and having other people notice his importance. It was why he had renamed the Lesser Towers apartment buildings the Sterling Towers, and the historic California Bank Building in Beverly Hills the Sterling Plaza. He soon moved the Clippers two hours north to Los Angeles, even though that city already had a basketball team. He wanted his friends to talk about him as the owner of a sports franchise, but nobody in Los Angeles cared about a team that played in the backwater of San Diego. The NBA objected to the idea of abandoning the growing San Diego market nearly as much as it hated the precedent the move set of encroaching on the domain of another team, in this case the Los Angeles Lakers. It fined Sterling $25 million, double what he'd paid for the Clippers. Sterling threatened litigation. The league then reduced the fine to $6 million. None of those numbers meant much in the context of Sterling's holdings.

If Sterling didn't run his team like a real business, it was because he didn't need to. Whether the Clippers won or lost, the financial structure of the NBA would make certain that they remained solvent. The stakes for the league's other owners were high; if one franchise failed, the value of everyone's investment would plummet. Television revenues and other income was divided among the teams, so even though their games were sparsely attended, the Clippers limped along. On the court, not surprisingly, they were terrible. For the first decade that Sterling owned them, they didn't manage a single winning season. In the 30 years from 1982 to 2011, they made the playoffs just three times, which is a remarkably awful run. In eight seasons during that span, they won fewer than a quarter of their games.

Yet, since the NBA operates like a single business with multiple branches, the price of its franchises is driven by scarcity. It doesn't matter how rich you are: if you want to own a basketball team that plays in the NBA, you must either buy an expansion franchise (and pay an inflated fee for the privilege) or a team that already exists. Each time a team changes hands, inevitably for more than the previous owner paid for it, the estimated value of all the others is recalibrated to reflect the current market. By 2010, the Clippers had moved to the heart of trendy downtown. They played in the glitzy Staples Center, which they shared with the Lakers. Sterling's original $12.5 million investment had grown to perhaps $500 million. Still, he refused to sell the team, even when offers came in for even more than that. His reasoning was entirely emotional: If he sold it, what would he talk about at the country club?

When he decided to buy a sports team, John Henry also made sentimental decisions without putting too much thought into the financial ramifications. He loved baseball, so he bought the Toros. He liked the idea of owning a piece of a big-league team, so he invested in the Yankees. When the opportunity came to get one of his own, he jumped at it and bought the Marlins. Only 30 franchises, 16 in the National League and 14 in the American League, played big-league baseball, and he was excited to have one of them. And two years later, when the chance came up to get one of the teams Henry had managed in his boyhood APBA games, he flipped the Marlins and upgraded to the Red Sox.

But now his team was literally worth billions. He was learning to treat it like a business because he had never owned a business that was anything close to it in value. He'd also learned, during the eight years he'd been running the team, to mistrust sentiment. He had no interest in standing on the sideline, watching the Liverpool Football Club go through a training session. (In truth, he didn't even have an interest in going to its games.) But however he felt about it, the club had a value. That value was likely to be higher, he'd learned during his time owning the Red Sox, if data analysis were applied to the decisions it made, both on and off the field. As with the Red Sox, that approach might even help turn a team that didn't win championships into one that did. And that would grow the value of the team even more.

In the rest of his life, Henry liked to make decisions by collecting as much information on the subject as he could find. Then he would analyze that information until it revealed its secrets. He did that with his stock market investments, with free agent signings, even where to have lunch in Italy, which meant a painstaking perusal of restaurant reviews across the internet, conversations with the hotel staff, and late-night immersion in guidebooks. By 2010, a similar relentless analysis of data had helped the Red Sox win two World Series on the field and evolve from a team with largely a regional following into one of the most popular sports franchises in America. But such dispassionate assessments were rarely applied to the business side of sports.

Lately, though, it had led New England Sports Ventures to make a handful of investments, mostly in the form of undervalued lots in the neighborhood around Fenway, that would either grow the value of the company or set the stage for future growth. It also had convinced Henry and his partners to reject some investments, such as the NBA teams, that on first consideration had seemed ideal for the growing portfolio. Whether Henry wanted to own a soccer team, he had come to understand, had little to do with whether his company should try to buy one.

It was far from the first time that a businessman had made a business decision about a sports team. But with that realization came a course change for Henry and New England Sports Ventures, and an inflection point for the industry of professional sports.

––––––––

SOME 10 HOURS later, long after the meeting at Fenway had ended, Henry launched another late-night email into the ether. This time, he admitted to Werner and Kennedy and the others that he hadn't been in favor of making a bid for Liverpool when he walked into the suite that afternoon. And he wanted to make clear that he still wasn't sure he was in favor of it. But the presentation *had* convinced him that Liverpool was a special place, at least in soccer terms—and that, as an investment, the Liverpool Football Club had much more in common with the Red Sox and even the Yankees than it did with the Florida Marlins. That didn't necessarily mean it was desirable for New England Sports Ventures to own. But whoever did end up buying it would, as Januszewski had surmised, be getting a property with a potential value that was far higher than they would be paying. With that in mind, Henry wanted to know more.

He devoted much of the next day to the task. His capacity for absorbing and assessing information was a source of wonderment for anyone who worked with him. He read and he sifted, traveling down the web's information highway and its side streets and more than a few blind alleys. And what he learned, about the structure of English soccer and Liverpool's history as a club and even the city itself, intrigued him.

Lately, too, Henry had felt constrained by the commercial restrictions imposed by Major League Baseball on its 30 franchises. He had constructed a superpower of a business group that was, in effect, banned from doing business anywhere outside New England, or selling anything too far removed from baseball itself. When Henry had broached the concept of Red Sox-themed pubs around Boston and the surrounding area, Selig had vetoed it. He had done that for Henry's own good, Selig explained, because anything the Red Sox might devise, the Yankees would eventually be able to do more profitably. Such a judgment, Henry believed, was not for Selig to make.

This was yet another restriction inherent in the singular calculus of North American sports. The success of owners or ownership groups is inevitably gauged by how much their teams win. Yet taking advantage of that success financially, either by investing more money in player salaries or extending the brand geographically or into related businesses in the way that any other company or corporation would attempt to grow, is made confoundingly difficult—and, in many cases, barred entirely by the leagues that run the sports. By contrast, Henry learned, the owner of Liverpool Football Club had the freedom to use its name and images in almost any way he desired. Not only could Henry open a pub branded with its name and logo across the street from Anfield, he could put one in Boston's Back Bay. Or Shanghai.

In baseball, the revenue from all merchandise sold around the world was pooled and equally divided. That meant the Red Sox earned no more from the replica jerseys and green St. Patrick's Day novelty hats they sold in the megastore across from Fenway than the Kansas City Royals or Tampa Bay Rays did. The restrictions on the Red Sox even extended to the internet itself; the commissioner's office not only controlled the club's digital rights, it designed and ran its website. Liverpool, which regularly sold more branded items that almost any other English club, kept everything it made. That was enticing to Henry. And Liverpool could do just about anything it wanted online, from nothing at all to creating original programming and even streaming exhibition games directly to subscribers for a fee.

Anfield, too, would be a remarkable asset. As Henry researched it, the parallels to Fenway became clear. In 2001, most of the bids for the Red Sox had included a new stadium as part of the pitch. But Lucchino, who had been deeply involved in the construction of a new ballpark on the Camden Yards site in Baltimore's Inner Harbor when he ran the Baltimore Orioles in the early 1990s, argued that the Red Sox didn't need to put a ballpark in a block of old warehouses somewhere. They already had a ballpark with a retro feel, and it was an original, dating to 1912. That outweighed its tiny seating capacity, the fact that some of the seats down the right-field line weren't even facing home plate, and other quirks. Werner, who had made a documentary about Fenway while a student at Harvard, agreed with him. Eventually, so did Henry. "You could never re-create the atmosphere that is the result of the history that resides within the walls," he explained.

The challenge had been to outfit Fenway with the same fan-pleasing—and income-generating—features of the latest genera-tion of stadiums without sacrificing that atmosphere. Fenway was already a revered piece of local real estate. After outfitting the build-ing with new seats, revamped concessions, and other improvements, and then marketing it as the best place in America to see a baseball game, it became as much of a national draw as the team itself. Tour-ists who didn't know the name of a single player lined up to tour the ballpark, buy shirts that featured it, and see a game there.

Anfield was equally iconic. Yet in terms of generating ancil-lary revenue, it was more like a high school football field. Install-ing, say, a café serving steaks and pizzas and cocktails for pre- and postgame dining, or a conference room with a view of the field that could be rented out by corporate boards, would add significantly to the bottom line. At Anfield, too, nearly every ticket was being sold for the same amount. There was something delightfully egalitarian about that, but it was like asking fans to pay the same for a piece of wooden bench in the bleachers as they did for a plushly padded seat directly behind the dugout. Imposing a multi-tiered ticketing struc-ture would enable the club to sell its best inventory for much higher prices, and ordinary locations for less than they currently cost. That would increase revenue while simultaneously getting a wider range of fans inside the grounds.

As Henry read up on the city, he realized it was actually an exciting place to have a soccer team. It wasn't London or even Manchester, sure—but then, Boston wasn't New York. In fact, Henry had grown to enjoy how his adopted home played the underdog. Boston was provincial, everyone always said, except that it had two of the best universities in the world, and superb museums, and more PhDs per capita than almost anywhere else. Liverpool was a center of progressive politics. It had the only branch of the Tate Museum besides the one in London, and a revitalized music scene that was building on the Beatles' legacy. It even looked like Boston: a coastal city along a sturdy river, white-marble buildings interspersed with glass-box skyscrapers, residents in long coats hustling through the winter chill over ancient, narrow streets. Like the Yankees, whom Lucchino had dubbed the "Evil Empire," Liverpool had a foil in nearby Manchester United, which had won the English title more times than any other club, and Henry appreciated the inherent value of that. Even the best teams can't win every year, he knew. But in a customer-satisfaction situation that only happens in sports, you could salvage something from a disappointing season by at least finishing ahead of your rivals.

Shortly after four o'clock that afternoon, Henry sent a third email to the working group. The equivalent of 37 pages in a Word document, it was a pastiche of articles, charts, financial information, even a video tour of Anfield. All of it was annotated by Henry's own commentary. In the meeting the previous day, the group had heard Henry announce that he didn't have an interest in owning a soccer team. "Now suddenly," Kennedy says, "he's saying, 'OK, if we're going to do this, we need to be able to beat Manchester United. And we need to win the league! And we need to get back into the Champions League!'" Considered dispassionately, a deal to buy Liverpool made sense. And by then, Henry was excited.

On October 15, 2010, New England Sports Ventures officially purchased Liverpool FC. The locals were understandably wary. They were ridding themselves of Hicks and Gillett, who had driven their team into receivership, but nothing they knew about the commodities trader and television producer who were replacing them made them confident they would be much of an improvement. Henry understood. "Two American businessmen who owned other sports teams and didn't know much about soccer," he said. "What could go wrong?"

In my conversations with team owners and executives that led to this book, the purchase of Liverpool by Henry, Werner, and their partners kept coming up as a watershed. Henry, a majority owner who had become rich by using a mathematical algorithm to trade commodities, presided over a due-diligence process for buying a team that relied heavily on research and analysis. The process ended up adding a complementary piece to the company's holdings, even though—unlike, say, Manchester United's Avi, Joel, and Bryan Glazer, who had grown up as season ticket holders of the North American Soccer League's Rochester Lancers—none of the major investors had even the slightest interest in the sport that the team played.

In the years that followed, more and more suitors for teams would use rational business judgments to examine the viability of buying them, including combining into groups of multiple investors to limit short-term risk. Sure, owning a sports franchise can be fun, but the scale of the industry had outgrown "fun" as the basis for an assessment. (There would still be a few aspirational owners who were wealthy enough to decide unilaterally that they wanted to acquire a particular team, whether as an investment or a bauble; those included the richest of the tech billionaires and, increasingly, the Russian oligarchs, Middle Eastern sheiks, and even the official investment arms of entire countries that were spreading their largesse around the soccer leagues of Europe. But as valuations began to reach and then routinely exceed $1 billion, that pool would get increasingly shallow.) Some of those potential owners might have had a previous passion for the sport they were buying into. Others didn't. What they had in common was an appreciation that, when run in an optimized way, sports teams were valid investment vehicles that had more in common with biotech firms or Silicon Valley software companies than with trophy purchases like yachts or collections of vintage racing cars.

It made sense. On the field, general managers such as Epstein were presiding over staffs of analysts who were changing the way decisions were being made inside the sports, including how to allocate tens of millions of dollars annually to sign players. Why wouldn't a potential investor use similar rigor to analyze whether buying a particular team was a prudent decision? By the end of the decade, many of the clubs that Liverpool played each season were being run by the same principles that Henry and his group used to purchase it. The same would be true of the opponents of the Red Sox.

Two days after New England Sports Ventures closed the deal, on a Sunday, Liverpool played a game against Everton, the city's other Premier League team. The distance between Anfield and Goodison Park, Everton's home ground, is less than mile, a brisk walk through a parking lot and then across a meadow. Everton scored a goal in the first half to take a lead and never relinquished it. The defeat dropped Liverpool to 19th place in the 20-team Premier League. If the season had ended that evening, the club would have dropped into English soccer's second league. "John W. Henry, owner of the visitors, surely arrived at this match eager to learn more about the

Anfield club he now owns," correspondent Kevin McCarra wrote in the *Guardian*, one of England's national newspapers. "But the reward was a thorough understanding of its inadequacies." Actually, Henry probably didn't understand those inadequacies nearly as thoroughly as McCarra assumed. It was the first live soccer game he had ever seen.

2

I KNEW NOTHING,
ABSOLUTELY NOTHING

IN MARCH OF 2002, I flew to Arizona to see Billy Beane, the general manager of baseball's Oakland A's. Beane's A's were a team that seemed to be on the cusp of success, but they kept getting thwarted by the economics of their sport. They were continually finding and nurturing talented players, only to have them leave for bigger markets. It seemed like a worthwhile topic for a magazine story. What I didn't realize, and wouldn't find out until months after my story was published, was that a revolution was afoot, one that was being fomented by the same executive I had come to interview.

Beane and I met behind home plate before a Cactus League game in Scottsdale. By then, he had been running the team for four full seasons. Although Oakland's annual payroll of around $40 million routinely ranked among baseball's lowest, that tenure had been uncommonly successful; in each of those seasons, the team had won more games than it had in the previous one. By 2000, the A's had managed to make the postseason, winning the American

League West before losing a five-game playoff series to the Yankees. The following year, they won 102 games. Again, they lost to the Yankees in the playoffs.

On the field in front of us was a 27-year-old shortstop named Miguel Tejada. The A's had discovered Tejada in 1995 in the Dominican Republic. Within two years, he was playing in Oakland. By the time I came to see him, he was entering his fifth season and was one of the stars of the American League. Beane knew that Tejada's next contract would be a prodigious one. He also knew that the A's would be unable to afford it. He would have Tejada for the 2002 season and, if he didn't trade him, for 2003. After that, Tejada would be able to sign wherever he wanted, and the A's would get no meaningful compensation in return.

The previous season, the A's had employed a first baseman named Jason Giambi. Hulking and unathletic, Giambi was an entirely different kind of player than Tejada. But he also could hit, and with power. In 2000, Giambi hit 43 home runs and was named the American League's Most Valuable Player. He followed that in 2001 with 38 homers. After that 2001 season, Giambi's contract expired. A month later, he signed with the Yankees.

In 2001, the A's had paid Giambi $4.1 million. During 2002, he would earn more than $10 million. (By the 2007 season, Giambi's contract with the Yankees stipulated, he would be making $23 million.) Losing Giambi was dismaying enough, but that he'd signed with the Yankees made it more difficult to accept. The A's had been unable to beat the Yankees in tight playoff series two seasons in a row. Now their best hitter was, in effect, moving across the field from one dugout to another. It hardly seemed fair.

That off-season had been an especially bad one for the A's. In addition to Giambi, two other crucial players had departed. Johnny

Damon, the starting center fielder, had left for the Red Sox. Jason Isringhausen, the club's top relief pitcher, had gone to the New York Mets. Beane understood that there was nothing he could have done to keep either player. Like the Yankees, the Red Sox and the Mets had far more money to spend than the A's did. And these were precisely the kind of talents—a slugging first baseman such as Giambi; a center fielder with speed and a quick bat; an elite closer—on which well-heeled teams were likely to spend their money. That was the way baseball worked, and the way it would probably always work, unless the teams and the players' union got together and agreed to put a cap on teams' spending. And that, everyone agreed, was unlikely to happen.

I had come there to learn what it felt like to be a general manager of one of those teams that couldn't generate enough revenue to keep its best players. But when I asked Beane about that, he shrugged. He said Tejada leaving wasn't what concerned him. Neither, he added, was the inevitable departure of all three of his starting pitchers. He waved his hand toward some guy who had just sat down on the other side of the aisle across from us. "That's who I worry about losing," he said. I laughed. I assumed he was pulling my leg. "That's my assistant," he said.

He told me the name, one I hadn't heard before: Paul DePodesta. Tall and thin, with glasses, DePodesta looked like he could still be in college. "Man," Beane said, "if he ever leaves me . . ." His voice trailed off. I still couldn't tell if he was kidding.

The previous November, the Toronto Blue Jays had hired Beane's director of player personnel, J. P. Ricciardi, to be their general manager. He was an unexpected choice. Ricciardi was relatively young, just 41. His playing career hadn't extended beyond the low minors. But the Athletics had been having success on a minimal budget, and the Blue Jays noticed. They couldn't coax Beane away from Oakland, so they figured they would get his lieutenant. That was what worried Beane. Tejada would be leaving soon, he knew—but if the team kept winning, DePodesta would leave, too. Beane explained that he would always be able to get another infielder. "Paul," he said, "I can't replace."

That struck me as absurd. I had no idea what DePodesta was doing for the A's, but I couldn't understand how special it could be. I did a little research and learned that he was a 29-year-old former Harvard football player who'd spent time scouting for Cleveland. His official title was assistant to the general manager. Now here was Beane, claiming that his value to the club over the coming years would be greater than that of the best shortstop in baseball. How could that possibly be right?

I was about to find out.

That 2002 season, the A's won 103 games, which tied them with the Yankees for the most in baseball. Tejada won a Most Valuable Player award by hitting 34 homers and knocking home 131 runs. The A's lost in the playoffs again. The following April, Michael Lewis's *Moneyball* was published.

———

TWO DECADES LATER, *Moneyball* has calcified into American culture as shorthand for an entirely different way of assessing sports, and particularly baseball. What those who read the book or watched the movie tend to remember are its definitive opinions on specific tactics, as derived by the laptop-toting DePodesta and promulgated by Beane. *Walks are good. Bunting is bad. Don't focus on what a player looks like, or even what his swing looks like, because appearances can deceive.* These were principles that underfunded teams like the A's could use to try to be competitive in the standings while still remaining solvent. But the book was really about finding hidden value. And unlike ball clubs, successful businesses had been doing that for decades.

After graduating from the London School of Economics, Lewis spent four years at Salomon Brothers. Then he published a best-seller, *Liar's Poker,* about the bond market. Most recently, he had been writing about the evolving tech scene in Silicon Valley. In those industries, as in many others, a gap between the actual and perceived value of an asset constituted an opportunity. The data was simply a means to figure out what the *actual* value of something was. That could mean the value of a relief pitcher compared with the other players on the roster, or of attempting to bunt a runner from first base to second with one out, compared with trying to construct a big inning. The effect of just about everything that happened to a baseball team on the field was theoretically knowable. It was hidden somewhere in the numbers. You just had to have the wherewithal to find it.

This kind of analysis had been around for two decades, ever since Bill James published the first edition of his *Baseball Abstract* in 1977. A security guard at a pork processing facility, James had time to spare, and a restless curiosity about his favorite sport. He would take truisms about baseball that were accepted as commonplace, such as the importance of a sure-handed, slick-fielding shortstop, and use statistics to figure out if they were actually true. Some of them were, it turned out. But many of them weren't.

James's academic analysis made for more informed arguments in chat rooms and bars, but for years the impact of such thinking on the way baseball was played was minimal. The game was run by the kind of people who had always run it—former players, who had been taught by coaches and managers in the way that they had themselves been taught. The tactics of the game went in and out of fashion, often based on which teams recently had won the World Series. But players were still being judged by the same metrics they'd been judged by since detailed records started to be kept at the end of the 1800s.

Until Beane. With the help of Ricciardi and DePodesta, and the innate sensibility of a contrarian stock picker, he understood that if he used the same information to evaluate players that the wealthier teams were using, he would end up coveting the same players. Not only would he never be able to outbid those teams for each year's free agents, he'd end up losing those he had, such as Giambi and Isringhausen and Tejada. What he needed was a different way to evaluate them. "In what amounted to a systematic scientific investigation of their sport," Lewis wrote in his introduction, "the Oakland front office had reexamined everything from the market price of foot speed to the inherent difference between the average major league player and the superior Triple-A one." Baseball people believed they knew the answers to those questions, and all the others. But those assumptions hadn't been tested in decades, if ever, so it shouldn't be surprising that many of them turned out to be wrong. From that gap between the assumed and the actual, Beane and his assistants were able to use their limited budget to construct division-winning teams.

The reaction to *Moneyball* was immediate. Inside baseball's orbit, it divided everyone—general managers, scouts, journalists, even fans—into warring camps. A small percentage of baseball executives instantly grasped the concept and set out to find additional opportunities hidden in baseball's vast storehouse of data. One of those was Epstein, the Yale graduate Lucchino had hired to run the Red Sox. (To enable Epstein to go all in on data analysis, the Red Sox hired Bill James to advise him.)

In the other camp was just about everyone else. That included the general managers of most of the bigger clubs, for whom the system was working. It included nearly all the field managers, baseball lifers who had come up following and then repeating all the unwritten rules about how the game was meant to be played. It included the dozens of scouts employed by every big-league club, who were tasked with spending month after month on the road, hunting down prospects, in search of what they called "intangibles"— aspects of a player's ability that only they could recognize. And, as Lewis would point out in a *Sports Illustrated* essay about the reaction to *Moneyball* in March 2004, it included the vast majority of journalists covering baseball. Because a big-league team is a coveted beat, many baseball writers were veterans in their 40s and 50s who had been watching the game—200 games every year, in fact, including preseason exhibitions and playoffs—for their entire adult lives. They didn't need numbers to tell them what good hitting was, or what an elite fielder looked like. They knew it when they saw it, didn't they? If not, what had they been doing in press box after press box for all those nights?

A handful of the men who owned or operated big-league franchises realized the book's wider implications. "Baseball people look at the bottom line differently," said Paul Godfrey, a former head of the Municipality of Metropolitan Toronto and publisher of the *Toronto Sun*, said when we talked in 2005. At the time, he had been serving as the chief executive officer of the Toronto Blue Jays for five years. He was still trying to figure out the lack of logic he saw all around him. "After every out, if there's nobody on base, they've got to throw the ball around. Everybody's got to touch it, like it's some mystical thing, though there's absolutely no reason why they should. In the same way, I don't think that even today half the organizations in baseball are run the way someone would run their private business, which is what earned them the money to buy a team in the first place. Baseball teams are looked at with a different set of principles. To me, that's a ridiculous situation."

In a real business, Godfrey understood, companies that were having success using unorthodox methods were studied, and often copied. In the case of the A's, who clearly had been mystifyingly successful, someone had gone to the trouble of spending an entire season with the team and then written a book that revealed exactly what they were doing differently. Not only was that methodology *not* being studied, it was excoriated by most rival general managers and team presidents, who couldn't get on the record fast enough that they had no intention of reading the book. That was annoying to Lewis, perhaps. But it was fortuitous for those owners and general managers who did understand what applying data analysis to the decisions made by a sports franchise could mean.

Because the methodology worked. And like most methodologies, it worked even better if you had money to put behind it. The Red Sox weren't a low-budget team in the abstract, but they were when compared with the Yankees, who earned more from their radio contract every season than some teams earned from local television. John Henry had embraced data analysis in his options-trading career, so it made sense for him to use it with his baseball team. Epstein, his general manager, hadn't played past high school, so he wasn't burdened with preconceived notions of how the game should look at the professional level. And you could hire a stadium full of young analysts with laptops for what the Yankees were paying Jason Giambi. "Theo was *Moneyball* with money," the Blue Jays' Ricciardi told me when I saw him in March of 2005, a few months after the Red Sox had finally won the World Series.

Even though few owners of MLB teams had taken the time to understand *Moneyball*, enough of them were intrigued by the concept that young general managers with gaudy degrees but little or no background as players were becoming trendy hires. One of those, as Beane feared, was DePodesta, who was plucked away from Oakland by the big-budget Los Angeles Dodgers. But while Epstein was perceived as the archetype of the successful use of analytics, DePodesta came to represent its failure.

When DePodesta arrived at Harvard in the fall of 1981, he had his future planned. Asked what he might like to major in, he handed his freshman adviser his schedule for the next four years. "Time slots, all the classes I was going to take, everything," he says. "And the guy stared at it, flipped it over to the back, then looked at me and said, 'Where's law school?'" Such certitude melted away as college progressed. In his senior year, DePodesta interviewed with banks and consulting firms, but realized he didn't have a passion for those professions. He decided to send letters to sports teams, only to wind up with a pile of rejections on nice stationery. Finally, he landed an unpaid internship with a Canadian Football League team, the Baltimore Stallions. (This was during the brief period when the CFL, bizarrely, included a division of US-based teams.) That fall of 1995, he started volunteering at night for a minor-league hockey team, trying to stay in sports. He knew law school lurked around the corner. About ready to give up, he used a distant contact to approach the MLB franchise in Cleveland. "Two weeks later," DePodesta says, "I was in spring training with the American League champions."

DePodesta thought he knew baseball. He had followed the game his whole life, then played for the Harvard junior varsity for a year. "It took me less than a week to realize I knew nothing, absolutely nothing," he says. From that humility came insight. "I don't have 30 years' experience," he says. "I didn't play in the big leagues. I didn't coach and manage in the minors for 15 years. I had to find a way to evaluate guys in order to make decisions. I knew I wasn't good enough to walk into a high school game, point to some kid, and say, 'He's going to be a star.'" He started exploring other methods to gauge the inherent value of a player. At one point, DePodesta's parents visited, and he explained to them what he did each day. "As I did, I realized that we were doing a lot of the same things as other businesses," he says. "We had to make the same decisions and deal with a lot of the same issues, at least in a parallel format." As he'd later tell Beane, "We're glorified human resources men. That's all we are."

Beane hired him away from Cleveland in 1998. Beane was headed in that direction, anyway, looking for clues to why terrific natural athletes like himself hadn't succeeded in the majors. But much of the innovative thinking that Beane gets credit for, DePodesta actually did. When the Dodgers came looking for a general manager before the 2004 season, the success that Oakland had managed with a tiny payroll—four straight postseason appearances—made them salivate over what the same approach might accomplish with money. The club's owner at the time, Frank McCourt, happened to have been one of the losing bidders when John Henry and Tom Werner bought the Red Sox. Perhaps in search of his own Theo Epstein, he asked DePodesta, who wasn't even a decade removed from Harvard at the time, to apply his magic to a well-funded ball club.

DePodesta, predictably, valued some players on the Dodger roster less than other general managers did. He made a series of unpopular trades, sending off several fan favorites in exchange for players who, DePodesta believed, had unseen value buried deep in their statistical profiles. Some of those, such as pitcher Brad Penny, worked out well. Others, such as first baseman Hee-seop Choi, didn't. To DePodesta, that was how probability worked. He'd made the best assessment he could with the information he had, but that didn't guarantee success, only the best possible chance of it. "Our industry is an outcome-based industry, but I focus on process," he told me. "A lot of times in baseball, people say, 'We'll see in five or six years if it was a good pick.' No! You had to make the pick today, so was it a good decision? Forget about whether it was a good outcome. Was the process leading up to it sound? If it was, you move on. That's how I judge what we do."

In 2004, most of DePodesta's bets came through. The Dodgers won 93 games and the National League West. In 2005, the Dodgers slumped to 71–91, their worst season in more than a decade. DePodesta understood that he was perceived as a failure, but he believed that perception was incorrect. He had a better sense of the value of players than the general managers of the San Diego Padres, Arizona Diamondbacks, and San Francisco Giants, all teams that had finished ahead of him in the division—not because he was so insightful, but because he had better information. Over that one season, a perilously small sample size, it turned out that the short-term assessments DePodesta had made had worked out poorly. That meant little, unless the owner of the team you worked for thought otherwise. Many of the baseball writers who covered the Dodgers or wrote columns about the team disdained DePodesta's emphasis on data analysis. They nicknamed him "Google Boy" and wrote that the disastrous season proved that DePodesta's way of appraising the game didn't work. McCourt read the criticism of his general manager in the *Los Angeles Times* day after day. When the season ended, DePodesta was fired.

AS AN EASILY quantifiable sequence of one-on-one confrontations between pitchers and batters, baseball was particularly susceptible to new strategies based on data analysis. But other sports, notably basketball, also generated plenty of data that could be collated, assessed, and used to question received wisdom.

Fortuitously, a new generation of owners, many of whom had become rich not in traditional business but in hedge funds and internet start-ups, had started buying NBA teams at the turn of the millennium. Unlike NFL teams, which are passed from one generation to the next like family heirlooms, NBA teams change hands fairly often. During the 10 years from 2000 to 2009, only five NFL franchises were sold. The new owners were old-school capitalists like Woody Johnson of the Johnson & Johnson fortune, Home Depot's Arthur Blank, and real estate magnate Stephen Ross. In the same period, twice as many NBA teams changed hands. In 2010 and 2011, seven more sales were consummated. That's 17 franchises, or far more than half the league, that welcomed new owners over little more than a decade.

Many of those new NBA owners had become rich not in manufacturing, the way the previous generation had done, but in the virtual realms of the internet and finance. Most of them were in their 40s or 50s and had made their fortunes in ways that owed at least as much to disrupting conventional wisdom as to following it. They understood the value of information—which was, in some form, what had made most of them rich. They had every intention of using it to run the new businesses they'd acquired for, in most cases, several hundred million dollars. "When I came in, many of the teams were family owned and had been for 20 or more years," says the Boston Celtics' Wyc Grousbeck, a venture capitalist. "They had been bought for $10 million or $12 million. But the technology revolution that began in the 1990s spawned new values for these teams. We used to be broadcast around Boston. Now we have a huge market in China." The same technology revolution, Grousbeck noted, had created a new class of American entrepreneur. "Many of us were college athletes, so we're competitive," he says. "Most of us became venture capitalists. We were interested in owning teams, but then the numbers involved became so large that we needed to create groups. But that's how VC works. You get a bunch of people together, you form a team, you make an investment."

At the time that Grousbeck started looking at the Celtics, most prospective owners still didn't regard a sports team primarily as an investment, and they weren't bringing analytics to bear on the purchase. "I could do better elsewhere, to be honest, managing my own money," said Jeff Vinik, a fund manager at Fidelity who invested $10 million in the Red Sox as part of Henry and Werner's group in 2002. Later, Vinik would buy the NHL's Tampa Bay Lightning and use his experience in finance to transform that team into one of the savviest across all sports. For the moment, though, he merely wanted something enjoyable to do with the second half of his career. "Like buying a boat," said Randy Vataha, the former NFL wide receiver who helps broker franchise sales. "'I have enough money, I'll get a boat.'"

————————

GROUSBECK LED THE group that bought the Celtics in 2002, the same year that John Henry's New England Sports Ventures group took possession of the Red Sox a few miles down Storrow Drive.

By then, the going rate for an NBA team was $280 million. That's what Mark Cuban had paid for the Dallas Mavericks in 2000, and that deal included a half-interest in the American Airlines Center, the facility the Mavericks would share with the NHL's Dallas Stars when it opened the following year. Grousbeck and his partners paid an astonishing $350 million for the Celtics, whose prime asset was history: at that point, the franchise had won 16 championships, an NBA record. "Our goal as an ownership group is to raise more championship banners," Grousbeck announced at the press conference, which is what new owners always say after they buy a team.

Grousbeck approached his stewardship of the Celtics like a fan; he was willing to lose money in the service of that next championship. The goal was to spread the losses around, so nobody had to lose too much. With that in mind, he and his partners—his father, Irv, and Bain Capital's Steve Pagliuca—corralled more than a dozen additional investors. As long as the team stayed solvent, he knew, any of those investors would be able to cash out, probably at a healthy profit. "We were overpaying," he says now. "But I wanted to get hold of the Celtics and go win the championship. I was convinced we would be able to do it without going broke if I had enough partners with me."

To help them consummate the sale, Grousbeck and Pagliuca hired a strategy consulting firm called EY-Parthenon. One of the two Parthenon employees who worked closely on the project was Daryl Morey, a 29-year-old statistical analyst. After growing up near Cleveland, Morey completed a computer science degree at Northwestern. Then he added a business degree at MIT's Sloan School of Management. He had consulted for one of the groups that had tried to buy the Red Sox. "I was the low, low-level guy," he says. That group's idea was to buy both the Red Sox and the Celtics and then construct a cable network around the two equities. Instead, Major League Baseball engineered the sale to Henry and Werner. "And we were ready to jump off the 20th floor of the building when we didn't get the bid," Morey says.

That's when Grousbeck emerged with an enticing offer for the Celtics. One Friday morning, Grousbeck convened his group of advisers, including the consultants from Parthenon, to discuss the week ahead. At the time, he was still seeking additional capital. He would be spending the following week in meetings with potential investors, explaining how he planned to run the team. To do that, he realized, he needed to know far more about restrictions that the NBA put on each team's player payroll than the little he'd gleaned by following the Celtics through the newspapers. "I really need to understand the salary cap better," he said to the assembled group. "And I guess I need to understand it by 9 a.m. Monday."

Grousbeck figured someone would spend the weekend Googling, "and then I'd learn something on Sunday night," he says. When the phone rang on Sunday, it was Morey. "I'm going to put you on speaker because I have some people here," Morey told him. Instead of using the internet, Morey had traveled to New York on Friday, talked his way into the NBA office on Fifth Avenue, and spent the weekend getting a crash course on the salary cap from the league executives who were tasked with implementing it. When he called Grousbeck, he was with several of those executives, including the league consul. Grousbeck was so impressed that he offered Morey a job. When the sale went through, Morey became the Celtics' senior vice president.

Grousbeck inherited a business that was being run essentially the way it had been the decade before, and all the decades before that. Season ticket information was stuffed into individual file folders

with notes such as "Be nice to this guy, he did us a favor." Grousbeck
set out to computerize the ticketing effort, but he didn't spend much
time on the tech side. "I was a history major," he says. "I'm a liberal
arts guy." Morey started on that project. Then he shifted to others as
the months passed.

When Grousbeck hired Danny Ainge as his general manager in 2003, it didn't occur to either the new owner or the former player, coach, and commentator to apply Morey's knowledge of
data analysis to the basketball side of the operation. But it occurred
to Morey. And when he suggested it, Grousbeck didn't object. So,
Morey began splitting time between the team's business offices on
Causeway Street, adjacent to Boston's North Station, and the practice facility, which was then in Waltham, a half hour's drive away.
Within a few weeks, he was providing the Celtics with the basketball equivalent of what DePodesta had done for the A's.

Ainge was an unlikely Beane. He operated intuitively, much like
an old baseball scout. But he was also a natural contrarian who was
open to alternative methodologies, especially if he felt they could
give him an edge. Morey started by analyzing the college draft. "If
you're in sports for more than two months," he says, "it becomes
clear that the biggest leverage comes in getting the right players."
He tried to understand which attributes correlated most directly
with doing well in the NBA. First, he had to define that success. He
sorted out the top third of draft picks, based on factors such as the
number of minutes they played once they arrived in the NBA, and
whether a player had become a starter by his third season. Then
he used a regression model to see which college statistics for each
position, as modified for the level of play in each conference, could
be used as predictors of future success. "You take out the noise level
and you say, 'Which are the things that really matter statistically to

determine whether you really have a successful draft choice in front of you?'" is how Grousbeck explains it. "'If you compare Player A and Player B, which are the elements that really matter?'"

What Morey learned surprised everyone. Take point guards, for example. Small differences in scoring average—18 points a game, compared with, say, 16—turned out to be irrelevant. Even more counterintuitive, since the most important skill a point guard can have is to distribute the ball to his scorers, the same was true about differences in assists. "And we're like, 'Of course they matter!'" Grousbeck says. "One guy has 18 points and 11 assists a game, another has 16 points and 10 assists. Why would I take the 16 and 10, assuming that they're from the same kind of school?"

Morey explained that putting too much emphasis on those numbers could easily lead a team in the wrong direction. Instead, the strongest correlation by far between college and pro success for point guards involved two statistical categories: rebounds and free throws attempted. The explanation he gave sounded convincing. As a point guard, how much you scored and how many assists you accrued depended on who your teammates were, and even what kind of offense your team was running. But for someone who is typically the smallest player on the floor, getting rebounds is evidence of a personal trait: the willingness to endure physical contact from the larger bodies around you. That willingness would serve you well in the NBA. "It means you're not afraid of getting your nose broken in there," Grousbeck says. Similarly, getting fouled frequently while shooting meant that you typically penetrated into the lane, but also that you were quick enough to get past the man who was guarding you, who then ended up having to foul you in order to prevent a basket.

Even a high number of turnovers, historically seen as a detriment, served to identify value. College coaches tend to want to control as much of the game as possible, Morey explains. "So, if there's a guy who is turning the ball over a lot, and the coach is still playing him, he must be hyper-talented."

When the Celtics applied these metrics to the 2006 draft, they highlighted an unheralded sophomore off a mediocre Kentucky team. His unlikely name was Rajon Rondo. The previous season, the scrawny Rondo, who stood just six foot one and weighed 170 pounds, had averaged 11.2 points a game, which ranked him below 25 other players in the Southeastern Conference alone. More relevant to Morey, he had managed to grab 209 rebounds, which put him just outside the top 10 among all SEC players. He had gone to the foul line more than 100 times in both his freshman and sophomore season. As it happened, Ainge had seen Rondo play and come away impressed. Whether Morey's analysis was reinforcing Ainge's existing perspective or whether Ainge used his visceral opinion of Rondo to validate the numbers is impossible to parse. Either way, the two methods of evaluating talent had converged on the same player.

On draft day, Grousbeck finalized a trade with Phoenix that moved the Celtics up in the draft order to 21st. Ainge chose Rondo. By his second season, Rondo was starting at point guard and playing just short of 30 minutes a game. That season, 2007–08, he helped lead the Celtics to their 17th championship.

———

ONE DAY IN 2003, one of Morey's former colleagues at Parthenon introduced him to Jessica Gelman, who was making the same kind of progress on the business side of the New England Patriots that

Morey was making with the Celtics. Gelman had played basketball at Harvard while majoring in psychology. As part of her studies, she ran an experiment on a local high school team that involved having them shoot free throws under casual circumstances, and then in the clutch. "I remember just sitting there running regressions, trying to determine whether there was anything that was statistically significant," she says. (There was: whether foul shooters' performance changed under pressure, either better or worse, depended on their psychological profile.)

She'd gone on to play professionally in Israel. Then she took a job in consulting, which she disliked. While at Harvard Business School at the end of 2001, she did a project for the Patriots. That led to a full-time job after she graduated the following spring. The Patriots' owner, Robert Kraft, had a background that was about as old-school as it comes. He had made his money by manufacturing and selling cardboard boxes. "But he was a disruptor," Gelman says, and Kraft liked the idea of hiring this obviously intelligent person with a unique skill set and then figuring out what to do with her.

Gelman started by looking at the ways the Patriots did business, from ticketing to retail to fan relationships. At one point, she realized that the team had thousands of fans in Canada whom nobody had ever reached out to, fans loyal enough to travel hundreds of miles to see a home game. They constituted an unrealized opportunity of some kind, if the team could figure out how to access it. "My entire life, I was like, 'Just because they say this is the way it should be done, doesn't mean it's the right way,'" she says. When *Moneyball* came out in 2003, she devoured it. It taught her that the way you perceive the world, with whatever biases you might have, was probably causing you to miss something. "If you cut the information a little bit differently, you get insights," she says. "And now we had the means, with computers, to crunch much more data than ever before." In some cases, that was likely to contradict the biases. As a basketball player, she was keenly aware that the player who feeds the scorer gets an assist, but the pass that initiates the play is lost in the statistical ether. "You don't get an assist, but you know you did something well," she says. That, too, she understood, was quantifiable.

The night they met, Morey took Gelman to the Celtics' practice facility, where they played two-on-two basketball. He invited her to join his fantasy football league, where he was applying everything he was learning about analytics to finding undervalued NFL players to draft. The two were kindred spirits, having each taken a roundabout route to the industry and arrived at it with a mind-set that was skeptical of anything that couldn't be validated. In the fall of 2005, Morey started teaching a class at MIT called "Analytical Sports Management." Gelman asked if she could sit in. "I figured I could learn something," she says. Within a few weeks, Morey had asked her to co-teach the class. He had started to make inroads on the basketball side of the Celtics' operations, but she was a step or two ahead of everyone else in the NFL on the business side.

The following February, Morey interviewed to become the assistant general manager of the Houston Rockets. (The job offered a path to the general manager's position after the 2006–07 season, when Carroll Dawson, who had been with the Rockets for more than a quarter century, would retire.) A few weeks later, Morey accepted an offer.

Morey insisted to Gelman that he would continue to teach the class at MIT, flying to Boston every other week, but she convinced him that trying to do that would be absurd. Instead, she suggested hosting an annual analytics conference with guest speakers. When months passed, Gelman figured Morey was submerged in his new duties in Houston and didn't have time for anything else. But in the summer of 2006, Morey called Gelman and said he'd been considering the idea of a conference and wanted to try to create one. He liked the idea of staying affiliated with MIT. Just as important to him, he felt an annual conference would help develop an analytics subculture within professional sports.

The first MIT Sloan Sports Analytics Conference was held on Saturday, February 10, 2007, in three classrooms. One was about half a mile away from the others. "Everyone had to put on their coats and walk for 10 minutes in the cold," Gelman says. Most of the 150 attendees came from inside the business, but some were friends of Gelman's who just thought it sounded interesting. Ricciardi, who had left Beane's A's for the Blue Jays five years before, was a keynote speaker.

During the third conference, in the winter of 2009, Mark Cuban participated. The owner of the Dallas Mavericks, Cuban had made his fortune with a company called Broadcast.com, an internet radio platform he sold to Yahoo in 1999 for $5.7 billion. Though the platform turned out to be nearly worthless for Yahoo, Cuban parlayed his take into ownership of the Mavericks, a chain of movie theaters, investment in high-definition TV, and a position in sports as an innovator, ready to listen to new ideas. Getting him to the conference was something of a coup.

At the conference, Cuban revealed he had been collecting data on his players since he bought the team. Analyzing that data, he found "repetitive elements that we can use to impact our decision-making, whether it's lineup combinations, lineups versus lineups, coaching influence, whether coaches put together the best lineups, and how often they do it."

Nothing about Cuban's comments was particularly astonishing. *Moneyball* had been published more than five years before, so it wasn't such a conceptual leap that someone was applying some of the same ideas to basketball. But the fact that it was Cuban, not just the insular group of quants at the Sloan conference, made news in mainstream media outlets—the NBA's most dynamic owner had publicly embraced analytics. The league would never be the same again.

———————

MOREY BECAME THE Rockets' general manager in May of 2007. During the previous season, as an apprentice under Dawson, he had started to shift the team's emphasis toward aspects of the game that weren't yet considered especially valuable, such as three-point shooting and defensive skills. In 2005–06, the season before Morey arrived in Houston, the Rockets attempted slightly more than 17 shots a game from outside the three-point arc. Morey innately understood the wisdom in taking as many of those shots as possible. (You don't need an MIT degree to figure out the math: you get three points for each shot you make, rather than two.) Rather than trying to work the ball inside for an easy jumper, lay-up, or dunk, he wanted his players to look for those slightly harder shots that were worth 50 percent more if they went in.

Eventually, Morey hired a Stanford Business School graduate, Sam Hinkie, as his own DePodesta. Together, they urged the Rockets' coaching staff to design plays that would get the ball to open shooters beyond the three-point line. Then they watched the records fall. By the end of Morey's tenure, the 2019–20 season, the Rockets were launching more than 45 three-pointers a game. They had created an entirely new architecture for an NBA offense.

To Morey, that was the low-hanging fruit. The more nuanced

impact came from using data to identify player attributes that contributed to winning games without showing up in the conventional
metrics. He needed a different way of evaluating the league's talent
for the same reason that Beane did with baseball's A's: the Rockets
didn't have as much money to spend as the teams they were competing against. Unlike baseball, the NBA has a cap on player salaries.
But by the time that Morey arrived, a huge percentage of the payroll
the Rockets were permitted to spend was already committed to two
players with long-term contracts: Tracy McGrady and the seven-
foot, six-inch Yao Ming.

Using a variation of the methodology he had first used in Boston, Morey identified Shane Battier of the Memphis Grizzlies as
an undervalued player who could help the Rockets. Battier didn't
score much, or gather many rebounds, or accumulate many assists,
the statistics that serve as the batting average, home runs, and RBIs
of basketball. But two months after Morey arrived in Houston, he
convinced Dawson to acquire Battier. "People knew of Daryl's
background," Battier told me in 2021. "But nobody knew what he
was actually doing, this mad scientist running an experiment. And
I was the first petri dish. I didn't understand exactly how Daryl
thought until probably midway through the year. But as I started
to spend more time with him and with Sam, I realized that the
way they approached the game and how they used their prepara-
tion and their scouting reports was much different than anything
I had encountered."

Morey understood that the unique attributes of Battier's game
were ideal complements to those of the Rockets' two stars. "Shane
was, like, engineered out of a lab to work with McGrady and Yao,"
Morey explains. Yao wasn't athletic, not even for a seven-footer.
Getting him the ball was an arduous task. It had to be placed per-

fectly, floated into his hands at the exact moment he reached out
for it. Battier, who was probably the best entry passer in the NBA
at the time, described it like scoring 100 on a Skee-Ball machine.
"Once Yao caught it, though, it was over," Morey says. By some statistical metrics, Yao was the most efficient NBA player ever from
inside five feet.

The challenge was that every team the Rockets played understood that. They knew that Yao was almost certain to score if he
could get the ball near the basket, so they would typically assign
another player to leave the man he was guarding and help prevent
that entry pass from getting through. The advantage for the Rockets
was that it would leave another player open, usually on the perimeter. In that situation, having a player who could dependably make
three-pointers when nobody was guarding him became crucial.
That, too, was Battier. In 2006–07, his first season in Houston, he
shot almost as well from beyond the three-point arc (42.1 percent)
as he did from inside it (44.6). "So he was almost a perfect fit on
offense," Morey says. "And on defense, he was like this program-
mable basketball machine."

Battier had majored in religion at Duke. "But I did take a
statistics class," he says now. "I understood probabilities." Morey
explained the game to him as a vast decision tree. At any
moment, every player had one optimal action he could be taking, and some number of others that were less than optimal. "So
I started to look at basketball in terms of 'there's a right answer
and a wrong answer everywhere you go on the court,'" Battier
says. "I have to do the best job I can of picking the right answer
as often as possible. That was true when we had the ball, and it
was true in terms of whoever I happened to be guarding." The
goal on defense, Battier realized, was to force his opponent to

make a suboptimal choice. If every player on a team could do that most of the time, that team was highly likely to win.

The Rockets had been a mid-level team before Morey arrived—fifth in the Western Conference in the regular season, first-round playoff losers. Beginning in 2009–10, they missed the playoffs for three seasons in succession. The conventional wisdom was that Morey was Billy Beane, except that instead of not being able to continue his magic in the postseason, his teams didn't even win enough to get there. "The Genius Who Outsmarted Himself" is how the headline in one SB Nation piece described Morey. But then something happened. In 2013, the Rockets finished eighth in the West and edged into the playoffs. In 2014, they finished fourth. The year after that, they were second in the West and lost in the conference final. No team in basketball was shooting, or had ever shot, more three-pointers. In 2017–18, in a little-recognized but nonetheless astounding statistical achievement, Morey's Rockets would become the first team in NBA history to attempt more three-pointers than two-pointers over the course of a season.

Unfortunately for the Rockets, another team understood Morey's insights, and was in the process of doing an even better job of applying them. For four of the five seasons between 2014–15 and 2018–19, the Rockets lost to the Golden State Warriors in the playoffs. Not coincidentally, the Warriors happened to have Steph Curry, who won consecutive Most Valuable Player awards largely by launching 10 or 11 three-pointers every game with an almost imperceptibly quick flick of his hands, and making nearly half of them.

Those same five years, from 2015 to 2019, the Warriors went to the NBA Finals every season, and won three championships. Along the way, they designed and built a $1.4 billion arena, the Chase Center, on the water in San Francisco—an arena that already had brought in $2 billion in revenue from suite sales and corporate spon-sorships by the time it opened shortly before the COVID-19 pan-demic hit. While Morey and Hinkie were extending the boundaries of analytics on the court in Houston, Joe Lacob and the Warriors had taken the best practices of Silicon Valley venture capital and applied them to the entire organization.

3

LIGHT-YEARS AHEAD

IT WAS STILL dark one morning in the early spring of 2016 when Joe Lacob drove his Mercedes station wagon through the Stanford University campus. He parked near the business school, then walked down a sidewalk through a drizzle to meet a group of Silicon Valley executives. The ex-CEO of OpenTable, now a partner at the venture capital firm Andreessen Horowitz, was coming. So were a founder of the online-learning start-up Curious and a managing director of Vanguard Ventures. On another morning, they all might have met at a charity event, or a TED Talk. But this was a Tuesday, and that meant basketball.

At the time, Lacob had been the majority owner of the Golden State Warriors for nearly six years. He had worked in venture capital for three decades, much of that for the Silicon Valley firm Kleiner Perkins Caufield & Byers. The previous night, he'd watched his Warriors play a home game in Oakland. Now he seemed tired. "The Tuesday mornings after we play Monday nights are the hardest," he said. The basketball court, which is normally used by students and faculty members, had a tidy, corporate look: gleaming hardwood surrounded by plexiglass walls. In his Warriors T-shirt and shorts, Lacob pushed his hands against the glass and stretched his legs. "Honestly, this is my favorite time of the week," he told me.

One by one, other players arrived. Most had known Lacob for years, since early in his career at Kleiner Perkins, which is when he helped start this pickup game. There was no reason for anyone to be deferential to him. But owning a basketball team has cachet, especially when that team had come to rank among the best in NBA history. Nobody mentioned his own business affairs, but everyone was eager to talk about Lacob's. "Joe, good to see Barnes back," someone said, referring to Harrison Barnes, a Warriors player who had missed games with an injury.

The group ran the court for an hour, playing games to 13 by twos and threes. Lacob, who was 60 years old, had an open, expressive face and broad shoulders. He was six feet tall, but seemed taller. He was one of the older players there, and he clearly had thought through his strengths and limitations. He would head to a particular spot—often one on the right side, about a third of the way around the three-point arc—and wait. When he saw an opportunity, he called for the ball or cut along the arc toward it. If he received a pass, he would usually shoot. His shot was peculiar, fluttering like a knuckleball, rotating only a few times before it reached the basket, but it went in more often than not. The first game ended with his sinking a three-pointer, then raising his arms in triumph. A few minutes later, his team moved in position to win again. Lacob stood at the top of the key with the ball. "Here comes the game winner," he said to nobody in particular. Then he sank the shot.

When he finished playing, Lacob wiped the perspiration from his hands with a towel. He pulled out his championship ring and passed it around for examination. "They've been asking to see it for two months," he explained. The ring had an extravagant and revealing design. One diamond had been inlaid for each of the 200-odd games the Warriors won from 2010, when Lacob and his investors bought the team, through that year's NBA Finals. "How much does this thing weigh?" asked Tom McConnell, the managing director of Vanguard Ventures, lifting his hand up and down as if trying to estimate its value.

After the pickup game, Lacob pulled on a sweatshirt and went to breakfast at a cafeteria on the ground floor. He was there so often that one of the smoothies on the menu, involving orange juice, vanilla yogurt, bananas, and strawberries, had been named for him. He pointed this out, then ordered one. When I asked him about the previous night's game, he could hardly contain himself. He boasted that the Warriors were playing in a far more sophisticated fashion than the rest of the league. "We've crushed them on the basketball court, and we're going to for years because of the way we've built this team," he said. But what really set the franchise apart, he said, was the way it operated as a business. "We're light-years ahead of probably every other team in structure, in planning, in how we're going to go about things," he said, a quote that would resonate around the league when it was published in the *New York Times Magazine*, earning him the derogatory nickname "Buzz Lightyear."

"We're going to be a handful for the rest of the NBA to deal with for a long time."

LACOB WASN'T THE first venture capitalist to buy a franchise, but he was the first to operate one according to what might be called Silicon Valley precepts: nimble management, open communication, integrating the wisdom of outside advisers, and continuous reevaluation of what companies do and how they do it. None of that typically happens in professional sports. Most franchise owners of previous generations became wealthy by mastering businesses that did one specific thing, if only because that was the way that people used to become wealthy in America. They ran their teams, for better or worse, in the same autocratic, hidebound fashion that they ran those companies. Lacob preferred to surround himself with expertise and exploit it.

Applying the techniques of high-tech venture capital to professional sports proved to be a brilliant strategy. When I first went to visit Lacob in May 2015, his Warriors had emerged as a basketball powerhouse, though they hadn't yet won an NBA title. By the time I saw him next, almost a year later, they were reigning champions. And I soon understood that this once-sclerotic franchise was being run at a level of imaginative efficiency that the industry of sports had never seen.

By the time that he bought the Warriors, Lacob had been thinking about how to be an owner for many years. "The first day that I met Joe, in 1998, he told me that he wanted to buy the Warriors," Warren Thaler, a former Cleveland Cavaliers director who served with Lacob on the board of Align Technology, told me. In fact, Lacob had been interested in becoming an owner since he walked into a Boys Club in New Bedford, Massachusetts, his hometown, when he was nine years old and saw his first parquet basketball floor. "It sounds crazy and stupid, but it's true," he says. "Anyone who knows me knows that, once I had a little money, I was planning for the day when I could own a team." The first in his family to attend college, he graduated from the University of California Irvine, then earned additional degrees at UCLA and Stanford. By then, his life's blueprint was complete.

He would use the first half of it to get rich, then devote the rest to acquiring and running a sports franchise.

As his first foray into sports ownership, Lacob invested in the American Basketball League. The ABL was the second of two women's leagues that appeared at about the same time in the late 1990s—the one not backed by the NBA. The league was essentially a start-up, trying to create room for itself in the crowded space of American professional sports. Lacob was still investing in and running companies for Kleiner Perkins at the time, and he treated the ABL as though it were one of them. "It was just fascinating to watch him go from evaluating an investment to 'How can we make this the best possible product it can be?'" says Gary Cavalli, who served as the league's chief executive. "What kind of ball? Quarters or halves? Short shorts or longer shorts? He's very, very smart and very, very rich, but unlike some rich people, he actually listens to other people. He does believe that other people have value. And he enjoys the exchange of ideas, however contentious that may be." As the league faltered, Lacob took over the process of finding investors and top executives. "He had done a lot of research to get to those names," Cavalli says. He paused. "He could have replaced me," he said.

Later, Lacob looked back on the experience with equal parts pain and understanding. "You need to fail at something to appreciate what it's like to succeed," he said. "I failed at the ABL. I lost a lot of money. I was the largest single owner." The lesson it taught Lacob was that start-ups succeeded even less often in sports than they did in other businesses. "If you're going to succeed, it takes a long time," he said. "And even then, it's very unlikely. That's why I wanted to join the big boys."

After Pagliuca and the Grousbecks bought the Boston Celtics, Lacob joined their group as a minority investor. But he never stopped looking for a team of his own. He had Randy Vataha, the franchise broker, on a retainer, searching for opportunities. Every so often, one would come close to happening, but either the price or the geography or the circumstances wouldn't be right. Lacob's life and career were in the Bay Area, and he felt strongly that he didn't want to be an absentee owner. "I believe that you need to be really involved," he says. "You need to live locally, and you need to be very, very involved."

In 2004, Lacob almost bought the Oakland A's. He had been working on the sale for three years. "I literally signed the deal," he says, but it didn't end up closing. Soon after, he came close to paying $180 million for baseball's Anaheim Angels. He'd worked seven years as a peanut vendor at Anaheim Stadium—"I can tell you everything about it, like it was yesterday," he says. But he'd always had a deeper interest in basketball. And he had a strong sense that he didn't want to own a team until he was done with venture capital. "I knew in my gut, even though I was looking at teams for years and years, that being an owner while I had a full-time job didn't feel right," he says. When he left Kleiner Perkins to buy the Warriors, he walked away from "a lot of money." The company wanted him to continue. "But I wanted to be great at this."

———

THE $450 MILLION that Lacob and his partners ended up paying Chris Cohan for the Warriors in 2010 was deemed wildly excessive by nearly everyone. Larry Ellison, one of the richest people in the world, was a losing bidder. It was more than anyone had ever spent on an NBA franchise, and this wasn't the Lakers or the Celtics or even the Knicks. This was the Warriors, a team that played in backwater Oakland and hadn't won a championship since 1975. It wasn't just a bad team, but a team that seemed permanently stuck in a state of irrelevance. "The little engine that couldn't" is how Nick Swinmurn, the founder of Zappos and a lifelong fan of the Warriors, described it. During Cohan's 16 years of ownership, the Warriors had reached the NBA playoffs only once. Sixteen of the league's 30 teams advance every season. "So, on an odds basis," Lacob notes, "you're supposed to make it half the time. Something was very wrong."

Such ineptitude had eroded interest. There were only 7,000 season ticket holders. The arena where the team played, in a vast parking lot beside a highway, was laughably outdated. Its corridors were narrow, its catering facilities rudimentary. It didn't have rooms that could be leased for corporate meetings. While the league's new-est arenas had been built with palatial home clubhouses the size of health clubs, the Warriors' facilities were austere and cramped. One look at them during a road trip was said to discourage players around the league from considering the team when they became free agents.

Other potential buyers perceived the institutional decrepitude as a drawback. Lacob and his most visible partner, the Hollywood entrepreneur Peter Guber, believed it represented an opportunity. In the Warriors, Lacob saw a start-up disguised as an underperform-ing business, a sports franchise that had been run autocratically— and therefore ineptly—as the industry evolved around it. Had he come across such a company while at Kleiner Perkins, he would have tried to figure out what a proper valuation might be under better management, with an infusion of capital and best practices gleaned from successful businesses in other industries. He would have brought on board members or additional investors with rel-evant experience and skills in areas that were needed most. He would examine the company against its direct competition and hypothesize what level of success might be expected in the next 5 to 10 years. In short, he would do exactly what he did after buying the Warriors.

Venture capitalists make large investments in companies that they don't necessarily control. Lacob brought the same mind-set to his basketball team. "In venture capital, I started 70 companies," he told me. "I also watched my partners' deals, maybe 200 of them. That's a lot of companies. I thought about the way we design a board of directors, the way we design the financing. There's an architecture to it. And I started thinking about the architecture I would use when I owned and built my own team someday."

Lacob gave Guber, who owns a far smaller share, all but equal standing because Guber brought four decades of connections in movies, music, sports, and media to the deal. Together, they hired a general manager who had never worked for a team before, let alone run one, and two coaches who hadn't coached at any level. At the time, these moves were perceived around the league as rookie mistakes. But Lacob was no rookie, not at building companies. And it turned out that they were not mistakes.

———————

ONE NIGHT DURING the 2015 playoffs, shortly before the Warriors won their first title, I met Lacob at the Bridge Club, just steps from the court inside Oracle Arena. There was a chef carving turkey and servers pouring all the Dehlinger chardonnay and Radio-Coteau pinot noir anyone wanted to drink. Lacob arrived late after fighting traffic from Menlo Park. He asked politely for a turkey burger, then found a seat at a high-top table.

Between bites, Lacob greeted a steady flow of friends and colleagues, mostly recognizable names in Silicon Valley. Many of them were limited partners in the Warriors. Mark Stevens, who was a partner at Sequoia Capital when the firm helped finance Google, PayPal, and LinkedIn, walked past. So did John Walecka of Redpoint Ventures, which had helped launch Netflix, MySpace, and Stripe. On another visit, I would meet Dennis Wong, Steve Ballmer's college roommate, who served as managing director of SPI Holdings, a privately held real estate firm, and YouTube's Chad Hurley. All were part of Lacob's group of investors.

At the time, the Bridge Club had become one of the best venues for venture capital networking in the Bay Area. It was a perk for the minority owners, but it served a purpose for Lacob. Before and after each game, he made himself accessible to any investors who wanted his ear. "It's the atmosphere of knowing you have a voice, knowing you're part of this," he explained. "One thing I didn't like when I owned part of the Celtics: Was I really heard? I don't know. I wanted to make sure that when I did this, everybody got heard."

The NBA demands that each franchise confer one owner, regardless of stake size, with nearly dictatorial power. Lacob wields his softly, just as he typically sits in the back of corporate board meetings without saying much, absorbing information, then guiding the discussion toward a decision. "I'm a professional listener," he told me. "The NBA isn't like the outside world. I can do whatever I want. But you don't treat people that way."

Lacob knew how the kind of people who invest many millions of dollars into someone else's business needed to be treated. The jump in franchise valuations had changed the population of investors and their expectations. "Being a part of any ownership group nowadays, $60 million will get you about 5 percent, based on the valuation,"

Billy Beane told me in 2016. (By 2022, that percentage for a $60 million investment had diminished to maybe 2 percent, depending on the franchise.) "So you also have to sell the vision of a business that has the ability to grow. People who have that kind of money are very, very bright people. They look at these investments with a squinty eye. So you have to sell them on it."

Stevens, who invested around $50 million in the Warriors, had previously put corporate money into Nvidia and Pixelworks, among many other start-ups. He liked basketball—he'd played point guard at Culver City High, near Los Angeles—but previously only went to Warrior games when the Lakers came to town. He perceived his investment in the Warriors as a certain amount of fun, but also a sound place to park his money. "This team," he said approvingly, "is being run like a real business."

The rise in franchise valuations has also served to narrow the pool of possible majority owners. If 5 percent of the Warriors suddenly became available and you decided to buy it, it would cost at least $250 million. That's not much less than Michael Jordan and a group of partners paid for the Charlotte Hornets in 2010. But that would only get you 5 percent—the other 95 percent would be owned by others. At that price, it's no surprise that potential investors insisted on competent corporate governance. "They're used to having boards of directors that matter," Stevens said. "They're used to crisp decision-making. They're used to environments in which inputs are taken, things are evaluated, and then you make the right decision with the best available facts. That's what they're going to expect."

Part of the sales pitch involved input. With so much money involved, few investors are content to sit quietly on the sidelines. And that, by extension, has started to change the executive structure and the decision-making process of pro franchises. "It's happening by necessity because the numbers are just flat-out bigger," Lacob told me. "It's moving toward the style of doing business in Silicon Valley, the way investors interact. It's far more open. It's very different than the old model of one guy saying, 'I'm doing this, I'm doing that.'"

It's no accident that Lacob surrounded himself with venture capitalists and digital executives whose skill sets complemented his. "To be successful going forward, this needs to be a media company, a real estate company," he said. He described it as a mutual fund of interests, under the Warriors umbrella. "It's technology, streaming video, all that," he said. "It's the entertainment face beyond having just the game itself. We've got to figure out how to monetize that, and the people in our ownership group have the expertise to do that."

So, after Wong advised Lacob on the real estate purchase for the new arena, Walecka helped with the financing. When I spoke with Swinmurn, he reeled off rapid-fire opinions on the design of the Warriors' branded attire, the type of food sold at the concession stands, and other disparate topics. "Before, it was only financial capital that gave you the imperative to run everything," Guber explained. "Today, unless the capital you're putting together is financial, intellectual, reputational, experiential, and you get the very best of that, you miss the opportunity to really realize the benefit."

Sports franchises were running gourmet restaurants and concert venues, and in some places entire streets of retail outlets. They serviced fans in distant cities through audio and video streaming and proprietary content. "It's very hard when someone has had great success in another business—the fish delivery business, the box cutting business," Guber said. "And then you come into this because 'I want to buy a sports team.' That just isn't a formula for great success in today's world."

Most of the Warriors partners had no basketball experience and

weren't involved in team operations. But every so often, those partners could influence what happened on the court. John Burbank
of Passport Capital, who used a deep knowledge of mathematics in
his own investments, contributed detailed memos applying complex
metrics to potential acquisitions. "I don't know if any of it has 180ed
us on a player," Bob Myers, the Warriors' general manager, told me,
"but it has certainly moved us in a direction, one way or another.
And he's done it enough that it's just the course of things now. It's
part of the process."

————————

ONCE HE BOUGHT the Warriors, Lacob started looking for the
same kinds of executives to run the team that he'd brought together
in his investment group. Rather than industry veterans, he sought
out smart, ambitious novices who didn't have preconceived notions
about how the business should be run. "I don't like people who have
sort of done and been in the whole NBA thing for 30 years," he said.
"I heard these guys. They were going to tell me what to do and how
to run this thing. And I had my own ideas."

In 2011, he hired Myers as an assistant general manager. He promoted him to general manager a year later. Myers, now 41, lettered
in basketball at UCLA as a walk-on, studied law at Loyola Mary-
mount in Los Angeles, then started a career as an agent, representing athletes. "The reason I'm sitting here now is because of that VC
model," he told me. "I had no track record. I had no past experience.
If you only believed in past performance, you're talking to someone
else. I mean, *I* wouldn't have hired me." That 2014–15 season, Myers
was named the NBA's Executive of the Year.

Lacob's experience building a diverse portfolio of businesses prepared him for the peculiarities of owning a franchise. "I want everyone to speak up," he says. "I don't care if we yell and scream. I want that. I want open dialogue all the time." Soon after buying the team, he supervised the removal of the walls inside its corporate offices, which at the time sat atop a parking garage in downtown Oakland. The team's lawyers protested, telling Lacob that they didn't want sensitive information on computer screens to be accessible to anyone who happened to wander past. He responded that people should turn their screens in the other direction.

Lacob also wanted his executives, and even other employees, to be involved in discussions that didn't directly impact his or her area. "You're here because you're a smart person who has a perspective on our business," explained Rick Welts, the team president at the time, who ran the Warriors' daily operations. "You're expected to share that, whether or not it happens to fall into your silo of responsibility." In the same way that Burbank would occasionally make player personnel suggestions, Myers, who presided over those player personnel decisions, sat in on meetings that only indirectly affected the business side of the franchise. "He's a bright guy with a law degree who has been around this business his whole life," Welts said. "It's a valuable perspective. And the fact that a Bob Myers can come in and have a suggestion on something we might offer as a season ticket holder benefit, that's pretty unusual in our world."

At Kleiner Perkins, Lacob was often forced to change entire management teams and restructure companies before he could make them profitable. He wasn't daunted by the challenge of turning around the Warriors. "You make highly contentious decisions in venture capital all the time," said Trae Vassallo, a former Kleiner Perkins partner who worked with Lacob. "But not everybody sees them."

During a game in March 2012, Lacob took the microphone at

halftime to honor Chris Mullin, who played for Golden State from 1985 to 1997. From the moment he began speaking, Lacob was booed. It had nothing to do with Mullin. The previous week, the Warriors had sent Monta Ellis, the team's most popular player, to the Milwaukee Bucks in exchange for Andrew Bogut. With time, that trade would take its place among the most effective in basketball history. The Warriors did more than acquire Bogut, a seven-footer who had missed half that season with a broken ankle. Trading Ellis allowed Curry, the point guard, to look for his own shots instead of mainly facilitating Ellis's. In truth, Lacob hadn't wanted to trade Ellis. His basketball advisers, including NBA legend Jerry West, urged him to do it, and Lacob was persuaded. "They made their case, especially Jerry," Lacob says, "and I accepted it. They were right."

Lacob understood that the Warriors, who had a losing record, needed to be dismantled before they could be rebuilt. He often had to implement a similar strategy with struggling companies. But the fans had been hearing about long-range plans for decades and had little confidence in them. And now they no longer had Ellis. The booing continued for so long that the popular former Warrior Rick Barry had to beseech the crowd to allow the ceremony to continue. By then, Lacob was shaking. The humiliation was so public, so raw, that Lacob's friends were moved to send messages of support. Many mention the episode now, four years later, as a rite of passage. "He made some amazingly tough calls with the Warriors," says Vassallo. "Highly public. Got booed by 20,000 people for the Monta Ellis trade. But for him, it was all about 'I'm going to invest in the right people for the long run of the organization and its ultimate growth over time.' And that mind-set is exactly the sort of mind-set you have to have when you're investing in an early-stage start-up company. If you don't have the right team, if you don't have the right pipeline of people, you're not going to do very well. And you have to take a long view and not be swayed by short-term public opinion."

That fall, the team had to decide whether to extend Curry's contract. The guard had shown flashes of exceptional talent, but he kept injuring his ankles. The previous season, which was shortened by a labor dispute, he had missed 40 of 66 games. "We had to make a decision in the margins, in the gray area," Myers said. "He was hurt at the time—he'd just sprained his ankle again. My first instinct was 'This is going to be a difficult decision. This is not clear.'" Lacob let everyone else speak first. He listened to both sides. Then he asked if anyone could recall an NBA player whose career had ended because of ankle injuries. "That was just a commonsense comment," Myers says. "You see knees, you see feet, back, but rarely ankles. Looking back at the history of the league, what player could not compete and was finished because of an ankle injury that couldn't be resolved?" Nobody could think of anyone. "And that kind of made the decision for us," Myers said.

What they did by offering Curry a four-year, $44 million extension, Lacob explained later, was rely not on the future stability of Curry's anatomy so much as the composition of his psyche—his determination to push through nagging discomfort to make himself great. "Now, if we were wrong, we'd just committed $44 million to a player who can't play basketball," Myers says. "So, the risk was there." Not only did Curry develop into the sport's best player, but his paltry (in terms of NBA superstardom) $11 million annual compensation gave the Warriors ample salary cap room to surround him with other talent.

In 2011, Lacob and Guber had chosen Mark Jackson, the former St. John's and Knicks point guard, to be their team's head coach. Jackson was an unusual hire; he had played for seven NBA teams and worked as a commentator, but had never coached. In his second and third seasons, he led the Warriors to the playoffs. "We were at the zero-yard line when Mark showed up here," Myers says. "And he got us to the playoffs, and we won a round and became respectable." So, when Lacob fired him in 2014, after a 51–31 season, and replaced him with Steve Kerr, the basketball world was dismayed. It seemed like another mistake borne from inexperience by a headstrong owner. But Lacob had decided that a different type of leadership was needed for the Warriors to make the leap from a playoff team to a championship team. Such noodling with success, replacing a leader with a limited strategic vision with another who is comfortable aiming higher, rarely happens in sports. But in venture capital, it happens all the time.

Lacob had known Kerr since the late '90s. They had been part of a social group that traveled to Scotland on golfing trips. Kerr won NBA titles as a player, first with Michael Jordan and the Chicago Bulls, and later with the San Antonio Spurs. Then he ran the Phoenix Suns' front office as their general manager. He had commentated on NBA broadcasts. What he hadn't done, as the man in charge or even as an assistant, was coach a basketball team. But Lacob had an intuition that Kerr would do better in the organization's structure than the more regimented Jackson. Kerr's willingness to at least consider suggestions from almost any source might have saved the Warriors during the 2015 championship series. They were behind Cleveland, 2–1, when Nick U'Ren—Kerr's assistant, whose responsibilities included constructing the musical playlists used during practices and splicing together highlight reels—happened to be watching a tape of the 2014 playoffs. Noticing how San Antonio had defended LeBron James, he suggested that the Warriors replace Bogut in the lineup with Andre Iguodala, who is half a foot shorter but athletic enough to at least force James to work to get good shots. Kerr took the suggestion, and the Warriors didn't lose another game. Kerr publicly gave U'Ren the credit.

When he bought the team in 2010, Lacob announced that it would win an NBA championship in five years. That is exactly what happened. Along the way, Lacob never hesitated to make the moves he felt were necessary, even if he knew they would attract criticism—a strategy that Beane, who had known him since the early 2000s, believed was crucial to his success. "Purchase price, Bob Myers, make a change at coach, extending Curry—every layer, there's a decision Joe made that only he believed in," Beane told me. Apart from ending up as the correct decision, each one sent a message to the rest of the organization, and the rest of the NBA, that Lacob wasn't content to operate in a particular way just because everyone else was doing it. "Put it this way," Beane says. "Joe was the first person I ever saw drive a Tesla. And he was so excited about it. I didn't even know who Elon Musk was. And I was saying, 'It's just a car, Joe.' But it really wasn't just a car. It represented an idea to him. That's the way he works. He's just ahead of everyone else."

————

AFTER THAT FIRST championship, the Warriors won two more. From 2015 through 2019, they were the flagship franchise in the NBA, and perhaps all of professional sports. Lacob presented winning as an inevitable result of the way the team had been constructed. "The great venture capitalists who built company after company, that's not an accident," he said. "And none of this is an accident, either."

By 2019, too, the $450 million investment by Lacob and his

partners was estimated by *Forbes* to be worth more than $4 billion. Among the emergent generation of investment tycoons, that hadn't gone unnoticed. "I knew what Joe had done," said Avenue Capital's Marc Lasry, the Moroccan-born billionaire who partnered with private equity investor Wesley Edens to buy the Milwaukee Bucks in 2014 and then guided them to an NBA championship in 2021. "We're trying to do the same." Lasry insisted that he loved basketball, but the way he described his intentions sounded less like *Hoosiers* than *The Big Short*: "We looked at it and said, 'The Bucks have huge potential. We think we can bring in the way we do business and do a huge turnaround.'"

In little more than a decade since Lacob and his partners bought the Warriors, the team had compiled one of the best records, on and off the court, in NBA history. Yet I also couldn't shake the idea that the story easily could have gone in a different direction. Without a transcendent star, it seemed to me, an organization could be run impeccably but still never manage to win a championship—or even, as with Morey's tenure in Houston, come especially close. In 2019–20, a season shortened by the COVID-19 pandemic, Curry broke his left hand and played in 5 of the team's 65 games. The Warriors won just 15 of them. The same ideas were being floated in the same meetings, and all those minority investors were continuing to add value on the business side. But from NBA finalists the previous season, the Warriors tumbled to a .231 winning percentage, easily the league's worst. By 2021–22, with Curry healthy, the Warriors had become champions again.

As with Jordan and the Bulls, a strong case can be made that Curry, not Lacob's ownership group, was what separated them from the rest of the NBA during the second half of the 2010s and into the 2020s. "They did what every really good organization should do with their star," the Bucks' Lasry said. "They nurtured him. But they got lucky in that Steph became far and away the best player in the league."

At the same time, though, Curry's mere presence wouldn't have created the means to overhaul a franchise. It takes an extraordinary player to do it, but that isn't all it takes. Plenty of perennial All-Stars, alone and in tandem, never managed to win championships. The decision to keep Curry, coupled with the good fortune that he remained healthy and grew into a transcendent player, gave Lacob and Guber's structural innovations the opportunity to have their desired effect. As Lacob perceives it, Curry's dominance on the court, though essential, is inextricable from everything else he's done with the franchise over the last few years, from knocking down the office walls to the Ellis trade. "It's not just Steph Curry," he told me. "It's architecting a team, a style of play, the way they all play together. It's all extremely thought through."

This confluence of good planning and luck reminded me of a conversation I had with Lacob over a glass of wine another evening at the Bridge Club, while we were waiting for a game to start. He told me that he considered himself one of the 10 best blackjack players in the world. "I shouldn't say this," he added, "but I've won over $1 million at one sitting nine times." As in gambling, there are no certain outcomes in sports, which is exactly what makes them worth watching. Whether you're playing pickup basketball on a Tuesday morning or hoping to turn a substandard NBA franchise into a champion, all you can do is try to increase your chances of getting the outcome you desire, the same insight that Paul DePodesta had explained to me a decade before. Lacob had a knack for process. For everything he did, he had worked out a system.

As an undergraduate at Irvine, Lacob took a calculus class

from Edward Thorp, whose 1962 book *Beat the Dealer* proved that a blackjack player could gain a slight edge on the house by counting cards. Thorp was banned by casinos, so he taught his students the system, backed them on trips to Las Vegas, and shared in the rewards. Lacob was one of those students. When he goes to a casino now, his blackjack sessions aren't certainties, but Lacob has far better odds of succeeding at them than anyone else at the table. His purchase of the Warriors was basically the same thing. He counted the cards and played the odds. And he won.

4

IF YOU ARE THINKING BIG, THINK EVEN BIGGER

AFTER 33 YEARS, Donald T. Sterling's incompetence finally caught up with him. Yet his team's dismal record—the .371 winning percentage during his tenure, the failure to make the playoffs in all but seven seasons—wasn't even the cause of his undoing.

In fact, at the time that Sterling was forced to sell the Los Angeles Clippers in 2014, they were a better team than they'd been in their entire history. In 2012–13, they won the NBA's Pacific Division, the first time they had finished first since the franchise was established in Buffalo in 1970. In 2013–14, they won 57 games, more than any Clippers team ever had, and repeated as division winners. Then they won a seven-game playoff series against the Warriors, who weren't quite ready for prime time. It was the same series that would lead Lacob and his Warrior brain trust to replace Jackson with Kerr.

During that Warriors series, the tabloid website TMZ released an audio tape of a conversation between Sterling and his girlfriend, who was known as V. Stiviano. (Sterling happened to be married at the time, but that wasn't even the scandal.) On the tape, Sterling can be heard admonishing Stiviano to stop bringing African Americans to Clippers games. "It bothers me a lot that you want to broadcast that you're associated with Black people," Sterling said.

At the time, the NBA's players' union was trying to find a new executive director. Chris Paul, a prominent labor leader within the league who happened to be the Clippers' starting point guard, asked Kevin Johnson to coordinate a player response. Johnson was a former NBA All-Star who had been elected mayor of Sacramento. He was perceived as an honest broker with ties to both players and management. What Johnson feared was a measured response by Adam Silver, the NBA's new commissioner, whose salary was paid by the league's owners. "If Adam had under-delivered, fined Sterling $1 million, and suspended him for a week, it would have gotten out of control in a hurry," Johnson told me in 2021. "There was a very high likelihood that the players would have used it as an opportunity to take a stand publicly and not play."

Silver happened to be in Oakland that week for the Clippers–Warriors series. Johnson drove down from Sacramento to meet with him. "My job was to make it clear: 'Adam, the players aren't playing chicken,'" Johnson said. Silver got the message. He spent the weekend that followed canvassing stakeholders, including owners and sponsors. Many advised a moderate approach: suspend Sterling indefinitely, perhaps, and then quietly encourage him to explore selling the team. After meeting with Johnson, though, Silver knew that wouldn't be enough.

Standing at a hotel lectern in Manhattan the following Tuesday morning, Silver announced he was banning Sterling for life, something no commissioner in the history of American sports had done to an owner. It was a bold move that laid the groundwork for the political activism and advocacy that would emerge from the league in the coming decade, first by the NBA's players and coaches, and eventually by some of its teams. It also removed perhaps the most anachronistic owner in sports and replaced him with one of the most progressive.

"One owner's out, a new owner's in," Kevin Johnson says. "And you look at the juxtaposition of what they wanted to do with the team, and it's night and day."

———

THE OFFER THAT Sterling eventually accepted from Steve Ballmer, the former Microsoft chief executive, was for $2 billion. It was a sum of money that, on the face of it, seemed absurd. Two billion dollars was more than four times what Lacob paid for the Warriors in 2010, and nearly four times what Edens and Lasry had paid for the Bucks earlier the same year. It was almost as much as the $2.15 billion that baseball's Los Angeles Dodgers sold for in 2012, and that deal had included Dodger Stadium and the right to develop nearby parking lots.

For his $2 billion, Ballmer was getting a franchise that ranked a distant second in its own market. The Clippers couldn't even rely on geography to provide them with a natural constituency. Baseball's Cubs and White Sox divided Chicagoland into north and south; hockey's Rangers, Islanders, and Devils were each based in different corners of New York's Tri-State area. But the Lakers, with their enticing Showtime branding and 16 NBA titles, played in the same building as the Clippers. "It wasn't even a team moving to a new city, starting fresh," says Gillian Zucker, a former auto racing

executive whom Ballmer installed as the Clippers' president soon
after buying the club. "It wasn't like he was starting with a clean
slate. He started with the most charged brand in all of sports."

Ballmer was perceived by many as a fool with more money than
he knew what to do with. But he had missed the chance to buy the
Sacramento Kings in 2013 and move them to Seattle, where he
lived, and he wasn't going to blow this opportunity. Sterling had
been threatening to challenge Silver's demand that he sell the team
by filing a lawsuit that could have kept the franchise in limbo for
years. By making an offer that large, an offer so outlandish that
Sterling knew he would never get anything close to it from anyone
else, Ballmer convinced him to go relatively quietly.

Nearly everyone around the NBA was happy to get Sterling out.
Yet the sale also seemed to reward him for decades of negligence
and ineptitude, not to mention those racist statements. Reaction
to the sale price outside the league ranged from dismay to outrage.
"Sterling to Reap 15,900 Percent Return on Sale of Clippers," read a
headline in the *New York Times*. "To say the least, the rate of return
is very impressive," wrote Josh Barro in the story beneath it. "It's a
much better performance than most of the ways Sterling could have
invested his money." The return, Barro noted, was four and a half
times what Sterling would have netted had he put the $12.5 million
he spent for the franchise into the S&P 500 index, even if he had
reinvested all the dividends.

This fact underscored two others, or seemed to. First, sports
teams *did* seem like the best place to park your money if you had
plenty of it and wanted to preserve it for the next generation. And a
corollary: the first point was true whether or not you had any interest in, or talent for, ably running your team. For all the vitriol that
Sterling's mismanagement had generated over the years, including

a *Sports Illustrated* cover story in 2000 that labeled the Clippers "The Worst Franchise in Sports History," he ultimately had done as well off the court as Jerry Buss of the Lakers. In 1979, Buss paid Jack Kent Cooke $67 million for three teams (the Lakers, the NHL's Kings, and the Los Angeles Strings of World Team Tennis) and an arena, the Fabulous Forum in Inglewood. Before his death in 2013, Buss's Lakers had won 10 NBA titles and revolutionized much about the way professional basketball was sold and marketed. Sterling, by contrast, had arguably the worst track record of any owner ever. Yet, by smashing the record for the sale price of an NBA team, Sterling appeared to have been rewarded for his penurious ways.

What wasn't evident at the time was how much money Sterling had left on the table during his time as owner. That only became clear a few years into Ballmer's tenure. By 2014, Ballmer liked to tell people that he was retired; what that actually meant was that he no longer worked for Microsoft, so he could spend time doing what he wanted. That included wading into the tall grass of running a sports team. It didn't take long before he began changing the way the Clippers operated by treating it like a mini-Microsoft. "He knows the story of a company by its math," Zucker explained. "He doesn't want words, he doesn't want adjectives. He wants an Excel spreadsheet. That tells him everything he needs to know, without people's opinions. It tends to be a much more unbiased way of looking at a business: Here are the facts. And now, let's talk about where we're going from there. What the strategy is."

As he did, it soon became clear to everyone associated with the Clippers just how much Sterling's mismanagement had cost him. Ballmer came from a professional experience that involved running one of the world's most influential companies and guiding it in a variety of new directions. He understood what Lacob and Guber had done with the Warriors, both on the court and off it, and the latent opportunities that existed for an NBA team in the internet era. During his 34-year career at Microsoft, where he served as CEO from 2000 to early 2014, a large part of Ballmer's job was to take stock of the ideas being generated around him and decide which to fund. He often cared less about the immediate return on a particular innovation—such as Xbox, which Microsoft developed during his tenure, or Skype, which it bought from eBay in 2011 for $8.5 billion—than its long-term prospects. "What Steve loves is big ideas," says Lisa Brummel, a former Microsoft executive vice president who left the company in 2014 and is now part owner of the WNBA's Seattle Storm. "If you're not thinking big enough, that's almost as bad as not having the proper analytical thought behind your idea. And if you are thinking big, think even bigger."

By thinking big, Ballmer grew the Clippers' fan base from a few thousand contrarian Angelenos to a national and even international following, tripling the club's revenue. He brought together two of the NBA's marquee names, Kawhi Leonard and Paul George, and constructed a team for the 2019–20 season that became one of the favorites for the NBA title. He began planning for a new arena, one that would utilize technology in different ways than any existing venue had done, without sacrificing the emotion and intimacy of live sports.

Most important, he ran the team like the large-scale business that it was. Not because he wanted it to make a profit, he is quick to point out, but because $2 billion is a significant amount of money, even to Steve Ballmer—and because treating a business like a business is the way that someone who accumulates so much money tends to think. "I mean, did I start out saying, 'How do I make more money in life?' No, of course I didn't," he told me before a game in

2020, only weeks before COVID-19 closed down the NBA. "I've been blessed. This extra blessing of more money I did not need. On the other hand, I want to be rational. I don't want to invest in things that lose money. And my motivation was, 'Let's see if we can change the world with this basketball team. Let's see if we can do it.'"

He was able to do all this because he was Steve Ballmer: one of the world's richest people, with a skill set and a background that allowed him to take advantage of the possibilities inherent in owning a sports team. But he was also able to do it because the landscape had changed from even a few years before. While John Henry had been an outlier when he bought the Red Sox, now there were owners who thought the way he did in all four major sports, and their numbers were growing annually. And in the same way that smart, young executives like Theo Epstein and Daryl Morey had been put in place by owners to make decisions on which players to sign and how to orchestrate team strategies, other smart, young executives were doing similar things in the back office, analyzing data to help the business side of the organization run as efficiently as in other businesses of similar size.

IN THE SUMMER of 2004, Tim Zue was hired by New England Sports Ventures as a business analyst. While an undergraduate student at MIT, Zue had won a prestigious robotics competition. After college, he worked as a consultant at Bain & Company. It would be safe to say that neither robot building nor experience at a major consulting firm like Bain was showing up on the résumés of many applicants for jobs with MLB teams in those days. If the chief financial officers of teams had come across potential employ-ees like Zue, most wouldn't have known what to do with him.

Not that the Red Sox had much of an idea. From 2004 to 2012, while Epstein and manager Terry Francona were winning two World Series with the help of an analytic approach as sophis-ticated as any in sports, the company surrounding the team was basically still being run as a more efficient, fan-friendly version of the one that had been selling tickets and advertising and sou-venirs out of Fenway Park for more than a century. Sitting at his desk on Yawkey Way, among the marketers and the human resources staff, Zue constituted a one-man analytics department. He accumulated data, then studied it in an attempt to optimize the various aspects of the club's business. But he seldom was able to get enough consensus to change much about the way it was being operated.

That was true throughout professional sports, even for teams like Beane's A's and Morey's Rockets that had identified data analysis as a means to gain competitive advantage. In their use of sophisticated business tools, sports franchises lagged significantly behind compa-nies of similar size in other industries. The teams knew they had loyal customers throughout their metropolitan areas and beyond, and they even knew who some of them were. Beyond that, they had accumulated almost no information about them. Maybe you were a Colorado Rockies fan who attended 10 or 15 games a year, walking up to the ticket window at the ballpark with a kid or two half an hour before game time. You typically threw down a couple of $20 bills for hot dogs, candy bars, and a beer around the fifth inning. Once or twice a year, you bought a team jersey, a hat, or a bobble-head. As of 2010, the Rockies probably had only a vague idea that you, your son, and your daughter even existed. They definitely had no idea that you loved to see the American League teams when they came to town, or that you usually bought upper-deck tickets along the first-base line, or that you lived in Littleton, a suburb southwest of the city, or that your work as an emergency room technician often gave you weekday afternoons off, which is why you sometimes also attended Wednesday matinee games on the spur of the moment. All of that was theoretically knowable, but the executives who ran MLB teams didn't yet understand the value in knowing it. Or, if they did, they hadn't figured out how to learn it.

Part of the problem was a lack of resources. There just wasn't anyone available to try to collect that kind of information. The number of employees on the business side of a big-league team, as opposed to the baseball side, was far smaller than at comparable companies in other industries. "Historically, teams had been structured as small businesses," says Royce Cohen, who became the head of analytics for the Los Angeles Dodgers in 2014 after working at Major League Baseball. That's because, for most of their existence, the teams *were* small businesses. The fact that many of them now had payrolls in the hundreds of millions of dollars hadn't yet changed the scale at which they operated. "The clubs' technology groups until maybe 2013 or 2014 were really more IT operations groups," says Brian Shield, who was hired by the Red Sox in 2013 to run their information systems. "They kind of kept the lights on at the games."

The larger issue was a mind-set that permeated professional sports, from the executives who chose to work in it (often at lower salaries than they might get in less enticing sectors) to the owners, most of whom had bought their teams as baubles to enjoy during the second half of their adult lives. In the minds of these men, sports teams weren't supposed to be actual businesses. The point of owning a team was that you could be frivolous with it, which meant doing things that wouldn't have made sense in another business setting, or not doing anything at all.

The owners who bought in beginning at the turn of the 21st century tended to have different expectations than those who had acquired their teams in years prior, often at one-tenth—or in some cases one-*fiftieth*—the capital investment. It took time for those new owners to learn the specifics of their businesses and gain influence within their leagues. Once they did, changes began to accelerate.

Early in the 2000s, a few professional sports teams started selling their ticket inventory using variable pricing, meaning they charged more for games against certain opponents and on desirable dates. This strategy had been used in other areas of entertainment for years; theater tickets for midday on Wednesday cost less than the same show on Friday night, for example, and that same nine-dollar cocktail you ordered at 7 p.m. would have been two dollars cheaper if you had come before 5:30. There was no reason that tickets to a ball game couldn't work the same way.

In 2009, baseball's San Francisco Giants became the first North American team to use dynamic pricing, in which the cost of a ticket often changed as a game approached. Not long before, Giants slugger Barry Bonds had broken Hank Aaron's record for career home runs. In the weeks leading up to August 7, 2007, when Bonds finally passed Aaron by hitting No. 756, interest in the team among casual Bay Area fans grew intense. Even if you hadn't been to a Giants game in years, and perhaps especially if you hadn't, you suddenly wanted to see the man who would soon be the most prolific home run hitter ever. (If you got lucky, you might even see him hit one.) The Giants had no way to take advantage of that surge of interest because ticket prices for those July and August home games had long since been fixed. But scalpers and other resellers did, and they made huge profits. This, the Giants realized, was a structural flaw in the way ticketing worked.

By then, software existed that allowed clubs to alter their entire pricing structures in real time to reflect demand. Under the system the Giants put into place for the 2009 season, a fan who purchased tickets in March for a game that summer was likely to get them for less than they would cost the week before the game was played. That incentivized fans to buy tickets months in advance. (Airlines had been selling tickets this way for years.)

For a long time, the Red Sox didn't do any of that. "We already had really high prices," Tim Zue explains. "And we were selling every ticket." In May 2003, shortly after Henry and Werner bought the club, the Red Sox began a streak of consecutive Fenway sellouts. By the end of the 2012 season, it had stretched to more than 800 games, the longest in the history of professional sports in North America. Heading into the 2013 season, 22 of baseball's 30 fran-chises employed both dynamic and variable pricing to sell their tick-ets, and seven others used one or the other. The Red Sox were the only team of the 30 with pricing that was completely static—all their games were priced equally, and that price stayed the same no matter when a ticket was purchased.

But at the end of that 2012 season, the Red Sox finished last in their division for the first time in 30 years. It was clear to everyone that the sellout streak would end, probably by the middle of April. Like every other club in baseball, the Red Sox would soon have to work to fill their ballpark. With that in mind, Zue set out to do a detailed analysis of the team's ticketing. The first step was to align admission to Red Sox games more closely with the marketplace. On the morning of a game, a grandstand ticket might be available at the team's box office for its $50 list price and on StubHub for $20—and guess which one most consumers would choose to buy. At the same time, a seat to see the Yankees on a gorgeous September evening in the midst of the pennant race cost the same as a game against the nondescript Seattle Mariners in chilly April. "We knew that wasn't right," Zue said. More than nearly any other ballpark, too, the seating map of quirky, angular Fenway was full of inefficiencies. "You have two seats next to each other," Zue said, "and the person sitting in field box 9 can hold hands with someone across a metal bar paying half the price."

StubHub is a Red Sox partner, so Zue had access to the company's data. He used it to generate heat maps that showed which seats most frequently sold for the highest markups, and which historically ended up selling on the secondary market for below list price. He then sorted that information based on a variety of factors, including the month when each game was played, the opponent, the day of the week, and even the starting pitchers. Zue knew that a ticket to a game on a Saturday night in July was more valuable than one for a Tuesday in April. The question was, by how much?

It turned out that, with one exception, the opponent barely mattered. That exception was the Yankees, of course. That rivalry drove pricing on the high end. Apart from Yankee games, and occasionally a prestige interleague opponent such as the Chicago Cubs or Los Angeles Dodgers, the majority of ticket buyers simply wanted to see the Red Sox, or perhaps simply to see a game at Fenway. There was a time in the early 2000s when putting future Hall of Famer Pedro Martínez on the mound would have meant a surge in interest and ticket sales; the same was probably also true about Roger Clemens in the late 1980s. But as of 2013, the Red Sox didn't have a pitcher of that stature. Other than the Yankees, only two factors had a consistent impact on ticket demand: the month when a game was played, and the day of the week.

As a precursor to implementing variable pricing, the Red Sox divided their schedule into five tiers, with Tier 1 games being the most coveted. With the data in front of him, Zue now could say definitively that an infield grandstand seat for a Saturday game in July against the Yankees, a quintessential Tier 1 game, was worth nearly double that of an average game, and four times more than a cold-weather game against a random opponent. At the time, though, the price for all three games was still the same: $52. "It turned out we were way underpriced for the Tier 1 games," he said. "And we were overpriced for the Tier 5 games, those April Tuesdays against the Rays. So we raised the price for the Tier 1 games and we lowered the price for the Tier 5."

Still, on November 1, when Zue and Ron Bumgarner, who ran the Red Sox ticket office, sat down with team president Larry Lucchino to present their findings to owners John Henry and Tom Werner, they made sure to recommend that the team *not* raise prices for the top-tier games nearly as much as the data indicated that it could. If you went on StubHub looking to sit in one of the rows of seats atop the Green Monster on Opening Day, for example, you would find seats costing in excess of $1,000. That's what Bumgarner would have charged if he wanted to optimize revenue, just as a promoter might do for a concert—the Rolling Stones or Springsteen coming through Boston and playing Fenway. But this was the opposite of a one-off purchase. Rather, the customer was part of a fan base that had a long and intimate relationship with the club. Pricing tickets strictly according to market demand would vastly alter the composition of the crowd at Fenway on those days. It would also alienate fans, even though similarly priced tickets were already being sold by StubHub.

The difference was that fans had a purely transactional relationship with StubHub, as consumers do with most businesses. By contrast, they routinely proclaimed their allegiance to the Red Sox.

They wore caps and jerseys. They shouted at the televisions in their living rooms, and passionately debated the decisions made by the manager. In some nebulous but important sense, they felt like part of the team. StubHub had a single product to sell them, in terms of the Red Sox: tickets to the games. But the Red Sox themselves were selling—or "selling"—a wide variety of products, services, and affiliations well beyond simply coming to a game. These included access to the Red Sox on television, on the radio, and on the internet; souvenirs and memorabilia; and a sense of affiliation that permeated through all of that and gave potential customers the incentive to come and watch the games. The team couldn't behave in the same way as a normal business. As much as everyone in that room appreciated the value of data analysis, they all understood that.

They also knew that many season ticket holders who had been attending games for years financed their increasingly expensive 81-game purchase by selling off the most coveted games to brokers. Rather than trying to stop the practice, Zue says, "we saw that as a good thing." If prices anywhere close to market value for those games were factored into the cost of a season ticket, selling those tickets at a profit would no longer be possible. In that case, some percentage of those fans were likely to abandon their season packages and only attend games occasionally, or not at all. Without the sales generated as part of season packages, a significant number of seats during those least-desirable Tier 5 games were likely to end up unoccupied, especially in years when the Red Sox weren't involved in the pennant race.

Sure, it was also probably the case that the revenue gained by maximizing the price of the top seats at the premium games would more than offset that loss—but, again, revenue wasn't the only factor that Zue and Bumgarner needed to consider. There was value in having fans sitting in seats at Fenway, no matter how much their tickets had cost them. That value was financial, in terms of ancillary income like hot dogs and beer and parking, but it also contributed to the harder-to-quantify atmospherics of having the ballpark close to full, game after game. And once someone attended a game, he or she was far more likely to develop an attachment to the team and return for more.

"That's the ecosystem," Zue says. "The analytics are certainly helpful, but what they're telling you isn't always the answer." So, while the StubHub data revealed that the same infield seat that had cost $52 in 2013 sold at an average of $96 for the 16 games that season they had designated as Tier 1, Bumgarner and the ticketing team chose to charge just $70 for those games in 2014. Most of that increase was offset by lowering the price of that same seat to $40 for the 16 games designated Tier 5. That meant the fan who wanted nothing more than to see the Red Sox play could do it from a seat between first and third base for $13 less than they could have during the previous season. They just had to be willing to do it on a weeknight, when school was still in session.

————

WHAT ZUE CONSIDERED his most important mandate with the Red Sox was to better identify who was following the team—both abstractly, in terms of percentages, and as individuals with specific backgrounds and predilections. Previously, the marketing of baseball teams had been rudimentary. If you don't know who your customers are, the best you can do is put up a billboard on a busy freeway and hope the right people will glance up and see it. But once you've zeroed in on your fan base, and can sort it by zip code, age, frequency of game attendance, and even the amount of money spent at the ballpark during an average visit, you can tailor offers to exactly the people most likely to respond to them.

Through electronic transactions, email, social media, and face-to-face encounters, the Red Sox had compiled various databases of names. All of them existed independently from each other. "I know, for example, that I was in the system 16 times," says Shield, who grew up in Andover, Massachusetts, and had been buying Red Sox tickets, in person and online, since the 1970s. Zue set out to integrate those databases and, in the process, find out who these people were. Where did most of them live? How did they get to games? How often did they visit the team's website?

Answering questions like these eventually led to a digital version of the index cards that had been posted on Charles Steinberg's wall, one that was both personalized and interactive. Rather than simply chronicling the fans' journey to and from Fenway, it became possible to engage with them in real time. Whenever someone tagged as a VIP arrived at the ballpark, whether it was a minority investor, a longtime season ticket holder, or a celebrity, a team employee could automatically be dispatched to offer greetings, press notes, or other amenities. If seats in prime locations became available before (or even during) a game, fans who had a history of sitting in certain locations would be given the chance to upgrade. And when games lasted late into the night, past the closing time of the rail station near Fenway, information on ride sharing could be disseminated by text based on home addresses.

Having accurate and almost infinitely sortable customer data at your disposal made even conventional marketing more powerful. One afternoon in October 2016, when the overhaul of the database was still in its early stages, the ticketing staff was sitting around the third-base conference room across from Zue's office, brainstorming ways to sell more season packages. At one point, an executive named Will Droste suggested sending out a mailer. Everyone laughed. "What are you talking about?" Zue remembers saying. "That's, like, 1980."

The difference was, by 2016 the database enabled them to identify and isolate likely consumers who fit a certain set of criteria. The staff culled through the database to compile a list of 70,000 Red Sox fans who might conceivably have an interest in a season package. They all had annual household incomes of at least $100,000. They all lived within 25 miles of Fenway Park. And all of them had attended a substantial number of games during the season that had just ended. The team sent out postcards to only those 70,000 households. Then they tracked season ticket inquiries, day by day, starting before the mailer arrived, and then in the days and weeks that followed. The mailer had cost $25,000 to produce. "And we can definitively say it made us $600,000," Zue says. "I remember it vividly because of how wrong I was."

Without analytics, it wouldn't have been possible to limit the cost to $25,000 by knowing exactly which 70,000 households in Greater Boston to target. And without tracking the responses, the impact of the mailer would have been impossible to gauge. But sandwiched between those uses of tracking and analyzing data was a marketing insight. "People get sick of getting emails," Droste had said during the meeting. "They like getting mail. And if they get mail from the Red Sox, they'll really like it." He was right.

———

BY THEN, THE Red Sox had finally hired an analyst to work under Zue. Jon Hay graduated from Harvard and the University of Chicago's Booth School of Business. He spent nearly five years at Morgan Stanley, managing a portfolio of government bonds and developing equities-trading strategies. In 2013, he went to work for the Red Sox—on the baseball analytics team under Bill James. He spent two years there, creating models that would more effectively predict future player performance. "There were about 20 people doing what I was doing," he says. Because of his familiarity with both finance and analytics, he was summoned to help Larry Lucchino with a business project. He immediately understood that he could make far more of an impact on the business side than as yet another quant assessing on-base percentage. "I can build a model that predicts our season ticket holders' churn rate," he told Zue.

At the time, around 2015, most MLB teams still had nobody doing business analytics as a full-time job. Those that did were in the biggest markets, with the notable exceptions of Cleveland and Tampa Bay. MLB franchises weren't competing with each other, as they were on the field, but rather with the wide range of leisure-time and entertainment options in megacities such as New York, Los Angeles, and Chicago. They also had far more to gain, in real terms, by running their businesses efficiently; if everybody's revenue could grow by 20 percent by simply learning how to better target their consumers, the additional income would add up to far more for the Dodgers than it would for the Padres or Mariners. Eventually, every team in baseball (and throughout big-league sports) came to understand the value of paying competitive salaries to smart young business analysts and empowering them to suggest changes. "The transition happened maybe five years ago," the Dodgers' Cohen told me in 2022, "from debating the merits to debating the methods."

In 2015, the Red Sox started hosting a business analytics conference for MLB teams. It was scheduled for the Thursday before

Morey and Gelman's MIT sports analytics conference in Boston. The idea was to bring together baseball's business-side representatives who would be attending the conference and let some of their ideas cross-pollinate. For that first conference in 2015, ten teams signed up. As of 2020, all 30 teams were represented. That 200 percent increase is a telling illustration of the growth of analytics in the back offices of stadiums and arenas around the country. "As of 2003, sports teams were way below the average in their use of data analysis in business, compared with all companies," Zue says. "As an industry, we are definitely above the average today. We are in the upper quadrant for sure."

The next steps involved the MLB Ballpark app that all ticket buyers used to gain access to big-league ballparks. By 2022, the Red Sox had started designing their own programs to interact with it—the only big-league team to do so. These included a mobile concessions function that could get hot dogs and beverages delivered to a seat; bingo games and other distractions for rain delays or between innings; and a loyalty program that could tie in with a music venue around the corner from Fenway that the club was planning to open later that year. "And I think we're still in the early stages of maximizing digital fan engagement value, the first third," Shield said. "There is much more to come."

———

ONE MORNING IN May of 2019, Zue was a featured speaker at the annual conference of the CFO Leadership Council, which annually draws a national audience to the Boston Convention Center. By then, he had become the club's chief financial officer. He presided over a seven-man analytics department, run by Hay, whose title of Vice President of Data, Intelligence and Analytics would have sounded appropriate at a diplomatic think tank. During his 15-year tenure with the team, Zue's calculations had helped annual revenue rise from of $152 million to $519 million. Some of that came from more lucrative media contracts. Still, the growth rate was compelling enough for him to get invited to address executives from some of the leading companies around the country, something that would have been almost impossible to imagine even a decade before.

Zue gave a presentation about the various ways in which the Red Sox had used data analysis to make their business more efficient. Sandra Clarke, one of the other speakers at the conference, was at the time the chief financial officer of Blue Shield of California, a nonprofit health-care provider. For years, Clarke told me, she would have laughed at the idea that she had anything to learn from a financial executive from a sports team. She described to me what her reaction would have been: "How in the world could people running around on a field have any insights to tell me about how to run a company?" But as she matured, so did the teams. In recent years, she had come to perceive their need to nimbly balance financial responsibility, competitive success, and a pleasurable customer experience as a business challenge unlike that in any other category. "In some ways, I can't think of another kind of company that would have more to teach me," she said.

At the same time, much of what sports teams can achieve with business analytics is a unique by-product of their relationship with fans. "Unlike most businesses, we have a thousand ways that our customers can raise their hands and tell us who they are," says Hay. After nearly a decade of concentrated effort by Zue and his team, Hay maintained that the Red Sox knew as much about the people who enjoyed their products and services as all but the biggest companies. "Maybe not as much as Google or Amazon," he said, "but certainly any our size. And the lifetime value of a Red Sox customer is just preposterous. If you become a fan at age five, you'll be one for the next 70 years of your life." Because of that, smart sports teams cultivate their customers in ways that might not work for other businesses, such as the Red Sox distributing free tickets through the Kid Nation construct that Lucchino and his staff created while in San Diego and perfected in Boston. "We'll do that for any game," Hay says, "and it's worth it. I don't care if you could sell that ticket for $200. If one out of every hundred kids becomes a fan, it's more than worth it."

The loyalty of those fans had initially been an impediment, the steady income they provided blinding teams to the advancements that were being made by the smart, young number crunchers on the baseball side. It took the growth in revenue of only a few teams to spur the others into action. "This is a copycat industry," Hay says. "You can imagine one owner telling another, 'We've got this nerd, he tells me how to price tickets, he tells me where to spend my money.' You can't help but think, 'Well, where's *my* nerd?' "

Something similar was happening with other leagues on the competitive side. NBA teams, such as Morey's Rockets, had been the first outside baseball to try to adapt *Moneyball* precepts to their sport. By around 2014, NFL and NHL teams were starting to wonder if perhaps they could gain an advantage by hiring number crunchers to test some of the previously unquestioned assumptions that governed player procurement, strategy, and tactics. Across the Atlantic, the first stirrings of an analytic movement had even started in soccer, which was considered singularly unsuited to the use of data collection and analysis. Progress was slow, even in England's Premier League—with one prominent exception. That club, one of the world's most visible, happened to share an ownership group with the Red Sox.

5

EVERY NOW AND THEN, THERE'S A BREAKTHROUGH

JÜRGEN KLOPP WAS in his third week as Liverpool's manager in November 2015 when the team's director of research, Ian Graham, arrived at his office carrying computer printouts. Graham wanted to show Klopp, whom he hadn't yet met, what his work could do. Then he hoped to persuade Klopp to actually use it.

Graham spread out his papers on the table in front of him. He began talking about a game that Borussia Dortmund, the German club that Klopp coached before joining Liverpool, had played the previous season. He noted that Dortmund had numerous chances against lightly regarded Mainz, a smaller club that would end up finishing in 11th place. Yet Klopp's team lost, 2–0. Graham was starting to explain what his printouts showed when Klopp's face lit up. "Ah, you saw that game," he said. "It was crazy. We killed them. You saw it!"

Graham had not seen the game. But earlier that fall, as Liverpool was deciding who should replace the manager it was about to fire, Graham fed a numerical rendering of every attempted pass, shot, and tackle by Dortmund's players during Klopp's tenure into a mathematical model he had constructed. Then he evaluated each of Dortmund's games based on how his calculations assessed the players' performances that day. The difference was striking. Dortmund had finished seventh during Klopp's last season with the club, but the model determined that it should have finished second. Graham's conclusion was that the disappointing season had nothing to do with Klopp, though his reputation had suffered because of it. He just happened to be coaching one of the unluckiest teams in recent history.

In that game against Mainz, the charts showed, Dortmund took 19 shots, compared to 10 by its opponent. It controlled the play nearly two-thirds of the time. It advanced the ball into the offensive zone a total of 85 times, allowing Mainz to do the same just 55 times. It worked the ball into Mainz's penalty area on an impressive 36 occasions; Mainz managed only 17. But Dortmund lost because of two fluky errors. In the 70th minute, Dortmund missed a penalty shot. Four minutes later, it mistakenly scored in its own goal. Dortmund had played a better game than Mainz by almost any measure—except the score.

In soccer, pure chance can influence outcomes to a much greater extent than in other sports. Goals are relatively rare, fewer than three per game in England's Premier League. So, whether a ball ricochets into the net or misses it by a few inches has, on average, far more of an effect upon the final result than whether, say, a potential home run in baseball lands fair or foul or an NFL running back grinds out a first down. Graham brought up another game to Klopp, against Hannover a month later. The statistics were weighted even more heavily in Dortmund's favor: shots, 18–7; balls into the box,

55–13; and 11 successful crosses from the wing to 3. "You lost, 1–0," he said. "But you created double the chances—"

Klopp practically shouted. "Did you see that game?"

"No, no, it's just . . ."

"We killed them! I've never seen anything like it. We should have won. Ah, you saw that!"

Graham had not seen that game, either. In fact, he told Klopp, he hadn't seen any of Dortmund's games that season, neither live nor on video. He hadn't needed to, unless he wanted to experience one of the breathtaking acts of athleticism that can occur in soccer, or the drama of two teams fighting to assert their will upon the other—the reasons, in other words, that most fans watch sports. To understand what happened, all he needed was his data.

Traditionally, soccer hadn't relied on statistics to figure out much of anything. Graham, who earned a doctorate in theoretical physics at Cambridge, built his own database to track the progress of more than 100,000 players. By recommending which of them Liverpool should try to acquire, and then how the new arrivals should be used, he helped that club, once soccer's most glamorous and successful, return to glory.

During the 2018–19 season, Liverpool constructed a season as compelling as any in the sport's history. It lost only one of its 38 games in the Premier League, yet it finished second. Manchester City, the defending champion, edged Liverpool by a single point on the last day after winning every one of its league games since January. At the same time as it was trying to catch Manchester City, Liverpool was competing against the top teams from other countries in Europe's Champions League. In the semifinals of that tournament, it overcame a three-goal deficit to defeat Barcelona, perhaps the era's best soccer team. Then it beat Tottenham Hotspur in the final. The following season, which was disrupted by the pandemic but ultimately completed that summer in empty stadiums, Liverpool won the first Premier League title in its history.

A few years after John Henry's group bought Liverpool, it started to incorporate data analysis into the decisions the club made, from the corporate to the tactical. By 2018, its ascent had started to make number crunching acceptable, even fashionable, in England and beyond. As more clubs contemplated employing analysts without soccer-playing backgrounds to try to gain a competitive edge, Liverpool's season served as something of a referendum on the practice.

At Dortmund, Klopp had analyzed no data. In this regard, he was like most managers. He was consumed by coaching his young team on the field. But by the time Graham left his office that morning in 2015, Klopp's epiphany was complete. He was convinced that Graham, despite having watched none of Dortmund's games, appreciated the unusually bad fortune that had befallen the team almost as keenly as if he'd been coaching it himself. Later, Klopp learned that without Graham's analysis of that season, he never would have been hired. "The department there in the back of the building?" he said recently, referring to Graham and his staff. "They're the reason I'm here."

IN THE FALL of 2016, as I traveled to England and around Europe, writing stories about world soccer, I started hearing that analytics were finally starting to permeate the sport. I knew that Tony Bloom, who had made a fortune as a sports gambler and poker player, owned Brighton and Hove Albion, a relatively small club on England's southern coast that would gain promotion to the Premier League that season after more than 30 years out of the top classification. Since his entire orientation of the sport had come through numbers, playing the odds, I was sure his team had embraced the collection and analysis of all kinds of information.

So had Brentford. That club had moved up from the fourth tier of English football, known as League Two, into League One and then the second-tier EFL Championship under the ownership of another professional gambler, Matthew Benham. But as of 2016, it had never played in the Premier League or its precursor, the old First Division. These were anomalies, lesser clubs outside the mainstream who were using every means possible to play above their level. But as I spent time talking with various executives and with other journalists before matches and over lunches and dinners, another term kept coming up. In the hands of mathematically minded Americans who also owned a baseball team, Liverpool had become "a laptop club," as one former sporting director disdainfully told me over drinks in London late one afternoon. It was why, he confided to me, they weren't winning.

In its first six years after New England Sports Ventures acquired it, Liverpool landed in the top quarter of the Premier League only once. An unexpected second-place finish in 2014 qualified it for the Champions League the following season, which meant an opportunity to earn the tens of millions of dollars of additional revenue from ticket sales and television rights (and many millions more in free worldwide marketing) that some of the biggest clubs around Europe had come to consider an annuity. But Liverpool won just one of six Champions League games that fall and was eliminated from the competition before Christmas.

Like that former sporting director, others both inside the sport and outside it believed that Liverpool's reliance on numbers was undermining the football men who should have been making its decisions. The main obstacle Klopp would need to overcome if he hoped to succeed there, the English newspaper the *Independent* wrote, was "the club's deep attachment to the theory that players' statistics—analytics—can provide most of the answers." The more conversations I had about analytics, the more I realized that the resistance to data analysis in English football was just as strong as, or stronger than, it had been across baseball the previous decade. But like Beane and the Athletics, or Joe Lacob and the NBA's Warriors, Fenway Sports Group and Liverpool had complete confidence in their approach.

The great Brazilian player Pelé once called soccer "the beautiful game." He didn't coin the phrase, but after he said it, the description stuck. Fluid and at times balletic, soccer isn't composed of discrete events, like baseball and American football. There aren't dozens of scoring plays to dissect in every game, as in basketball. Rather, much of what happens seems impossible to quantify. Talent is often judged exclusively on aesthetics. If you look like a good player, the feeling is, you probably are.

For many years, nobody in soccer kept track about much beyond which players scored the goals. Part of the reason was, there were no other statistics to shed light on what was actually happening. By the middle of the last decade, fans were getting updates on how many shots different players had taken, what percentage of the time each team had controlled the ball, and plenty of other metrics. But almost none of that provided a clearer explanation of what was happening on the field, including which team ended up winning.

For example, a ball deflected by a defensive player over the end line gives the opposition a corner kick—a goal-scoring opportunity. In theory, corners are good, and getting more of them than your opponent would seemingly indicate a successful strategy. Except that corners are more helpful to some teams than others. Teams with attackers who are skilled at redirecting centering passes work to create them, but teams with finishers who have the talent to elude defenders often prefer to take their chances in open play. Those teams don't try to create corners, and they aren't especially pleased when they happen.

Or consider time of possession. Teams rarely score without the ball, so having it more than the opponent sounds desirable. Yet some teams don't want possession of the ball. If you don't have it, you can't give it up deep in your own end, a member of Iceland's defensive-minded national team once told me. Iceland's ball handlers aren't especially adept, so its coaches prioritized keeping the ball far from its goal. In 2016, Iceland advanced to the quarterfinals of the European championships, beating countries many times its size, including England, and tying the tournament's eventual champion, Portugal. In none of those games did it come close to controlling the ball even half the time.

For these sorts of reasons, soccer was assumed to be unsuited to an analytical approach. Much of the game involves probing and assessing, moving the ball from player to player while waiting for an opening. And then the only goal might come from a winger who has done little else—after, say, a faulty clearance by a team that otherwise has been entirely dominant. "Our game is unpredictable," Sam Allardyce, who has managed 14 clubs over three decades, told me when I reached him at home during one of those brief spells when he was between jobs. "Too unpredictable to make decisions on stats. We're not talking about baseball or American football here."

Chelsea created the Premier League's first analytics department back in 2008. Arsenal later bought a statistical analysis company, StatDNA. But the managers of those clubs apparently didn't see enough advantage in applying data to the sport to actually do it, or else they were too busy trying to keep their jobs to figure out how. A few years ago, the OptaPro analytics conference, a sort of single-sport version of MIT Sloan, emerged in London as a way for the tiny band of soccer quants to present papers to one another. Still, all those charts with arrows and heat maps revealing where most of the action takes place seemed to have little effect. As new metrics emerged, in fact, many commentators and coaches took pride in repudiating them. When ESPN's Craig Burley, a former Premier League midfielder, was asked on the air to comment about a team's "expected goals," a formula that calculates how often a team should have scored as opposed to how often it actually did, he replied with disbelief. "What an absolute load of nonsense that is," he shouted. "I expect things at Christmas from Santa Claus, but they don't come."

Chelsea, Arsenal, Manchester City, and other wealthy teams that are owned by multibillionaires, or even the investment arms of entire nations, have resources at their disposal that allow them to accumulate the best talent. Compared with them, and the European clubs such as Barcelona, Real Madrid, and Bayern Munich that could count on those remunerative Champions League runs every season, Liverpool was essentially in the position of Beane's early A's teams. A different approach was necessary for it to keep up with the biggest clubs.

And all those players running around the soccer field were clearly doing *something*. Every now and then, too, goals were scored. "Everything depends on everything else in football, which is what makes it so difficult," Graham said. But if collecting and

analyzing data could help divine a connection, wasn't it foolish
not to try it?

———

GRAHAM GREW UP an hour's drive from Cardiff as a Liverpool fan.
His childhood in the 1970s and '80s coincided with Liverpool's era
of dominance. It didn't hurt that one of the club's best players, Ian
Rush, happened to be Welsh. Before each game, Graham and the
three analysts who worked under him compiled a packet of information. By the time Klopp decided which of their insights were worth
passing along to the team, the equations were long gone; the players
were only dimly aware that some of the suggestions were rooted in
doctorate-level mathematics. "We know someone has spent hours
behind closed doors figuring it out," the midfielder Alex Oxlade-
Chamberlain said. "But the manager doesn't hit us with statistics
and analytics. He just tells us what to do."

Often, the advice contradicted what someone merely watching
videos of the games might come to believe. Graham and his team
could report that a club's strong-footed left winger sent booming
crosses over the defense toward the goal. But the data indicated
that the less impressive crosses coming from the right wing, often
accurately placed, resulted in goals far more frequently. That sounds
rudimentary. In soccer, it was practically a revolution.

Graham's weightiest responsibility was helping Liverpool decide
which players to acquire. He did that by feeding information on
games into his formulas. What he didn't do was make evaluations
by watching those games. "I don't like video," he told me. "It biases
you." Graham wanted the club that he worked for to win, but he
also wanted his judgments to be validated. "All of these players,

there has been discussion of their relative merits," he said. "If they do badly, I take it as sort of a personal affront. If I think someone is a good player, I really, really want them to do well."

Naby Keïta was one of Graham's finds. Born in Guinea, in West Africa, he was playing for the Austrian club Red Bull Salzburg when Graham noticed the data he was generating; it was unlike any he had seen. At the time, Keïta was a defensive midfielder, positioned in front of Salzburg's defenders. Occasionally, over the course of a career, defensive midfielders will evolve into central midfielders, who play farther forward. Keïta did. Rarely, if ever, will they emerge as attacking midfielders, whose role is largely offensive. Keïta did that, too.

Keïta's shifting roles made a muddle of the conventional statistics used to quantify a player's contribution to his club. The position you play in soccer has a significant effect on your chances of putting the ball into the goal, or how frequently you leave your feet to nudge it from an opponent. But Graham disdained those statistics anyway. He had only slightly less contempt for some of the more evolved metrics, like the percentage of attempted passes that are completed. Instead, he spent months building a model that calculated the chance each team had of scoring a goal before any given action—a pass, a missed shot, a slide tackle—and then what chance it had immediately after that action. Using that model, he could quantify how much each player affected his team's chance of winning during the game. It was the closest anyone had come to applying machine learning to soccer.

Inevitably, some of the players who came out best in the familiar statistics ended up at the top of Graham's list. But others ended up at the bottom. That gave Graham a strong indication of which players were overvalued, undervalued, and valued correctly by others in the sport. It was the same arbitrage opportunity that Beane had been seeking in baseball. And like Beane, Graham had the advantage of working within an industry that largely disdained the use of data.

Naby Keïta's pass completion rate tended to be lower than that of some other elite midfielders. To some observers, including many who worked for other clubs around Europe, that diminished his value. But Graham's proprietary figures showed that Keïta often tried passes that, if completed, would get the ball to a teammate in a position where he had a better-than-average chance of scoring. Everyone agreed that Keïta was a versatile midfielder, but what Graham saw on his laptop was a phenomenon. Here was someone continually working to move the ball into more advantageous positions, something even an attentive spectator probably wouldn't notice unless told to look for it. Beginning in 2016, Graham recommended that Liverpool try to get him. Keïta arrived at Liverpool in 2018.

In January 2019, I watched a game with Graham at Anfield. At that time, Liverpool, which was playing Leicester City, still held a lead over Manchester City in the Premier League table, one that it would soon relinquish. Before the game, Graham met a friend, a sports scientist named Paul Balsom, in the Anfield lobby. Balsom was helping Leicester establish its own analytics department, and Graham had recommended some names of analysts who might be a fit. They shook hands and Balsom thanked him. "We're really excited," Balsom said. "We don't know where it's going, but it's going."

At his seat, Graham scanned the team sheet. He was excited to see that Keïta was in the lineup. At the time, Keïta's play hadn't seemed to justify Graham's endorsement. The calculations insisted that Keïta was doing as well as ever, but few fans realized that— and some of Liverpool's executives probably didn't, either. For Keïta's sake, and for the sake of Graham's peace of mind, some easy-to-quantify goals or assists would help. About half an hour into the game, Keïta received the ball from his left and started to dribble forward with elongated strides. From his seat, Graham exhorted him. "Go on, Naby," he said in his deep Welsh accent. "Go on!" Keïta passed two Leicester defenders. Then he hesitated for a moment and lost the ball. Graham sighed. "Ahhhh, Naby," he said.

In the second half, Keïta dribbled the ball through several defenders. Somehow, he emerged with nobody between him and the goalkeeper. As Graham lifted himself halfway out of his seat in anticipation, Keïta shot. At the same time, a Leicester player careened into him. The ball went wide, and to the displeasure of Liverpool's fans, no penalty was called. Graham groaned. Soon after, Keïta was removed for a substitute. Graham clapped enthusiastically as Keïta left the field, but when I asked if he thought Keïta had played well, he wouldn't give me a definitive answer. He would tell me tomorrow, he said, after he looked at the data.

———

GRAHAM WAS LABORING through a two-year postdoctorate at Cambridge when he realized he didn't want to be a scientist. Most of the breakthroughs in his area, polymer physics, had been made years before. "The classic papers had been written in the 1970s," he says. "So, you're searching around for something you can maybe make a little progress on." When someone forwarded him a notice for a job at Decision Analysis, an analytics start-up that was hoping to consult for soccer teams, he was intrigued. He quit his postdoctorate program, landed the job, and was told to read *Moneyball*.

At the time, the mathematical models needed to be relatively intricate because the data was so rudimentary. You knew which team won, and in most European leagues you knew which team had more shots and more corners, and sometimes even which had possession of the ball the most. "The challenge was, you've got this data that doesn't tell you much," Graham says. "And a sophisticated model was needed to kind of wring the information out of that."

For the next four years, from 2008 to 2012, Graham advised Tottenham, which hadn't won a league championship since 1961. The club had a French director of football, Damien Comolli, who declared himself open to new ideas. Comolli had even made a pilgrimage to America to meet with Beane. In 2007, he offered Decision Analytics a contract. "I got absolutely demolished by the football people, but I didn't care," Comolli says. "I wanted to find a competitive advantage." That sounded promising to Graham. But that October, Tottenham hired a new manager, Harry Redknapp. Redknapp had run five different teams and would go on to run three more. "Harry had his way of working," said Tim Sherwood, who served under Redknapp as an assistant, and that didn't include taking advice from theoretical biophysicists. "When that happens," Comolli says, "you're stuck as a sporting director. You know there's value, but the manager just doesn't want to hear it." Comolli gave up and returned to Paris.

Comolli's successor would prove crucial in getting Graham to Liverpool. Michael Edwards, a former apprentice player for Peterborough, had worked under Redknapp at Portsmouth. Then he followed Redknapp to Tottenham. The first time that Edwards met Graham, they talked for three hours. "Three hours of hollering," Graham recalls. "He just battered me." Over time, Edwards would become Graham's strongest supporter, but in 2008 he didn't understand analytics, and didn't want to. When the meeting ended, Graham quietly left the building. He called his colleagues at Decision Analysis from the parking lot. "I think our contract with Spurs is about to be canceled," he said.

During the next two years, Edwards's opinion of analytics evolved dramatically. Eventually, he would take Graham's recommendations on both game strategies and potential recruitment targets and try to sell them to Redknapp. He didn't often succeed, but by the time Comolli landed back in the Premier League as Liverpool's sporting director, Edwards had gained a reputation as a bright young executive. Eventually, Comolli brought him to Liverpool. Then they set out to hire Graham, who they both had come to feel had the best analytics mind in English football, and probably anywhere in the sport.

Graham was dubious of Comolli's renewed interest in his work. As analytics had become more accepted in soccer, Decision Analytics suddenly found itself in demand. The company wasn't fending off clubs that wanted to hire it, but from what had been almost a subsistence living, Graham finally felt he had some security. He also knew that the average tenure of an English soccer manager is less than a year. If Liverpool's next hire was someone like Redknapp, Graham wouldn't just be out a consulting contract, he would be out on the street. He eventually agreed to an interview because he respected Edwards. "But I wasn't planning to accept an offer," he says.

Graham was heading north, on the train from London to Liverpool, when Comolli was ousted by the owners and replaced with Edwards. "I'd been expecting to meet with Damien," Graham says. "Instead, John Henry walked in the room." Graham knew what Henry and his executive team had done with the Red Sox. As he talked with Henry, he realized he would be in a position to implement the soccer version of *Moneyball* with Liverpool. "To do the same thing from the inside," he says. He left Liverpool with the conviction that if he was ever going to try working for a club, this was the one.

———————

GRAHAM WAS HIRED to build the equivalent of the Red Sox' research department. The reaction, almost uniformly, was scorn. "'Laptop guys,' 'Don't know the game'—you'd hear that until just a few months ago," says Barry Hunter, who runs the club's scouting department. "The *Moneyball* thing was thrown at us a lot." Graham hardly noticed. He was immersed in his search for inefficiencies—finding players, some hidden in plain sight, who were undervalued.

In 2014, Chelsea had acquired the contract of the Egyptian attacker Mohamed Salah. Salah arrived in the Premier League with a reputation as a rising star, though in two years with a Swiss team he scored just nine goals. At Chelsea, he had what was by all accounts an undistinguished tenure, playing in 13 games over two seasons and scoring twice, while spending much of his time being loaned out to other clubs. Eventually, his contract was sold to AS Roma, in Italy. At that point, Salah was considered to have little chance of ever succeeding in England.

Playing in the Premier League is unique, according to the English soccer community. Competition is more balanced than elsewhere; nearly every match is a struggle. English players learn the game in frosted conditions that tend to thwart precision passing, fostering a rough, overtly physical style of play. The intensive media attention is distracting. The weather is often terrible. Some players, the assumption holds, just aren't suited for it. But others don't get the chance. "There's this idea that Salah failed at Chelsea," Graham said. "I respectfully disagree." Based on Graham's calculations,

Salah's productivity at Chelsea was similar to how he had played before coming to England, and after he left. And those 500 minutes he played for Chelsea constituted a tiny fraction of his career. "They may be slight evidence against his quality," Graham said, "but they are offset by 20 times the data from thousands and thousands of minutes." In the conventional notion that playing in England is different, Graham saw an opportunity for those who could prove that it wasn't—another inefficiency in the system.

Graham recommended that Liverpool acquire Salah, who by then was thriving in Italy. In American sports, the team might have offered another player in exchange. In soccer, players' rights are bought and sold in a worldwide marketplace. Once a sale price is reached, negotiations begin with the player. If he isn't satisfied with the salary being proposed, or if he dislikes the city where the team plays or the manager he will play for, he can remain where he is. Grooming emerging talent and then selling the rights to it for a profit can help smaller teams stay solvent. Even some clubs playing in their countries' top leagues, such as Germany's Bayer Leverkusen and Holland's PSV Eindhoven, use the process to generate enough income to remain competitive. "Transfers are where the money is," Graham said. "They are a huge component of financial performance."

That July, Liverpool paid Roma about $41 million for Salah, which is a substantial fee but not nearly as much as would be expected for a world-class goal scorer. "People weren't battering down the door for his services," Graham said. It was also true that Salah might mean more to Liverpool than he would to a different club. Graham's data suggested that Salah could pair especially well with Roberto Firmino, another of Liverpool's attackers, who creates more expected goals from his passes than nearly anyone else in his position. That turned out to be the case. During the season that followed, 2017–18, Salah turned those expected goals into real ones. He broke the Premier League record by scoring 32 times. He also became the symbol of Liverpool's revival. His crown of curly hair, infectious grin, and stubby legs that somehow ate up ground as he raced across the turf made him one of soccer's most recognizable players. In what turned out to be a harbinger of the club's progress, Liverpool made an unanticipated run to the final of that season's Champions League before losing, 3–1, to Real Madrid. That provided the first tangible evidence that the strategies put in place by Henry and his Fenway group were working. In 2018–19, Salah was one of the three players who led the Premier League in goals. Before the pandemic roiled the marketplace, the website Transfermarkt, which tracks crowdsourced player valuations, estimated his value at $173 million.

Another acquisition might have been even more important. Soon after arriving at Liverpool, Graham was asked to research a left winger at Inter Milan, Philippe Coutinho. His data strongly endorsed Coutinho. Liverpool bought Coutinho's rights for about $16 million. Over the next five years, Coutinho's play contributed to Liverpool's revival. But his most important contribution to the team was to accrue value. In 2018, Barcelona paid Liverpool about $170 million for Coutinho. Soon after, Liverpool spent more than $200 million on three new players: Alisson Becker, a goalkeeper; the Brazilian midfielder Fábio Henrique Tavares, who is known as Fabinho; and the stalwart center back Virgil van Dijk. All became crucial contributors. These were known commodities, and none came at a bargain price. But without the profit made by selling Coutinho, Henry later stressed to me, those players would not have been acquired.

UNTIL THE CLUB opened a sprawling new training complex in 2020, it was based at Melwood, an understated compound set in a residential neighborhood a 10-minute drive from downtown. Graham worked down a corridor from the coaches and the cafeteria. Tim Waskett, who studied astrophysics, sat to Graham's left. Nearby was Dafydd Steele, a former junior chess champion with a graduate math degree who previously worked in the energy industry.

The background of the newest analyst to arrive at Liverpool, Will Spearman, was even less conventional. Spearman completed a doctorate in high-energy physics at Harvard. Then he worked at CERN, in Geneva, where scientists verified the existence of the subatomic Higgs boson. His dissertation provided the first direct measurement of the particle's width, and one of the first of its mass. When he was hired by Graham, and even after months at the job, Spearman knew so little about the sport that he spent much of his downtime playing the video simulation game Football Manager, not just to learn about players around the world, but even some of the names of the positions. "I'd never heard of a mezzala until I started playing Football Manager," he told me. "I'd never heard of a box-to-box midfielder." Another club might conceivably have hired an analyst like Graham, or Steele, or Waskett, and maybe—though it's highly unlikely—even Spearman. But Liverpool, it is safe to say, is the only club that would have hired all of them.

As often as possible, the analysts arrived in time for breakfast. Players sat at one of two tables with coaches and trainers. The analysts, who looked like nobody else in the building, sat at an adjacent table. Greetings were cordial, even friendly. But there was little evidence that the players knew one analyst from another.

The morning after that game against Leicester, Graham sat with his back to Keïta, their chairs touching. Hours before, he'd been shouting at Keïta from the stands. Now he was within a foot of him, eating the same poached eggs, yet there was no interaction between the two of them. "If he wants to talk about the game to me, he can initiate that, and I'd be delighted," Graham said. "Otherwise, I'll leave him in peace."

At one point, Spearman went for coffee. He returned with a question rooted in the intersection of breathless fandom and mathematical geekiness: Who would be the most accurately regarded player in soccer? Not the most underrated or overrated, but the one conventional wisdom comes closest to gauging correctly. His choice was Leo Messi, the generational talent who, at the time, had been playing at Barcelona for his entire professional career. (Messi later moved to Paris Saint-Germain.) "It has to be Messi," he said. "Because if he isn't the best player in the world, he's second. So, the most that opinion could be off is one place." As if to punctuate his point, Spearman suddenly spilled his coffee so that it streamed down the middle of the table. The analysts erupted in good-natured jibes. "You're not doing a good job at convincing anyone that you're not a nerd," Waskett said.

Spearman was raised near the campuses of Northwestern, Georgia Tech, and Texas A&M, where his father taught industrial engineering. He graduated high school at 16 and went directly to college. He looks slightly unkempt, and a lot like Nate Silver, the statistician who created the FiveThirtyEight website for political prognostication. Like Silver, Spearman also has a consuming interest in sports. After finishing his studies in December 2014, he took a telecommuting job with Hudl, a Nebraska-based company that packages videos for high school football and basketball coaches. From his apartment in Brookline, Massachusetts, Spearman wrote code to facilitate the tagging of specific highlights, and even sifted through footage himself. "A lot of it was very rudimentary," he says.

Not long before, the Premier League had started using specialized cameras to track player movements. Clubs were provided with the data, but none seemed to know what to make of it. Some of it found its way to a company that Hudl owned that had a relationship with the league. Someone working there used a mathematical construct called a Voronoi diagram to divide the field into zones controlled by each player. Spearman found that simplistic. "I could do better," he remembers thinking.

Spearman knew nothing about soccer. But he did understand electromagnetic fields. The players' movements struck him as weirdly similar. "You have two particles," he explains. "And how do you know what control they exert on some space in the vacuum? It's their charge. So, the speed each is traveling effectively becomes its charge." He spent a weekend working out how to shape the data into a more accurate model. By that Monday, he was able to calculate exactly where on the field each particular player exerted control at any moment. In early 2016, Spearman presented his findings at London's OptaPro conference. After watching Spearman's presentation, Waskett called Graham. "We have to hire this guy," Waskett said. "We have to take him off the market."

The ready availability of tracking data had exponentially increased the amount of information available to analysts. Not all of the European leagues have equipped their stadiums with the necessary camera system to capture player movement, and the vast majority of young talent that Liverpool scouts plays in leagues around the world that don't have the capability to track players, and may never get it. But enough leagues do have it that patterns inherent to the sport can be identified. "We've now got the trajectory of all the players at 25 frames per second," says Graham. "So, the data exists that we can start to ask the question, 'Why don't we try to play football in a slightly different way?' That was one of the rationales behind hiring Will."

The use of that data has also started to make its way into the mainstream, in the same way that the speed of a ball off the bat and even the spin rate of pitchers' curveballs are now routinely referenced during telecasts of baseball games. In a game during the 2016–17 season, Liverpool kept possession of the ball 80.6 percent of the time at Burnley, yet Burnley somehow managed to win, 2–0. It was revealed by the Premier League in a press release to be the highest possession rate ever recorded for a losing team in its history, and only the second time that any team had managed to keep the ball more than 80 percent of the time. "It's announced from time to time as 'and here's this interesting thing,'" Graham says. "Most commentators are still highly skeptical of it. But from time to time, you'll hear something like that presented, and there's more of it every year."

———————

LATER THAT WINTER, I attended the OptaPro conference with Graham, Waskett, and Spearman. We gathered across the street from London's Euston Station, one floor below ground level in an exhibition space. The vibe was a mix of Silicon Valley and the high school math team, though about half the attendees were wearing tracksuits. About 60 clubs from around the world were represented, but the only one from outside England I saw on a name tag was FC Barcelona.

The seminars, which were all held in the same lecture hall, were so mathematically based that most were incomprehensible to an outsider—and even, Graham confided, to many insiders. But much of the activity took place between seminars, during long interludes that were meant for social interaction. Since even the few dozen analysts employed by English clubs almost never traveled to games, this was one of the few times all year that they were able to have contact with each other. For these analysts, most of whom spent their days doing obscure mathematical calculations that would end up having little, if any, bearing on how the football clubs they were working for would be run, those hours in between the seminars were an opportunity to validate their entire professional existence.

The Liverpool analysts appeared to hold the status of minor celebrities, not so much for the exact nature of the work they were doing, which remained mostly secretive, but for the fact that they were actually getting the manager and even the players to listen to it. Many of the teams there, Graham told me, had started employing analysis in recent months because they had come to believe it was necessary to do so, but much of their work was routinely ignored. I was surprised to see that Wolverhampton Wanderers, a recently promoted club from the industrial Black Country in the heart of England, had five analysts registered at the conference. It turned out they were surprised to be there, too. "The club has made a big commitment," said Will Sanders, who had worked at Brentford, Rangers, and Nottingham Forest before getting hired by Wolves to lead the analytics effort the previous summer. The problem, though, was the club's manager at the time: Nuno Espírito Santo, an inscrutable, taciturn, old-line football man from Portugal. It was hard to imagine him sending an email, let alone sifting through analytical data. Much of Sanders's time was spent angling to find a conduit who would present the findings of the analytics team as his own. Some-times, it was a Scottish assistant; other times, it was one of the Por-tuguese assistants who was closest to Espírito Santo. "We try, and every now and then there's a breakthrough," he said.

And those Wolves analysts were comparatively fortunate. At least they had jobs. More than half of the attendees of the confer-ence, including many of the presenters, did football analysis on a freelance basis, or as a hobby. They would pick a topic and do a study on it, as Spearman had done with player movement. Then they would present it at the conference in the hope that a club would see the work and hire them. Spearman was the ultimate suc-cess story, someone who had come in with no soccer experience and ended up in the back room at Liverpool. When I told one of the aspiring analysts that I was there with the Liverpool contingent, his eyes widened. "Will Spearman," he intoned, almost in a whisper. "I think Will is brilliant."

Spearman had little to do with Liverpool's emergence as one of the world's best clubs. He did almost none of the work that Klopp saw, and he was rarely involved with discovering players. His man-date was more ethereal. Spearman knew just enough about the sport, or just little enough, to try to change it. Soccer is the sum of thousands of individual actions, but the only ones Graham's model could evaluate were the passes, shots, and ball movements that are downloaded from the official play-by-play. "There are still funda-mental limitations in the data we have," Graham said. "It's still like looking through a very foggy lens." By working to get the mathemat-ical rendering closer to reflecting what actually happens on the field, recording not just that a defender kicked a pass to a midfielder but how hard it went and what happened when it was received, Spear-man was looking to find a path through the fog.

Most of his time was spent creating a model that employed video tracking. It assigned numerical scores to everything that happened to everyone, even when the ball wasn't involved. That included a fullback racing down the sideline, forcing a lone defender to choose between two players to cover, or a striker getting into position to receive a cross directly in front of the goalkeeper, even if the pass sailed over his head. "Every action, how much value it adds, how well it was performed," Spearman said. "Once you have that, you can start to create new approaches." One of those eventually might be to script plays, as in the NFL, radically altering the nature of a game that has resisted change for more than a century.

Liverpool's success helped make analytics more palatable in the Premier League, at least publicly. Still, in my discussions with managers and executives in the months that followed, I rarely found anyone who understood the concept. At one point during the OptaPro conference, I snuck away to take Steve Walsh to a late lunch. As an assistant manager at Leicester City, Walsh had been responsible for scouting many of the players who won an unexpected Premier League title in 2016.

Walsh, who was unemployed when we met, had been scouting for various English clubs since the 1970s. He had the amiable, slightly gruff demeanor of someone who had been inside the game for a long time. He knew I was there to talk with him about analytics, and he started the conversation by telling me that they "don't measure character, they don't measure desire. They can't measure passion." But he also said that, more than most scouts and sporting directors, he understood analytics and had come to appreciate their value. "You've got to move with the times," he said.

I knew that Leicester City didn't have an analytics department when Walsh was there because Balsom, Ian Graham's friend, had been in the process of helping the club start one when we'd met a few weeks before. I couldn't help wondering whether Walsh, who was aware as he talked to me that he might be quoted in a magazine story, had potential future employers in mind. It seemed possible that he was positioning himself to me as more forward-thinking than he actually was. When I asked him whether analytics played much of a role in finding some of his most important discoveries on that Leicester City team, such as the midfielder N'Golo Kanté and the striker Jamie Vardy, he nodded vigorously. "Oh, yes," he said. "Kanté, you have to say that was an analytic signing. We knew that he was playing in one of the top five leagues in Europe, and playing well."

I must have looked at him quizzically because he immediately segued to Vardy. He pointed out that Vardy had led a glorified semipro league in goals as an unknown 24-year-old in 2011. A year later, Vardy did the same in a slightly higher league, but one still several rungs below the level at which someone could make a living playing football. "And that," Walsh said triumphantly, "is what led us to decide to scout him."

This didn't sound like advanced analysis to me. "You were just following him in the newspaper and tallying his goals?" I asked him. "Or occasionally looking him up on some club website?" Walsh nodded.

I told him that he could have done essentially the same thing half a century before. "There's nothing revolutionary about that," I said. "That's not data analysis. That's just simple addition. That's counting."

He looked astonished that I would make such a distinction. "What do you mean?" he said. "It's numbers, isn't it?"

6

WE HATE ORTHODOXY

IN 2011, THE Canadian author and journalist Jonah Keri wrote a book about how the Tampa Bay Rays were using analytics to overperform, year after year. The title of the book, *The Extra 2%*, made it sound like the Rays' devotion to data analysis involved incremental gains, like putting healthier food on the training table or a massage jet in the shower.

Actually, it wasn't about that at all. With a former investment banker named Andrew Friedman as their general manager, the Rays had taken a systematic, organization-wide approach to baseball. They gathered and analyzed more data than any team in any sport had previously dared, and then applied it to every aspect of their business. The Rays were Beane's A's taken to the logical extreme. They had almost no natural fan base. They played in a terrible stadium—a dark, echoing dome on the St. Petersburg waterfront that felt like an empty warehouse with Astroturf in the middle. They had very little money and not much hope of ever making any. They didn't just need to be smarter. They needed to be revolutionary.

Keri made these points in his book, which chronicled the Rays' 97-victory season of 2008 that won them the American League pennant. (They lost to the Phillies in five games in the World Series.) Then he made them again and again, on the website Grantland and on ESPN's website and its podcasts. In the years that followed, Keri's life would spiral precipitously downward; as a result of a domestic abuse conviction, he would be sentenced to 21 months in prison in March 2022. At that point, he had long since disappeared from the media landscape. But as of 2015, when we met for lunch at a gourmet burger bar near where he was living in Denver, Keri had standing as the most articulate mass-market spokesman for the analytic approach to baseball. He disdained strategies that were rooted in baseball's distant past, when a far higher percentage of runs were scored on singles and doubles than from home runs, and he wasn't reticent about letting the world know how he felt.

Most of baseball had figured out by then that, in all but a few specific strategic situations, advancing a runner from first to second base in exchange for an out (with a sacrifice bunt) or even the chance of an out (an attempted steal) was a losing proposition. According to data compiled through that season by Greg Stoll, putting a runner on first base with nobody out would lead, on average, to 0.87 runs. Giving up an out by bunting that runner to second base decreased the number of runs the team should expect during that inning to 0.68. Maybe more important, the odds that the team would score more than one run diminished from 23.8 percent to 16.2. To put it another way, if a lineup's goal is to construct a big inning—"put up a crooked number," in the parlance of yesterday's players and today's sportscasters—bunting a runner to second lowered the chances of that happening by more than 30 percent.

I had gone to see Keri to try to understand why the Kansas City Royals, who seemed to play as though they were unaware of the changes that data analysis had brought to baseball, had advanced all the way to the seventh game of the World Series the previous season before losing to San Francisco. The Royals were managed by Ned Yost, a former backup catcher for the New York Mets and Milwaukee Brewers. If you conjured up an image of an old-school baseball man, someone who told his players to rub spit and dirt on their spike wounds and who had utter disdain for an analyst with a laptop, he would look and sound exactly like Yost.

Because of Yost's apparent obliviousness to data-based thinking, he had become the most criticized manager in the major leagues. In fact, as a consequence of the reach of social media and the herd mentality that pervaded it, he may have been the most criticized baseball manager ever. The criticism occurred not merely at the margins, in bars and man caves and on Twitter and fan websites (where the verb "Yosted" had emerged to describe what happened when his choices led to a Royals loss), but squarely in the media mainstream. It fixated on Yost's batting orders, his team's tendency to bunt and try to steal, the way he handled his pitching staff— nearly everything that could be plugged into a formula and rendered as a number. The *Chicago Tribune* suggested that Yost was "a bumbling idiot." A *Wall Street Journal* headline referred to him as a "dunce." Pedro Martínez, a Hall of Fame pitcher, disparaged one of his decisions on national television as "another panic move."

Yet the Royals won. For four consecutive years beginning with Yost's first full season in 2011, they won more games than they had the year before. Their trip to the World Series in 2014, which happened after they qualified for the playoffs as a wild card, was only the franchise's second in more than 50 years of existence, and its first since 1985. By the time of my lunch with Keri in July 2015, the Royals were on track to win their division for the first time in three decades. Either the Royals were somehow able to succeed despite Yost, or the analytic approach that was taking over baseball had missed something important.

Keri strongly believed it was the former. When I asked him about Yost's relative standing among major-league managers, he responded that Yost was one of the worst. He explained that the Royals' success the previous season had been a product of good relief pitching by the deepest bullpen in baseball, coupled with luck that came at the right times. Before the 2015 season, he had predicted that the Royals' luck was likely to even out, as luck tends to do. Of the 30 major-league teams, he ranked them 23rd. He predicted a fourth-place finish for the Royals in the five-team American League Central.

Instead, the Royals were 52–34 at the time of our lunch. They had a four-and-a-half-game lead in the division. Keri admitted that their ongoing success confounded him. "When you have close games, weird things can happen," he said. But he felt confident that the statistical analyses he had built his journalistic career expounding would ultimately prove correct.

As we were getting ready to leave, he added something that surprised me. As anyone who had read *Moneyball* or seen the movie was well aware, Beane's epiphany was that baseball people put too much stock in appearances. Beane himself had looked exactly like a major leaguer was supposed to look. Except that, once he advanced to the majors, he turned out to not have the elite skills needed to succeed. If that were the case, Beane surmised, perhaps the opposite was true: that baseball talent was hidden in players most executives were disregarding only because they didn't look like standouts. From that came the entire concept of questioning baseball's received wisdom—from where a shortstop should play against a given hitter to the situations in which your best relief pitcher should be used— upon which Keri had built his career.

Yet, as I spoke with Keri, I couldn't help feeling that he was making the same mistake that the baseball lifers who had scouted Beane had made. The Rays were led by Joe Maddon, the epitome of the enlightened, post-*Moneyball* manager. Maddon wore funky glasses and cultivated a hipster persona. If he enjoyed anything more than talking baseball tactics with reporters who had made the effort to fully understand the Rays' approach, it was talking about topics other than baseball—literature, philosophy, wine. During the season he spent with the Rays, Keri enjoyed long sessions with Maddon in the dugout during batting practice, in Maddon's office at Tropicana Field deep into the night after games, in hotel bars, and anywhere else they found themselves together. Keri came away entranced.

Yost's interests, on the other hand, were as stereotypical as a baseball man's could get: hunting, stock car racing, and how to play the game. Yost's conversations with reporters were brusque and basic. He sounded like every grizzled manager since the Deadball Era. And that, as much as anything else, was the reason that Keri disdained him. "We hate orthodoxy," he told me, speaking for the emerging school of analytically savvy baseball writers. "We hate it. And Ned Yost is a pretty orthodox kind of guy. He goes in, he's old-school, no flowery words. He's not reading psychology books. He's not giving a seminar on wine." Keri had made a career of arguing that ball clubs should ignore their biases and focus on the data. But had his own biases about what a good manager should look like blinded him to Yost's true value?

EARLIER THAT YEAR, a new product called Statcast had been introduced at MIT's Sports Analytics Conference. It won the Alpha Award, which is given annually to the best new analytics innovation or technology. Statcast was owned by Baseball Advanced Media, known as BAM, a spinoff of Major League Baseball that had been created back in 2000 as a way to standardize the websites of the 30 teams, and which took on a life of its own as the virtual universe expanded.

The purpose of Statcast, which had been beta-tested in three stadiums during the 2014 season, was to record the movement of every player on a baseball field during every play, in relation to the ball. It was the first step toward trying to solve a mystery that had eluded baseball people since the game began, throughout the 20th century, and into the analytics era: How can you tell how proficient a player is at defense? "To this point, it has been what my eyes see," said Jeff Bridich, a former Harvard baseball player who was the general manager of the Colorado Rockies at the time. "Which might be different than what your eyes see."

To track a moving object like a ball, you typically set two cameras perpendicular to each other. A computer program then hunts through the images from each camera for something that, based on its shape and movement, seems likely to be a ball. By triangulating the two views, you can figure out where that ball was at a given moment. In 2006, BAM started using that approach to gauge the velocity, movement, location, and spin rate of every pitch. It called the system "PITCHf/x." But PITCHf/x doesn't work nearly as well with forms that don't have a predictable shape, like people. And when you try to follow those forms as they come together and then split apart in seemingly random patterns, which happens in baseball on nearly every play, it doesn't work well at all.

In 2012, at the International Broadcasting Convention in Amsterdam, the Swedish company Hego introduced a technology that used two cameras to simulate how the eyes of a person coordinate to gauge distances. "It could see the depth of the field inherently," recalls Joe Inzerillo, baseball's chief technology officer. Unlike PITCHf/x, this new technology couldn't pick up balls, which were too small and moved too quickly. But Inzerillo believed it would have no trouble tracking players.

BAM had been trying to capture data on player movements since its start more than a decade before. At the Amsterdam conference, Inzerillo sensed that he and his team were close. He proposed the idea of trying to integrate Hego's system with a second technology so that they could follow the ball and the players simultaneously. That second technology wouldn't be PITCHf/x, he knew; in a large space like the entire field, the prospect of the ball getting lost entirely amid the background clutter would increase drastically. But he wondered about TrackMan, the modified Doppler radar system that was starting to be used to measure the trajectory of thrown and batted balls. "Radar, on the other hand, does not really see the background," Inzerillo says. "And one unit can cover the field pretty well. We literally sat down and sketched it out on a piece of paper and figured out how these two systems could talk to each other."

Hego's two camera pods were eventually installed, 70 to 150 feet apart, along the third-base line in all but two major-league ballparks. (In Boston and Milwaukee, they were put along the first-base line because of architectural quirks.) The TrackMan system, adapted from technology used for missile defense, traces the ball as it would any moving object. Statcast was programmed to layer the information generated by one atop the other, creating a representation of what's happening on the field. Usually, it worked.

Sometimes, though, it didn't. Nearly three years after an initial trial run in the Arizona Fall League, Statcast was still committing rookie errors. Chopped grounders that bounded high into the air eluded the radar. So did high pop-ups. The system was precise at the middle of the field, less so toward the foul lines. And even though the vast majority of the Statcast data was accurate, its sheer volume—millions of lines of digital output from every day of the baseball season—remained difficult to process. Merely coming up with a program to unpack the pages of computer coding was beyond the wherewithal of most teams. "It's nice to say that we have the technology, the means of capturing data," said Bridich. "But now we're plowing through it, trying to understand it. What does all of this mean?"

That's not to say Statcast wasn't already having an influence. Kevin Kiermaier, Tampa Bay's center fielder who was known for his acrobatic catches, spent much of the 2015 season in a debilitating batting slump. His manager, Kevin Cash, wanted him to understand how much he was contributing to the team despite his offensive struggles. "What he was doing was helping us win games more than anyone picking up a newspaper could tell," Cash said. Using wins above replacement, a somewhat arbitrary (but increasingly popular) statistic that amalgamates the output of various offensive categories into a single number, he showed Kiermaier how well a particular All-Star outfielder was hitting. Then he used Statcast data to quantify Kiermaier's value into an approximate defensive equivalent. "I said, 'Here's what you're doing—not with home runs, not with batting average, just on defense,'" Cash said. "'You're impacting our club in a huge way.'" Relieved of the pressure to hit, Kiermaier relaxed.

He finished the season batting .263. He also won the Gold Glove Award as the best center fielder in the American League.

It should be axiomatic that a run prevented is as important as a run scored. Yet perhaps because accurately validating defensive contributions is so difficult, baseball people tend not to think that way. "It starts when you're young," Kiermaier told me. "When you're done with a Little League game and your parents say, 'How'd you do?' you say, 'Two for four with a double,' not 'I held a guy to a single with a great throw.'" If you're an outstanding hitter, a manager will keep you in the lineup no matter how you field. If you're an outstanding fielder—well, you'd better be able to hit a little, too. "There's a huge difference in perception between a guy hitting .200 and .240," Kiermaier told me. But that huge difference only amounts to four hits out of 100 at-bats. On the other hand, if you were to replace Kiermaier with a subpar outfielder for 100 at-bats by the opposition, it's likely that his team would surrender more than four additional hits. And that doesn't take into account extra bases taken by runners, extra batters faced by pitchers, and other hidden consequences.

Baseball's analytics experts understood that fielding had eluded them. "Everything we do is trying to predict the future," said Zack Scott, who was the assistant general manager of the Red Sox until 2020 and then, briefly, the general manager of the Mets. "We build predictive models. And that's far easier to do with hitting." After graduating with a statistics degree from the University of Vermont in 1999, Scott went to work for the owners of Diamond Mind, a baseball simulation game. Its inventor, Tom Tippett, had been attempting rudimentary analyses of outfielders' range. Scott, whose job was to produce player ratings, tried to advance the discipline. Using hitters' spray charts, which showed where each ball was hit, he could figure out where batted balls went and whether they were caught. But he had no idea where the fielders had been standing when the pitch was thrown. And even if he could estimate how often a fielder made a certain play, he had no idea why. "Instincts?" Scott asks. "Speed? The routes he was taking to the ball? You couldn't answer that question."

The Red Sox hired Scott in late 2003, in part to help figure out how to gauge defensive prowess. Progress was slow. "We felt like we had an advantage because we were into this stuff so early," Scott says. "We had the most experience using defensive metrics. But we weren't where we wanted to be." So, when a 22-year-old named Jackie Bradley Jr. was promoted to Boston's major-league roster in 2013 with a reputation as the best defensive outfielder in the organization, he was judged the same way as every fielder before him: "The eye test," as John Farrell, who was Boston's manager at the time, called it.

Bradley was clearly a superior defensive player. The problem was, he didn't hit. He had been productive during his college and minor-league careers, but he struggled in Boston. He batted .189 in 37 games in 2013, and .198 the following season. In 2014, because of a paucity of other options as much as any other reason, Bradley became the team's starting center fielder. "But he was at .180, .190," Farrell says. "And that was subjectively outweighing the defense. I didn't have the ability to say, 'What is he saving us defensively?'" Before the 2015 season, Farrell decided that Bradley needed to hit .240 in order to remain in the lineup. That number, which would govern Bradley's fortunes—and, to some extent, the team's—was little more than a guess. "It was arbitrary," Farrell told me. "We just didn't know."

———

AT LEAST FARRELL was trying to figure it out. In Kansas City that same summer, Ned Yost seemed to be managing almost entirely on instinct, the way someone might play a game of Monopoly, disregarding not just advanced analytics and Statcast data but all statistics entirely. Yost grew up in California's Livermore Valley as an undersized striver seeking a sport in which he could excel. Cut from the high school soccer team, he struggled for a semester as a five-foot, two-inch hurdler. Then he turned to baseball, which he hadn't played since Little League. In 36 junior varsity at-bats as a sophomore, he couldn't muster even one hit. Nevertheless, Yost decided he was going to play—not merely in high school, but for a living. "I just knew it," he says. "When I sat down with my counselors and they said, 'What are you going to do?' I said, 'I'm going to be a professional baseball player.' And they looked at me like I was nuts."

Such certitude, based on no discernible foundation, informed Yost's decision-making processes all his life. "I often wonder, 'Do other people have that same feeling and then it doesn't happen?'" Yost told me. "Because I *knew* it was going to happen." He made the varsity team, had a growth spurt, then eventually landed at Chabot, a community college in Hayward, near Oakland. After he starred on a summer team, the Mets drafted him as a catcher. In 1980, he reached the majors, just as he had predicted. He seldom played, though. Over six seasons, Yost accumulated just 605 at-bats, a number that some starters exceed in a single year. He was wondering what to do next when the Braves asked if he would work with young players at their minor-league outpost in Sumter, South Carolina. He ended up as the manager there for three years. Then he was hired onto Bobby Cox's staff in Atlanta, where he remained for more than a decade as a bullpen coach, and later a third-base coach.

Along the way, he cultivated an unconventional relationship with players, one that made them eager to get to the ballpark. "He'd throw a belt into the whirlpool when I was in there and pretend it was a snake," recalls the former major leaguer Eddie Pérez, who was in Sumter and Atlanta with Yost. "Not many managers would do that."

Yost can be prickly in news conferences. But in an intimate set-ting, he's engaging, even warm. One afternoon, he shared memories with me about a friend he considered a mentor, the legendary racer Dale Earnhardt Sr., whom he met in the early 1990s. Yost wore the number 3 to honor Earnhardt, who died in a crash in 2001. "We hit it off," he said. "Hunted together every year." In 1994, when a labor dispute truncated the baseball season, Earnhardt invited Yost to travel with him on the NASCAR circuit and serve as "rehydration engineer" (in other words, water fetcher). At one race, Earnhardt roared back from a huge deficit and nearly won. When Yost con-gratulated him, Earnhardt grabbed him by the shirt and pulled his friend nose to nose. "Never, ever, let anybody who you're around, anybody you're associated with, allow you to settle for mediocrity," Yost says Earnhardt told him.

Later, Yost would be criticized for not replacing erratic infield-ers when he had late-inning leads and allowing untested pitchers to compete—and often fail—in crucial situations. The critics didn't understand, he told me, that he wasn't necessarily trying to win those games. "The difference between 72 and 76 wins doesn't mean a damn thing to me," he says. It was the same as the difference between second place and last place, which, Earnhardt had stressed, was no difference at all. "I wanted to put those young players in a position to gain experience, so that when we could compete for a championship, they'd know how," Yost said. "You can't do that when you're pinch-hitting for young guys. You can't do it when you quick-hook starting pitchers. They'll never learn to work themselves out of trouble. People would say, 'What's he doing?' They didn't under-stand. I'd rather lose a game on my watch so they could win later."

In Milwaukee, Yost was hired to nurture a group of young players learning to be major leaguers. He inherited a 56-win team, the worst in franchise history, and a legacy that was equally dismal. The Brewers hadn't had a winning record in more than a decade. In their first two seasons under Yost, they won just 68 and 67 games. But in 2007, they remained in contention until the season's final week before finishing 83–79, narrowly missing the playoffs. That week, an increasingly agitated Yost was ejected from games three times for arguing with umpires. The consensus was that he'd cracked under the pressure. The next year, the Brewers were 16 games above .500 with two weeks remaining in the season, but they were mired in a slump. They had lost 11 of 16 games and appeared to be collapsing again when Yost was fired. The Brewers wound up winning 90 games, but they would be remembered as the playoff team that dumped its manager down the stretch.

The knock on Yost as an unsteady hand returned in 2014, after the Royals qualified as one of the two American League wild card teams. In the single-game elimination against Oakland, James Shields, the Royals' starting pitcher, held a 3–2 lead after five innings. Then he allowed a single and a walk to start the sixth. Yost had three standout relievers in his bullpen in Kelvin Herrera, Wade Davis, and Greg Holland, but they had been earmarked to work a single inning each at the end of the game—in succession, the seventh, eighth, and ninth. Seemingly oblivious to the fact that his team's season was on the line, Yost instead turned to Yordano Ventura. A 23-year-old starter, Ventura had worked as a reliever once all season. He also had thrown 73 pitches two days before.

The criticism of Yost, on television and online, began when he lifted Shields. Then Brandon Moss hit a three-run homer, giving Oakland the lead. When Yost left the dugout to replace Ventura, the reaction from the home fans was hostile, bordering on homicidal. For 29 years, they had longed for the playoffs. Now, it appeared, the obduracy of an already unpopular manager was ending the Royals' postseason when it had barely begun. Their frustration manifested itself in a deafening outpouring of disapproval. "I'd never in my life heard anything like it," says the broadcaster Ryan Lefebvre, whose father, Jim, played and managed in the major leagues.

"It didn't bother me," Yost told me. "I still felt like we were going to win the game. I had no doubt that we would." They did, in 12 innings. Then they swept their series against the Angels and the Orioles and advanced to the World Series.

———————

YOST ARRIVED IN Kansas City in 2010 with the mandate to develop young talent, just as he had in Milwaukee. Dayton Moore, the Royals' general manager, had worked with Yost in Atlanta. When the Royals' losses mounted during Yost's first few years on the job, Moore didn't flinch. "A lot of people were saying we needed to make a change," he says. "It never crossed my mind."

Moore had spent enough time in the clubhouse to notice how Yost and his charges interacted. Yost, it turned out, had hardly changed since Sumter. Instead of data points to be plugged into an equation, he treated players with sportive affection, like favored nephews. "I love these guys," Yost told me. "I really love them. You have to, in order to understand them. And you have to under-stand them in order to manage them. If you understand their back-grounds, why they are the way they are, you can understand what motivates them."

Like most modern clubhouses, that Kansas City team was

an eclectic mix. Chris Young was a cerebral Princeton graduate. Lorenzo Cain was raised by his mother in rural Florida and didn't play baseball until high school. Drew Butera's father and Mike Moustakas's uncle were major leaguers. There were Dominicans and Venezuelans, a Puerto Rican, a Nicaraguan, a Cuban, and some-times even a Brazilian. "This is a very culturally diverse team," said Ben Zobrist, a utility player who arrived in Kansas City from Oak-land that July. "But these guys for sure feel comfortable with each other. When a clubhouse is that comfortable, it has started with the manager." To Zobrist, an ideal clubhouse was one where you couldn't tell whether a team had lost or won four games in a row. That's possible because of the steady, accretive cadence of baseball, a sport in which alternating games of no hits and three hits will win you a batting title. "Most managers don't let you do it," he says. "You pick up clues from the manager. If he's worried, you need to be wor-ried. Here, you have the freedom to think that whatever happened yesterday doesn't matter."

The Royals' success wasn't all about intangibles. A decade of high draft picks paid off with a cadre of homegrown stars. And the team's roster of line-drive hitters and fleet fielders was tailored to the capacious dimensions of Kansas City's Kauffman Stadium. (It was also analytics-friendly, in the sense that it was ideally suited for the economics of playing in the sport's second-smallest metropolitan area. Building a team around outfield defense and middle relief is cheap compared with the marquee expenses of power hitting and starting pitching.) Still, it was telling that castoffs and prospects on downward trajectories had, one after another, righted themselves under Yost.

In 2014, the burly third baseman Moustakas, the second pick in the amateur draft, was struggling, his batting average lower than his weight. "I kept hearing: 'Why are you playing him? Why are you playing him?'" Yost said. Moustakas would arrive each day wondering if he would be dropped from the lineup. Finally, it dawned on him that no matter how badly he performed, Yost wasn't going to remove him. The effect was liberating. His five postseason homers would lead the team. "He finds a way to get each of us to believe in what he's doing," Moustakas said later. "For me, it really helped to get out there, struggle and learn how to work through failure. It made all the difference." In 2015, Moustakas was named an American League All-Star. When Yost made the announcement, he beamed like a proud uncle.

Yost was criticized because his players bunted and stole excessively, risking outs in misguided attempts to move runners up a base. But most of those decisions, it turned out, weren't made by him. Perhaps alone among big-league managers, he allowed his players to run and bunt on their own. The few games that such ill-considered tactics might cost during a season, he decided, were more than mitigated by a lack of inhibition that would encourage looser, more productive play. "He allows us to be ourselves, on and off the field," explained Cain, the center fielder. "And we have a blast doing it. We laugh together, have a great time. The chemistry on this team is amazing. That reflects on a manager. And it matters."

That chemistry also appeared to have offset the construction of curious batting orders. Alcides Escobar, who hit leadoff for much of the season, historically had reached base less often than the league average. The potent Alex Gordon was hitting sixth before he strained a groin muscle in early July. This especially annoyed the analysts. "Batting order is something a manager very clearly has control of," said Dave Cameron, the managing editor of the widely read website FanGraphs. "It's something Yost has done particularly poorly."

Yost dismissed such criticism. But others in the organization felt compelled to respond. "We have information that the fans and analysts don't," said Yost's bench coach, Don Wakamatsu, who previously managed the Seattle Mariners. When he was in Seattle, Wakamatsu said, he occasionally put the slugger Russell Branyan fourth, in the cleanup spot. "When I did, he'd break out in hives. But I'd put him at two, or five, or six, and he was a world-beater. Can the numbers account for that?"

If Yost never wavered in support of Moustakas, Cain, Escobar, and others, it was because he saw their future, just as he had seen his own. "I knew it when I saw them playing as Class A ballplayers, that they'd be All-Stars," he says. "I've never really had a guy that I strongly believed in not make it. I just knew it, don't ask me how." In 2014, the Royals were foundering at the All-Star break. "Then we were swept by Boston," Wakamatsu says. "Ned told us: 'Don't worry. We'll be 10 games over .500 soon.' And we said, 'What?' And we were. And then he said, 'We'll be 20 games over.' And we were. There's a calmness and a confidence about it that eventually makes you not question it."

The problem with attributes such as calmness and chemistry, at least to commentators like Keri, was that you couldn't quantify them. They *knew* what the Royals were giving up every time Cain squared around to bunt—it was right there in the numbers. But Moustakas's epiphany that Yost wasn't going to replace him? Yost's eerie certitude that his young players were destined to succeed? How do you plug such nebulous factors into a calculator? Was Yost such an incisive judge of talent that he correctly identified a lineup's worth of future stars, or did his belief in them help make them that way? Did he see something in his team that others didn't, or did his confidence provide inspiration? These are all questions that analytics cannot yet answer.

Yet the same unpredictability that confounds those who try to explain the game through statistical formulations is, paradoxically, what makes it so enjoyable to follow. Accumulated data may suggest shifting the shortstop to the other side of second base against a particular hitter—when baseball rules allowed that, until 2023—and that particular hitter might oblige by hitting a ground ball to exactly that spot. The strategy has worked—except when the grounder hits a pebble and bounds past. And there's the batter, safe at first base.

And there was Yost, when I saw him last near the end of that season, standing by the rail in the Royals' dugout, leading his team to the World Series again for reasons that seemed impossible to validate. It wasn't important to him why the grounders kept getting past the shortstop, only that they did.

———

THOSE 2015 ROYALS kept on winning. They won their division. They beat the Astros in the first round of the playoffs, and then the favored Blue Jays to advance to the World Series against the Mets. By then, their success was being seen as something more than an ongoing coincidence. Still, most observers rated the World Series a toss-up, or even gave the Mets a slight advantage. Their veteran manager, Terry Collins, appeared to have evolved in ways that Yost had been unwilling to. "The scouting report used to be this thick," Collins told me at one point, moving his thumb and his forefinger perhaps half an inch apart. Then he widened them to maybe two inches. "Now, it's *this* thick. If you can use it right, it can help you win a game." Instead, Yost and the Royals won four out of five to become champions.

And then Yost effectively disappeared. He managed for four more years, but it was as though he'd made his point and could retreat in peace. In 2016, after improving every season under Yost, the Royals suddenly became irrelevant. They won 81 games, exactly as many as they lost. They finished third in their division and missed the playoffs. In 2017, they had almost exactly the same season, losing one more game to finish 80–82. After that, Yost presided over two seasons of rebuilding, winning just 58 and 59 games. Following the 2019 season, he retired.

Baseball, it seemed, had learned nothing from Yost's success—if, in fact, there was anything to be learned. Rather, the game continued its shift decisively away from Yost's relationship-based style of leadership and toward one that positioned managers as essentially intermediaries between upper management and the players. Between the 2017 and 2018 seasons, five veteran managers who had combined for 8,946 games of experience over 58 seasons lost their jobs. The casualties included the Mets' Collins, two seasons removed from winning the National League pennant, and Joe Girardi, who had just guided the Yankees to within a game of the World Series. The Red Sox and the Washington Nationals won their divisions, yet their managers were also fired. All of them had been criticized, overtly or obliquely, for being unwilling to fully implement the data-based recommendations that were being generated by their teams' analytics departments.

If anyone needed more evidence that the value of managerial intuition was plummeting, none of the men chosen to replace the five deposed managers had managed even a single day in the majors. Three of the five new hires—Mickey Callaway (who replaced Collins), the Yankees' Aaron Boone, and Washington's Dave Martinez—hadn't managed at any level, from Little League to the high minors. In December, at baseball's annual winter meetings, each of the novice managers sat before an arc of digital recorders in a ballroom of an Orlando hotel for question after question about analytics and their applications. The reporters might have been interviewing currency traders.

In a way, that made sense. Many decisions that managers previously made by instinct, from filling out lineup cards to choosing relievers, were now being worked out across baseball at 10 a.m., if not during the previous week, in an office that probably didn't even have a view of the field. The back end of the process had become important—the translating of all those data-driven decisions into wins by coaxing players to actually do what the data was suggesting they would do: to help managers overcome their instincts in order to optimize their teams' performance. In this structure, the job of a manager had evolved into a corporate *middle manager* who received orders from above and implemented them below. "The information you have might be terrific information," Callaway explained when we discussed his approach. "But no matter how good it is, if they're not going to buy into it and have confidence that it will help them? You might as well throw it out the window."

The Yankees, Mets, Red Sox, Nationals, and Philadelphia Phillies all sought the same kind of manager. It's hardly surprising that each compiled a similar list of candidates. "I had five calls asking me to interview," Alex Cora, who had been a successful conduit between players and management as the Astros' bench coach in 2017, said. "I couldn't even get to all of them." Cora ended up getting hired by the Red Sox. In an effort to find different names, the Mets' general manager, Sandy Alderson, a former Marine with a Harvard law degree who had run baseball teams on and off since the 1980s, even called baseball writers for their suggestions. He eventually asked six prospective hires to have preliminary discussions. He envisioned a process similar to the one a major corporation might use to recruit and hire an executive: a series of interviews that would winnow down the candidates until a clear choice emerged.

To prepare for it, Callaway wrote a 7,000-word manifesto outlining his managerial vision. "Collaboration and communication," he stressed, "will be the biggest key to our success." As manager, he promised, he would utilize every possible resource, "whether it be a coach . . . with 40 years' experience or an analytics intern that we just hired out of college." He would nurture relationships with players, but he rejected the traditional notion of the "player's manager." "I will always be good about having the front office's back when it comes to players," he wrote. He listed books that had helped his philosophy coalesce, including Carol Dweck's *Mindset*, which preaches the doctrine of dedication triumphing over innate talent. Callaway's manifesto was not something that Ned Yost ever would have bothered to read, much less to write.

Callaway didn't give his manifesto to Alderson before their discussion because he wasn't certain how such an intellectual approach would be received. So, he was astonished when Alderson asked him questions, one after another, on many of the topics that were in his memo, including how Callaway would communicate with players and how he planned to balance his players' desires with what the organization wanted them to do. As he was leaving, he told Alderson: "I have this document that I'm going to give to you. And what I think you're going to find is, this document is almost exactly the same as that paper in front of you that you're using to ask me questions." Alderson read it. Then, after consulting with Fred and Jeff Wilpon, who owned the Mets at the time, Alderson called off his search and offered Callaway the job.

As well as he'd planned for it, Callaway didn't succeed while managing the Mets. He was fired after winning almost exactly half his games—163, against 161 losses—over two seasons. (Later, he would be suspended by Major League Baseball after accusations that he sexually harassed multiple women, while managing the Mets and in previous jobs.) But Cora, who also had been on Alderson's interview list, fared differently. In his first season in Boston, his lightly regarded Red Sox won the 2018 World Series in five games. The team the Red Sox beat, the Dodgers, were managed by Dave Roberts, who was nearly as analytically inclined. The following year, another of those novice managers, Dave Martinez, shocked Roberts's Dodgers in the National League Division Series. Then he led the Nationals to their first championship.

———————

IN 2014, THE Dodgers had raided Tampa Bay's staff to hire Andrew Friedman as their head of baseball operations. Friedman's mandate was to layer into the corporate culture of one of baseball's biggest and wealthiest franchises the same analytical approach that Keri had chronicled in St. Petersburg. It wasn't easy. Despite their valuation at the time of more than $2 billion, and some of the richest sponsorship and local media contracts in the industry, the Dodgers hadn't won a championship since 1988, long before the analytic era. Friedman, who was 37 at the time, inherited a team that had won consecutive division titles under Don Mattingly, a manager who seemed nearly as oblivious to the data revolution as Yost. Mattingly lasted one season under Friedman. He won yet another division title for the Dodgers, but lost in the playoffs to the Mets. A few days before the Mets and Royals opened that 2015 World Series, Mattingly agreed to leave with a year remaining on his contract.

The Dodgers then won their division for the next five seasons—

2016 through 2020. They lost to Houston in one World Series in 2017 (the Astros turned out to be illegally stealing signs from Dodgers catchers), and then to Cora and the Red Sox in another World Series, a year later. In 2020, the season that was truncated by the COVID-19 pandemic, they advanced all the way to the World Series for the third time in Friedman's tenure.

This time, their opponent was the Rays, Friedman's former employer. Despite a $28.3 million payroll, second-lowest among the 30 MLB teams, the Rays had fashioned another winner by once again relying more heavily on analytics than any other team. (The Dodgers' payroll, by means of comparison, was $105.7 million.) It helped that the Rays had a talented pitching staff led by Blake Snell, who had been drafted in 2011 out of a high school near Seattle and nurtured through the Rays system. In 2018, Snell emerged as one of baseball's best starters by both the old metrics and the new ones. He won 21 games and lost 5, with a 1.89 earned-run average. His WHIP, or combined walks and hits allowed per inning, was 0.974. And over nine innings, on average, he allowed a league-low 5.6 hits.

His numbers in the COVID-ravaged 2020 season weren't quite as gaudy. But when Snell took the ball for Game Six of the World Series, with the Dodgers just one victory away from finally winning one in the 21st century, he was clearly the Rays' best hope of extending the season to another game. On that evening, Snell was nearly unhittable. Through five innings, he shut out the Dodgers and allowed only one single. Entering the sixth inning, protecting a 1–0 lead, his velocity was as good as it had been at the start of the game. He showed no signs of tiring.

A basic tenet that emerged after two decades of baseball analytics is that a starting pitcher's success diminishes dramatically with every time through the opposition's batting order. Each pitcher has a somewhat different arc over the course of an average game, but even the best of them start to degrade when they face hitters for the third time in a day. It's a function of the number of pitches they've thrown by that point, coupled with the hitters' growing familiarity with their repertoire. When Snell gave up a second single with one out in the Dodger sixth inning, it brought up Mookie Betts, the leadoff hitter. Betts was hitless in the game, but now he would be facing Snell for the third time. In addition, Snell hadn't pitched six innings in a game in months. Cash, the Tampa Bay manager, wasn't sure Snell had the stamina to do so under the pressure of a potential season-ending game that left no room for a mistake. He called for a reliever, Nick Anderson, to replace him.

It was a decision that never would have been made before analytics—and probably wouldn't have been made, at that moment, by the manager of any other team in baseball. But the Rays had advanced all the way to the World Series by making decisions almost exclusively by accessing the information at hand. Cash wasn't going to make an exception now, merely because the world was watching.

High above the field in the Dodgers' suite, Friedman understood. Changing pitchers in that situation validated everything he had come to believe about baseball. As the Rays' general manager all those years, he was the one who had pushed Maddon to not manage by instinct but *always* to use the insights that data analysis was providing. That philosophy had worked in 2008, the year Maddon's scrappy Rays advanced to the World Series, and it had worked again for Cash and Erik Neander, the Rays' current general manager, during the 2020 season.

But Friedman also understood what was happening in front of him at Dodger Stadium. Snell was pitching the best game of his life. The Dodgers had shown little capacity for hitting him, and nothing Friedman had seen indicated that the next few innings would be any different. He had constructed his entire baseball career on a foundation of factoring out instinct and emotion and making decisions based on the data at hand. Now he could only hope that, by strictly adhering to that same doctrine of analytics, Cash and the Rays were making a mistake.

They were. Betts greeted Anderson with a double. A wild pitch followed, and then a ground ball sent Betts home. In barely the time it took for Snell to grab a jacket and settle into a seat in the dugout, the Dodgers had a 2–1 lead. The final score would be 3–1. The season was over. After 32 years, the Dodgers had won another World Series.

The following February, Friedman appeared on a panel at the MIT Sloan Sports Analytics Conference, which was being held virtually because of the pandemic. Daryl Morey could hardly wait to pose the question that had been looming over all of baseball. "When they took him out of the game," Morey asked, "were you happy?"

It was a question freighted with the weight of the entire analytic revolution. The decision to remove Snell was an indication of just how deeply analytics had permeated the sport. In that sense, it was a triumph for Friedman. Yet Friedman had been working to bring a championship to Los Angeles for six seasons. Of everyone who benefited from Cash's decision, Friedman ranked near the top of the list.

Friedman hadn't played at a very high level, but he had worked in baseball long enough to understand his good fortune when he saw Snell head off the field. About that, he and Ned Yost would have agreed. He didn't hesitate to answer Morey. "I was very happy," he said.

7

WE'RE ACTIVELY GOING TO DO SOMETHING

ONE AFTERNOON IN the spring of 2021, a lanky, youthful-looking 42-year-old named Ryan Smith walked into a conference room at the Utah Jazz's practice facility south of downtown Salt Lake City. He was wearing a baseball cap turned backward, a hoodie, and midnight-blue jeans, and carrying three boxes of fast-food tacos. He had no socks on and his sneakers were untied. He might have been a mid-career point guard. In fact, he owned the team, or a hefty percentage of it. He cracked open a Diet Mountain Dew. "Anyone want tacos?" he asked.

By the time Smith bought the Jazz in October of 2020, most owners of professional franchises had at least grown comfortable with the internet economy. Smith's immersion in it was far deeper than that. While still in graduate school, he co-founded Qualtrics, an online information-gathering company. Then he ran it for nearly two decades. Apart from internships, he'd never held another job. At the time he became an NBA owner, his entire professional career had been filtered through the lens of data accumulation and analysis.

Smith didn't invent the phrase *experience management*, but Qualtrics co-opted it. Created in 2002, the company used analytics to translate customer feedback into actionable advice. Qualtrics was immediately successful, though for years it wasn't widely known. Smith resisted bringing in outside money or selling out to a large corporation or an investment group. "Had we walked away after year 3, year 5, year 11, year 15, we would have missed out," he said. Finally, in January 2019, the German software company SAP bought Qualtrics for $8 billion. Smith stayed on to run it. In an unusual maneuver, he then convinced SAP to spin off the company in an initial public offering less than two years later. That tripled its value to $24 billion. Smith remained the executive chairman.

Now he had mock-ups of alternate Jazz logos in a dozen colors mounted on a wall. Photos of various uniform iterations decorated another. "I care about weird stuff," said Smith, whose group had paid $1.66 billion for 80 percent of the franchise. "I care about the clothing we wear. I care about the entry that the players use to go through at the stadium."

He also had come to care deeply about social justice. So had a few other majority owners and prominent investors spread across the four largest North American leagues. But as of 2020, Smith's willingness to use his billion-dollar franchise on behalf of provocative social causes made him unique. Though he characterized himself as apolitical, Smith had donated money to both Republican and Democratic candidates. In an increasingly bifurcated America, and especially in a state that Donald Trump had won by more than 20 points just a few months before, that also set him apart.

Through Qualtrics, Smith had amassed more than enough

money to last him the rest of his life. He wanted to do something significant with it. "I see the world through experiences," he said. "I like good experiences and creating good experiences for people. I care about every single group that makes up our stakeholder base. You can't make everybody happy all the time, but you can have a plan for each. My punch list is long."

For every game the Jazz won, Smith and his wife, Ashley, offered to fund the entire college education of a local student of color. For Black History Month in February, Jazz players were given the opportunity to name and discuss their heroes on Zoom feeds made available to schools. Later that month, Smith appeared on ABC's *Good Morning America* to announce a $4 million initiative to build safe-haven homes for LGBTQ youth.

To a businessman in ultraconservative Utah, such progressive activism constituted a significant risk. Yet, surprisingly, Smith believed that his social activism was also a form of optimizing the franchise, both on and off the court. Perhaps these programs, and others he was planning to implement, would attract players who might not otherwise consider Salt Lake City a place where they wanted to live. Less directly, it could influence young innovators to move to the region, which in turn would eventually help it prosper, and therefore have a positive effect on the quality of life of Jazz players and their families. The inner rings of that ripple effect were quantifiable, and the outer rings probably were, too, if someone had the time and inclination to do the math.

It wasn't out of the realm of possibility that Smith's activism contributed to the success of the 2020–21 season, during which the Jazz won 52 games and the NBA's Northwest Division title and finished with the league's best record for the first time in their history. Several players said that the scholarships Smith awarded gave them the sense that they were competing for something beyond basket-ball. "When you're in the game, there are moments when you're like, 'This is changing somebody's life,'" guard Donovan Mitchell said. When I visited the Jazz shortly before the start of the playoffs that season, I asked Quin Snyder, the head coach, whether the team's social justice advocacy made him proud to represent it in the Salt Lake community, and in conversations with coaches and players around the NBA. He replied that it did. "I think it does for our play-ers, too," he said. "And for the people in the state."

Predictably, though, not everyone approved. Since the recipients of the scholarships were all minorities, some observers described the program as racist, both on social media and in communication with the team. Right-wing provocateurs, including Ann Coulter and the Fox host Tucker Carlson, who railed against it as "totally immoral," were harsher. Other owners would have perceived such opposition as a warning that a chunk of the team's fan base was likely to be offended. Smith remained unbowed. "If Ann Coulter is against something we're doing, that's probably a pretty good sign," he said.

THE SMITHS TOOK control of the Jazz at an inflection point. Salt Lake City, formerly a tidy state capital surrounded by farmland, had matured into a thriving tech hub. "The story that gets told about Salt Lake is 15 to 20 years old," Smith says. "Why don't we start talking about the new Utah? Three of the top 10 cities for fastest-growing economy are here. That's 30 percent of the fastest-growing economies in America, within 30 miles."

As we talked, Smith and I were heading down I-15 in his luxury SUV. Traffic was light, as usual. "This is the beauty of Utah," he gushed. "It's easy to get around." We were heading from the Jazz facility to the Qualtrics corporate headquarters, half an hour south. On the way, we passed Goldman Sachs's largest office outside New York, and a massive regional headquarters for Adobe. We passed the so-called Silicon Slopes, where much of the entrepreneurial growth is centered. Ten minutes south of downtown, Smith started calling my attention to buildings on either side of the highway. "Billion-dollar company," he said, pointing to the headquarters of a software firm called Lucid, in South Jordan. And then, moments later, "Billion-dollar company" as we drove past Ivanti, another software innovator. "Every week, there's a billion-dollar company standing up and being sold here," he said. "It's crazy."

Back in 1983–84, when the Jazz outsourced 11 home games to Las Vegas to help make ends meet, the idea of putting an NBA franchise playing in the old American Basketball Association market of Salt Lake City seemed a failed experiment. The Jazz were bound for Miami when local car dealer Larry H. Miller intervened and bought them in 1985. For years, Utahns assumed that if Miller ever decided to sell, the team would leave for somewhere else. After Miller died in 2009, his wife, Gail, assumed control, aided by her sons. As of 2020, the Miller family had owned the Jazz for 35 years. By all appearances, it planned on 35 more. On October 28, the day the sale to Smith was announced, Utah ground to a halt. "Everyone's phone blew up," said Dan Hanks, a principal at Peterson Partners, a local investment firm. "It was the kind of thing where everyone in the state will know where they were when it happened. I called my boss and said, 'Hey, we need to get season tickets. Like now! Ryan Smith just bought the Jazz!'"

It wasn't just about the Millers cashing out. Smith had unique standing in Utah's business community. "The common thread in

Utah even five years ago was to look next door and see what they're doing, and that's your measuring stick," said Eric Rea, the chief executive of Podium, a Provo-based online communications firm. Smith ran Qualtrics differently, Rea explained. "Ryan tells his employees, 'We should be looking at the best software companies anywhere and trying to emulate them and compete with them.'" Across the state, fans started imagining what the same attitude might mean when applied to basketball, especially in conjunction with Qualtrics's emphasis on analytics. "The vibe of all the messages I was getting was 'Something's going to happen,'" Hanks said. "'This guy is going to bring something new and exciting.'"

In the car, Smith and I passed PluralSight, in the town of Draper. "Online tech learning platform," Smith said. "They employ thousands of people." In December of 2020, Vista Equity bought PluralSight for $3.5 billion. When Smith reached Lehi, Utah, the companies started coming faster: Entrata, Lendio, Canopy Tax, Purple, Owlet. "You're watching what Mountain View looked like 25 years ago," he said.

He pulled into the Qualtrics parking lot. When we went inside, I found myself standing on a basketball court. Smith had modeled it after the NBA's headquarters on New York's Fifth Avenue, where he remembered stepping off an elevator onto hardwood. The atrium design of the rest of the building felt non-hierarchical. "That's because it is," Smith said. "No offices! Everything's out in the open."

A few years ago, Smith noticed that many of his female employees were leaving to start families. True to its mission, Qualtrics managed its own experience. The company constructed the biggest day care facility in Utah, measuring some 40,000 square feet. STEM-focused, Smith calls it "the MIT of day care." Only available to the sons and daughters of Qualtrics employees, it is offered free as a perk of employment. For Qualtrics, the day care facility was merely an incremental gain. The equivalent for the Jazz might have been the new player entry from the parking lot that Smith had redesigned, as opposed to, say, the signing of some All-Star power forward.

But Smith has built a career on the insight that all those marginal advancements add up to something significant. It's a matter of nudging the odds further and further in the direction of success, which is in the same philosophical realm as using Statcast data to figure out when to move your center fielder eight steps to the left during a baseball game. On any given play, the positioning is probably going to be insignificant. On some plays, it might even cost the team. Eventually, though, it will end up having a positive effect.

He felt the same way about his team's relationship with its region. "Utah should be one of the most lucrative places to play," he said. That struck me as unlikely. With all its recent growth, the state is still perceived by many to be a backwater. But Smith explained that if he could make it a more appealing area not just to be a player, but also a wife, a sponsor, a fan, one of his employees, or even a resident who might not have any interest in basketball, the Jazz would prosper.

He started to talk me through that punch list. He'd added carpeting, heaters, and a seating area to what had been a depressingly drab arena entrance. Now it resembled the lobby of a luxury hotel. That would make families and friends more comfortable while they waited for the players after each game. He introduced former Heat standout Dwyane Wade, who had no previous ties to the Jazz, as a minority owner, which gave heft and a touch of celebrity to the executive team. He signed standouts Donovan Mitchell and Rudy Gobert to contract extensions, though that meant the team's payroll would be so high that it would be subject to a luxury tax. (Mitchell was later traded.) He made himself available to players, at practices and at games. "We have an issue about something or an idea, he's all ears," says point guard Mike Conley. "You can walk right up to him."

Smith had spent two decades immersed in consumer feedback about how to improve companies—and, by extension, he believed, the world they inhabited. He had convinced one company after another that it was good business to make their customers more content. Now he was doing the same with his new acquisition, which happened to have wide-angle reach.

On the surface, what he was doing with the Jazz didn't seem like data collection. If anything, it was the opposite—Smith imposing his values on his ticket buyers. He didn't care. "Look, we want to get rid of all the sucky experiences," he said. "Systemic racism is a horrible experience. Lack of equity is a horrible experience. When we took over, I was pretty direct that we were going to be actively antiracist. And active means not passive. It means we're actively going to do something."

———————

ATHLETES HAVE LONG used the stage of sports to advocate for social change, perhaps most famously during the 1968 Olympics, when the American sprinters John Carlos and Tommie Smith made a stand for racial justice with fists thrust skyward, and the gymnast Věra Čáslavská subtly protested the occupation of Czechoslovakia by lowering her head during the Soviet anthem. But professional sports franchises were careful to distance themselves from any activity that could be perceived as political. They had little to gain, they figured. Every issue had two sides, and sports teams wanted fans on both of those sides to be customers. By taking a stand on any issue that was even vaguely controversial, a team would almost certainly alienate a percentage of its following and scare away potential sponsors. It also might upset ticket buyers who looked to sports as an escape.

David Stern, the NBA's commissioner before Adam Silver, was politically left of center. But when Stern took control of the league in 1984, he felt the wolf at its door. CBS owned the broadcast rights for the NBA Finals, but many of that network's affiliates chose to show the games on tape delay after the late news, when the potential audience was far smaller. "Red Ink and a Bleak Future," a *Washington Post* headline about the NBA screamed in March of 1983.

The article that followed was nearly as pessimistic. It mentioned four franchises, including Utah, that were in such serious financial trouble that they were likely to be consolidated or folded. Only seven franchises were reported to be profitable, despite the league's $88 million, four-year television deal. Much of America remained uninterested in the league, which was perceived as too urban. That meant too disconnected from white, suburban America, which preferred college basketball. Stands at NBA games were often nearly empty. Perhaps as a result, players didn't seem to try very hard; their languid pace of play often didn't pick up until the final quarter. In the years that followed, even as Stern guided the sport to unimaginable prosperity, he never felt confident that the NBA was more than one reversal away from disaster. The idea of a team alienating fans by taking a political stand was a risk he stood firmly against taking.

Within months of Stern's retirement in 2014, the prospect of Donald Trump as president emerged as at least a theoretical reality. With that, the low-risk social activism that athletes had typically engaged in—visits to schools in poor neighborhoods, photo ops at hospitals—made a marked turn toward the political. In September 2016, Colin Kaepernick, then a quarterback for the San Francisco 49ers, rested on one knee as the national anthem played before a preseason game, protesting what he called "a country that oppresses Black people." Though he wasn't officially punished by the NFL, which ultimately decided that players were encouraged but not required to remain standing, the response to his gesture was clear enough. Coaches and executives around the sport spoke out in a chorus of reprobation. The sport's elder statesmen, such as former linebacker Ray Lewis, advised Kaepernick to keep his politics private. Fans tweeted insults. Kaepernick, who had led the 49ers to the Super Bowl during the 2012 season, was 28 at the time. Though he was coming off three surgical procedures, he remained in the prime of his career. After his contract expired the following January, no NFL team showed any interest in signing him. Through the 2022 season, he hadn't played in another game.

But Kaepernick's statement struck a chord inside the NBA, a league in which more than four-fifths of the players are non-white. Already, a sense of social responsibility had started to permeate its locker rooms. When training camps opened that fall, some of its best-known personalities were quick to weigh in. "You have the right to voice your opinion, stand for your opinion, and he's doing it in the most peaceful way I've ever seen someone do something," LeBron James said at the time. James expanded on that when I met him in the visitors' locker room at Denver's Pepsi Center a few months later. "Times have changed," he said. "Athletes feel like there's more than just sports."

In fact, momentum had been building for most of the decade. In 2012, James and his Miami Heat teammates had posted a picture on social media that showed them wearing hoodies, with their heads bowed and their hands in their pockets. It was a symbolic reminder of Trayvon Martin, who'd been murdered by a would-be vigilante in Florida one month earlier. In 2014, the year that Donald Sterling was forced to sell the Clippers, players around the league wore "I Can't Breathe" T-shirts to memorialize Eric Garner, who died after a New York City police officer put him in a chokehold. And after Freddie Gray died in police custody in Baltimore the next year, the New York Knicks' Carmelo Anthony traveled to the city and joined a street protest. James, who publicly supported Hillary Clinton's presidential campaign, stood onstage at the ESPY Awards in 2016 and urged players to speak out on issues of the moment.

Like everyone else, NBA players and coaches were getting streams of information at a pace that would have been hard to imagine even a decade ago. "You have these images of shootings around the country that you can literally pull out and see on your phone," said Steve Kerr, the head coach of the Golden State Warriors. "And you've got this presidential campaign going on with all these shenanigans. It's all right there for you to see, on a minute-by-minute basis."

In the weeks after Kaepernick's protest, more NBA players and coaches went public with their opinions. The league issued no fines or even reprimands. Gregg Popovich, who coached the San Antonio Spurs, mentioned Kaepernick in a team meeting. "Here's our stance on the flag," Popovich told the Spurs players. "We have no stance. You're grown men. Do what you want."

At the time I spoke to James, it seemed like another voice was joining the chorus every few days. When I asked him if he considered himself responsible, he said he wasn't trying to serve as a model; it just felt good to speak his mind. More important, it felt wrong *not* to. "I don't do it to get other people behind me or give them more courage," he said. "If that happens, so be it. But what I do, I do for me. If I'm knowledgeable about something and I have a passion for it, I'm going to speak up."

The Warriors' Steph Curry agreed. The sporting gear company

Under Armour was paying him several million dollars a year in 2016 when Kevin Plank, its chief executive, described Trump as an "asset" to America. Curry responded that he agreed, but only "if you remove the *e-t*." In what many read as a response to Curry, Plank bought a full-page newspaper advertisement in which he said that his previous choice of words "did not accurately reflect" his intent. The mea culpa was an astonishing reversal. It had always been assumed that an overtly political statement by a player, especially a statement as personally denigrating as Curry's, would harm his reputation—and maybe the league's with it. Instead, here was Under Armour doing damage control, even as Curry gained respect around America for his candor. For the first time, NBA players could be confident that they wouldn't be punished for expressing and acting on their beliefs.

What had been isolated actions of James and others coalesced into something that looked a lot like a movement among NBA players. Social media enabled them to be easily heard in their own voices, while the erosion of credibility suffered by both elected officials and the media created space for others to wield influence. Crucially, too, contracts in excess of $100 million allowed the league's biggest names to ignore any financial risk inherent in becoming politically active. If a sponsor responded by canceling an endorsement contract, it no longer meant that the player would be unable to pay his rent. The increased affluence of even marginal players let them be opinionated, even controversial, without the fear of a backlash. By 2018, the average NBA salary had jumped to $8.5 million, from around $325,000 in Michael Jordan's rookie season. "I remember how everyone worried about offending Nike," James Worthy, the former Lakers star, said of his time in the NBA. "But these days, it's flipped the other way. Under Armour wouldn't dare go against Steph Curry and his values. Superstars carry more weight than any company."

What made the insurgency even more remarkable is that the existing power structure was helping to facilitate it. Silver encouraged the league's athletes to take a stand. "Critical issues that affect our society also impact you directly," he told them in a letter to the players' union. "You have real power to make a difference."

The NBA's franchises, like those across the other professional leagues, were moving far more slowly. If any team appeared immune from fan backlash, it was Curry and Kerr's Warriors. They played in the Bay Area, one of the country's most liberal regions. Their market included the solidly Democratic Silicon Valley; according to one report, the largest tech companies contributed 60 times as much to Clinton in 2016 as they did to Trump. And like nearly all NBA teams, the Warriors roster was firmly left of center. "I've very rarely been around a player who was hardcore conservative to the point where there were political arguments," Kerr told me.

Yet Joe Lacob, the Warriors' majority owner, quietly supported Trump, as did many other wealthy white men in the NBA's ownership suites. That made Kerr pause. "I'm very sensitive to the fact that I'm representing an organization where maybe not everybody shares my beliefs," he explained. "I don't want to go overboard. I want people to understand that I'm speaking from my own personal background. But that's a blurry line, because I speak for the Warriors every day about basketball. I'm one of the faces of the organization."

As it happened, the Spurs' Popovich also worked for someone who didn't share his political beliefs. Peter Holt, who owned the team at the time, had contributed $500,000 to the presidential campaign of Rick Perry, the former Texas governor, who later became the Secretary of Energy under Trump. He gave $250,000 to Restore

Our Future, a GOP SuperPAC, and $33,000 to the Republican National Committee. And he donated $250,000 to Trump's Victory Fund, even as Popovich was doing all he could to stop Trump from getting elected.

That the Spurs' head coach was fanatically opposed to the causes and candidates backed by the team's owner (and much of the state's population) emerged as an ongoing story in Texas. Yet Holt managed to separate his personal political beliefs from his business investments to an extent that Popovich, for example, would have found impossible. At one point, Don Rackler, the owner of an air conditioning and heating supplier called Jon Wayne Service, pulled some $300,000 in advertising and sponsorship money in response to Popovich's public statements. He also vowed to never attend another Spurs game. Popovich didn't find out until weeks later. "The owner didn't say a single word to me," he said, "and they've given nearly a million dollars to the Republicans this time around. Not a word. I give them credit."

Why would owners such as Lacob and Holt *not* use the power of their teams to help disseminate their own political beliefs? Part of the reason, surely, is rooted in the political composition of the NBA. By openly supporting Trump, or by not allowing players and coaches to state their own opinions, Lacob and Holt risked losing their locker rooms. And just as Ryan Smith believed that the activism he championed could help attract like-minded players, aligning a club too publicly with right-wing causes could scare away potential free agents.

The difference in mind-set may also be generational. Both Lacob and Holt are decades older than Smith. Their business instincts are rooted in another era, one closer to Stern's. In their minds, using a team as a tool to enact change was *bad* business.

The safest way to maintain the value of their franchises was to keep them politically neutral.

———————

UNTIL SMITH AND the Jazz, in fact, only one modern big-league team had knowingly incorporated activism into its brand. On July 18, 2018, the Seattle Storm of the WNBA donated $5 from every ticket sold for their game against the Chicago Sky to Planned Parenthood, a not-for-profit organization that was under siege from conservatives. The Storm made merely buying a ticket to the game a political act. "We took a turn," said Ginny Gilder, who owned the Storm with the former Microsoft executives Lisa Brummel and Dawn Trudeau. "We made a conscious decision. We did something we had not done before." The total contribution to the regional chapter that included the Seattle area amounted to the relatively modest sum of $45,000. But the money was the least of it. The impact, both for Planned Parenthood and for the team, was far greater. "It was a big thing, what we did," admitted Gilder. "But for me, it was just a logical next step."

As of 2008, when the Storm seemed set to move to Oklahoma City with the NBA's Seattle SuperSonics, the three women were season-ticket holders. Trudeau had been a major investor in the Seattle Reign of the defunct ABL, the league Lacob had helped to run. She knew Gilder because they'd served together on the board of a local girls' school. And Gilder and Brummel had overlapped at Yale, where Brummel was a four-year basketball star and Gilder a rower headed toward an Olympic medal. After coming together to save the team for Seattle, they had grown to perceive its place in the community as, in Gilder's words, "a corner at the intersection of business, sports, and social justice." Even in a heavily Democratic market, aligning with an organization perceived to be as progressive as Planned Parenthood carried risks. But the Storm's ownership felt the risks were mitigated because the club was playing to its base.

Gilder comes from an activist family, but on the other side of the political spectrum. Richard Gilder was a retired money manager and renowned philanthropist. He helped found the conservative Club for Growth, and for years donated large sums to right-wing candidates.

His daughter was an avowed feminist who participated in the 1976 "strip-in," a protest staged during her freshman year at Yale in an effort to get women's showers added to the coed boathouse. Gilder viewed the strip-in as part of an ongoing struggle against a gender disparity that seemed outdated even in the 1970s. "We'd walk into the weight room to lift weights and the guys would say, 'Those are our weights,'" she says now. "I mean, it was insanely stupid."

Gilder also had an abortion at Yale, facilitated by Planned Parenthood. As the organization came under assault during the 2016 campaign, she contemplated ways to help. She brought the idea of a Planned Parenthood Night to Trudeau and Brummel with some trepidation. Early in their ownership, the three had agreed to never use the franchise to endorse a politician. "You want everyone to feel comfortable when they come into the arena," Trudeau explains. "You don't care who they are or how they think or how they voted. They need to be welcomed."

The owners viewed Planned Parenthood as a cause, not an affiliation with a candidate or a party. They believed that it stood for the same issues of women's empowerment and opportunity that had motivated the creation of the WNBA a quarter century before. Gilder found a sympathetic ear in Trudeau, who had gone to Planned Parenthood for contraception before she'd even started dating. And if the economics of the gesture were risky, well, the three of them hadn't bought the team in order to play it safe. It wasn't as though they were selling out KeyArena anyway. Brummel told her partners that taking a stand was unlikely to hurt their business. And, potentially, it might even help.

The Storm's only appearance on national television of the season, Planned Parenthood Night drew 8,358, about 2,000 more than a typical weeknight game. It included a pregame rally outside what was then KeyArena, complete with protesters and a rousing speech by Trudeau. A raffle raised additional contributions. The night's events gained the Storm national publicity, from the *New York Times* to talk show host Samantha Bee. The team also received hundreds of emails, voicemails, and letters from those who disagreed with the idea of bringing politics into sports. Suddenly, the Storm and its actions were in the news, garnering the attention of industry insiders and even fans across America. And that didn't happen often to a WNBA team.

The activism became incorporated into the Storm's identity. The owners estimated that about 60 percent of their fans were women, and 80 percent were politically liberal—basically the opposite of Smith's Jazz constituency. "The Seattle Storm stands for progressive support for issues that matter to girls and women," Brummel stated unequivocally. "I don't know that we have a plan, but we do have a brand. The question now becomes: What do we do with it?"

One drizzly morning in 2019, she sipped coffee at a café inside KEXP, the University of Washington's public radio station. The station was celebrating International Clash Day, so the guitar riffs of Joe Strummer filled the room, making foot-tapping easy but conversation hard. But don't be fooled by the unconventional setting Brummel had chosen for an interview, or the gym-teacher shorts she wore during almost every occasion: when it came to running a company, the UCLA business school graduate was a by-the-book pragmatist. She understood that the affiliation with Planned Parenthood had likely closed the door to some potential sponsors, who had national shareholders to consider, even as it had opened the door to others.

As Strummer sang about police and thieves taking to the streets, she mused about what the Storm's activism could mean for the team's future. "The only way we're ever going to expand the exposure for this business, the only way we're ever going to draw new fans, is to try new things," she said. "Things that other teams in other leagues may not be able to do because they're constrained, they're too big, or because of their owners or their sponsors. We have to do things like this to test the boundaries of where this business can go. Otherwise, how will we ever know?"

Brummel was well aware that no WNBA team had developed a nationwide following, or even gained significant visibility outside its market. The Houston Comets won the first four WNBA championships; eight years later, they'd ceased operations. At the time we spoke, at least half of the league's franchises were losing money, and most of those that weren't were sharing operational costs with an NBA team, which meant they didn't need to hire their own ticketing staffs or sponsorship salesmen. Against that backdrop, taking risks with a franchise seemed logical. "From a revenue standpoint, there isn't a whole lot of upside to a WNBA franchise," David Carter, a former consultant for sports teams, organizations, and venues who later served as executive director of the University of Southern California's Sports Business Institute, told me. "So why not use the franchise in the way you want to?"

For Brummel, Gilder, and Trudeau, that meant using it to support a cause they all supported. Not long after I spoke with them, another WNBA team took a leap further.

IN THE SUMMER of 2020, the WNBA gathered inside what it hoped would be a COVID-free bubble at IMG Academy in Bradenton, Florida, to try to stage a basketball season. At the time, America was roiling again. It wasn't just the pandemic. On May 25, George Floyd had been murdered by a Minneapolis police officer. Earlier in the year, Breonna Taylor was killed in her bed in Louisville. They were the latest African Americans to lose their lives at the hands of local law enforcement officials. By summer, the largest protests against racial injustice since the Civil Rights movement had erupted around the country.

At the time, the WNBA's rosters were composed of around 80 percent women of color. When teams gathered for the first time since the pandemic started in March, their conversations quickly led to general agreement that the league needed to participate in the protests, even from inside the bubble. "As players, you want to be part of what's going on," says Renee Montgomery, who had been playing professionally since 2009 and had spent the previous season captaining the Atlanta Dream. "You want to be able to take a stand. And you want to make sure that you're standing on the right side of things."

To the Atlanta team, which had been named after Martin Luther King's "I Have a Dream" speech when it was founded prior to the 2008 season, the idea had special urgency. One of its co-owners, Kelly Loeffler, had been appointed to the US Senate the previous December. That summer, Loeffler was running for reelection. In the weeks following Floyd's death, Loeffler publicly criticized the Black Lives Matter movement in an open letter to Cathy Engelbert, the league's commissioner. Black Lives Matter, she later told the Fox News commentator Laura Ingraham, was "based on Marxist principles." It was a threat to "destroy" America. The Dream's players were determined to respond with a public gesture. But should it be a direct repudiation of Loeffler, or simply in support of Black Lives Matter? And what form should it take?

Eventually, their strategy coalesced around support for Raphael Warnock, with whom Montgomery had developed a friendship. A reverend who served at Ebenezer Baptist Church, where King had presided, Warnock was bidding to be Georgia's first African American senator—by running against Loeffler. At the time, his standing in the polls was low, only about 9 percent. On Tuesday, August 3, the Dream's players came out on the court with T-shirts emblazoned with the message "VOTE WARNOCK." (Players on two other teams, Chicago and Phoenix, showed their support by doing the same.) "We knew the risk," said the Dream's Tiffany Hayes. "But we were like, 'Gotta do what you gotta do.' It's you walking into work one day and giving it to your boss—'Hey, that's not OK.'"

The protest gained immediate national attention as an astonishingly daring act. "We saw a team getting involved in a political campaign and speaking truth to power," says Larry Gottesdiener, a commercial real estate developer who owns the $10 billion Northland Investment Corporation, based in Newton, Massachusetts. "What could be more truth-to-power than 'Vote for the Other Guy?'"

Gottesdiener had watched the situation in the WNBA bubble with fascination. He'd made his fortune, estimated at $500 million, by identifying, buying, and redeveloping undervalued real estate in precisely the kinds of neighborhoods where many WNBA players

were raised. Over the years, he had researched the viability of investing in an NBA team, as either a majority or minority owner. He
inquired about the Philadelphia 76ers, the Atlanta Hawks, the Sacramento Kings, the Oklahoma City Thunder, a piece of the Boston
Celtics. Recently, he had started thinking about the WNBA. As a
progressive, the league's inherent values—racial and gender equity,
empowerment, gay rights—appealed to him

Gottesdiener had come of age as a shareholder capitalist. "That
means you make as much money as you possibly can, without regard
for anyone else," he says. "But at some point, I had to figure out
my values." Northland's president and chief operating officer was
Suzanne Abair, an openly gay attorney. Gottesdiener's daughter,
Laura, had wrestled against boys and run cross country at Milton
Academy, then walked onto Yale's crew team. (She later wrote a
sports column for the *Huffington Post*.) Talking through his beliefs
with the two of them, and with his wife, led him to decide that his
priorities for the rest of his life would be "to empower women, to
promote social justice, and eradicate homelessness." He did that by
contributing to progressive candidates and attempting to run his
company as benevolently as possible. But as the summer of 2020
unspooled, he realized he couldn't continue to be passive. "You can't
just try to have a good heart," he says. "You need to stand up and
take a position." Then he saw the Dream do exactly that.

To Gottesdiener, the T-shirts were an inflection point for the
role of sports in American society. They also had created a Donald Sterling moment; clearly, the Dream could not continue under
the current ownership. As it happened, Gottesdiener had recently
started talking with Engelbert, the commissioner, about another
WNBA team, one that turned out to be unavailable. The Dream,
on the other hand, now seemed eminently available. His son, Mat-

thew, who works with him at Northland, told Gottesdiener, "Their values are *your* values. If you're going to do something in that space, this is the team.'" That January, he bought the Dream from Loeffler and her co-owner for a sum that the sellers insisted remain undisclosed. Both Abair and Montgomery signed on as limited partners.

From its inception before the 2008 season, the Dream had been challenged in the crowded Atlanta sports market. When I spoke with Loeffler, she said that despite her best efforts during the decade that she owned it, most Atlanta sports fans weren't even aware that the city had a WNBA team. Many who did know about it were uncertain when and where it played, a problem that had been exacerbated by its failure to find a permanent venue. By supporting Warnock in 2020, even Loeffler admitted, the Dream had done more to promote awareness of its existence than all those years of marketing.

The T-shirts made buying a ticket to a Dream game a partisan act. Going forward, Gottesdiener and Abair believed, the team's success would be determined by how deftly it balanced its core product of professional women's basketball with that political identity. Was political activism a good business strategy for a sports team? It could be, they felt, as long as it didn't come to *define* the business. In 2022, Warnock ran for reelection. His opponent was the Trump-affiliated former football star Herschel Walker. Another endorsement, I was told, was definitely possible.

At the same time, Abair stressed the investment opportunity inherent in owning the Dream. Her frame of reference was that of an investor, not an activist. "This was not a throwaway, philanthropic, 'We need to go rescue the team in Atlanta,'" she said. "When we model this out, we do have a break-even point, and then a point where we begin to turn a profit." She was clear: the Dream was a business. It was a business that had the capacity to change the world around it, perhaps—but a business first. That December, Warnock defeated Walker in a runoff election. No endorsement was ever made.

———

IN TERMS OF his own financial exposure, Ryan Smith had quite a bit more on the line than those two groups of WNBA owners: about $1 billion of his own money. The only big-league team in the state for most of its history, the Jazz had served to unite a polarized population—urban and agricultural, University of Utah and Brigham Young University, Mormons and the other 35 percent. The Miller family had appreciated the value of broad appeal. The state was red, but Salt Lake was a dot of blue. The older generation was insular, while young professionals welcomed transplants. Development clashed with conservation. But everybody loved the Jazz.

But Smith understood that the Jazz were no longer primarily a local business. By 2020, NBA teams had more fans across Europe and Asia than they did in their own markets. The success of Qualtrics, which he had based down the highway from Salt Lake City in Provo, had taught Smith that a company's location became irrelevant when its customers were everywhere. That made him wonder why Utah's Jazz couldn't become a worldwide brand. And as the pandemic had made abundantly clear, NBA arenas were in a sense little more than a stage set for video feeds. If you were watching from Lisbon or Lagos, the hometown of each franchise was just a name across a jersey. As Snyder, the Jazz head coach, put it, "In the digital world, everything is the same size."

On the Zoom calls that meetings of the NBA Board of Governors had temporarily become during Smith's first months of owning the team, Smith proselytized that perspective. Since the league had reached its maturity in the 1970s, it had been bifurcated into one group consisting of New York, Los Angeles, Chicago, Boston, the Bay Area, and later Miami, and one of everywhere else. Smith wondered why those few major cities should necessarily wield the most clout these days, and why the smaller cities should ask for special consideration. "There's a traditional way in the NBA that owners think of small markets versus big markets," Silver says. "Ryan has made it clear that he doesn't accept that way of looking at it. Technology has been a great equalizer."

As Utah's flagship sports team, it made sense for the Jazz to stay neutral. As the owner of a multinational brand, Smith found that neutrality hard to justify. He knew that Atlanta-based mega-companies Delta Airlines and Coca-Cola, both Qualtrics customers, had felt compelled to speak out against the new voting laws that Georgia's legislature passed in early 2021; the stakeholders of those businesses, from investors to customers, expected them to take stands on the compelling issues of the moment. And those companies operated on a scale that he wanted the Jazz to emulate, in the same way that he'd looked outside Utah, to Silicon Valley, for comparisons with Qualtrics.

Nevertheless, the Jazz's activism had local repercussions. Some customers called or wrote the team to say they were dropping their season tickets. Others stated publicly that they would never again attend a game. During the pandemic, when the Jazz insisted that fans provide either proof of vaccination against COVID-19 or a negative test to enter the arena, Congressman Chris Stewart, a Republican, announced he would boycott the team. He expressed his disappointment on Facebook. "In a world where so many things have turned contentious or divisive, the Jazz were an opportunity to bring us together," he wrote. Smith responded with a tweet: "Scratching my head at those who believe the recent rain is an answer to prayer for a drought . . . but that the vaccine is not for the pandemic."

The Smiths' sense of mission helped insulate them from critics, like Stewart, who couldn't understand why the Jazz weren't sticking to basketball. "That's what gives us the energy and the enthusiasm," Ashley Smith said. "I don't care about the haters. I don't care about the negative feedback. Because we're so clear on the stewardship and what it means to us, and on exactly what we want to do."

For better or worse, the Jazz's willingness to help foment change had become part of its brand. As with the Storm and the Dream, that quality would inform perceptions of the franchise going forward. It would have an impact on which companies might choose to partner with it and which wouldn't. It would attract fans who might not otherwise have bought tickets, while repelling others.

Smith professed to be comfortable with that as an unavoidable side effect of aspiring to do more than provide entertainment. He continued to believe in the long-term benefit of the strategy to the team and to the community around it, even though he'd done no Qualtrics-style assessment of what that community actually wanted. He was confident that those benefits would also redound to him and his family, but even that wasn't the point. "I'm just trying to use the platform of the NBA to do the right thing," he said. "That's the platform I have, and I'm going to use it."

8

WHAT ARE YOU SO AFRAID OF?

THE SCENE AT Wrigley Field would have been inconceivable for nearly the entire history of American professional sports. On a sweltering June morning in 2022, five men lined up on dusty white gravel at the corner of Addison and Sheffield to sign a ceremonial girder. One of those men, Crane Kenney, was the president of the Chicago Cubs. Another, Jason Robins, was the co-founder and chief executive of DraftKings, a sports betting firm. DraftKings had pioneered the business of daily fantasy sports a decade before. In 2018, it had segued into handling bets made on smartphones and other devices as wagering on sports became legal in one state after another. Kenney and Robins were accompanied by catering and construction executives. They posed for pictures, pens in hand.

The ceremony commemorated the official groundbreaking for a joint venture between the Cubs and DraftKings. The Cubs were building a multi-level addition to Wrigley Field, a National Historic Landmark where the team had been playing baseball since 1916.

DraftKings had agreed to transform the space into a 22,000-square-foot betting parlor, paying the team to brand it with the company name and run the bookmaking operation. The Cubs would receive a percentage of the income from food and beverage sales, though not the gambling revenue. "We're a landlord in this process," Kenney explained. He assured fans that profits generated by the new addition would be available for use by the baseball team, which was struggling through another losing season.

DraftKings Sportsbook would be open not only during Cubs games, but every day of the year, even Christmas. Someone asked Robins why a DraftKings customer, who could make bets from the comfort of his living room or a bleacher seat, would bother to stop in. The answer, he said, was the communal experience of gathering with other fans, watching games on an absurdly large, 2,000-square-foot television screen, enjoying the food and drink, and participating in special promotions that would be made available only to those present. With taxes, rent, and the Cubs' take of food and beverage sales, DraftKings wouldn't make a killing on the new venture, but the idea was to drive business back to the mother ship, which was the company's digital presence. "Maybe someone has two apps on their phone, and they need to figure out which one they're going to pull out and make a bet," Robins said. "I want them to think back to what a great time they had when they came here." If that customer brought along a friend or two who weren't already DraftKings loyalists, well, that would be even better.

The Cubs' motivation was strikingly similar: to entice gamblers to make the trip to Wrigley Field with the expectation that they would spend money there on more than just the sports book. Those bettors might only be casual Cubs fans. They might never have been inside a big-league stadium. Maybe they'd be coming to watch college basketball, or the NHL playoffs, or the Kentucky Derby. Once they were there, though, Kenney was confident that many of them would walk around the corner and buy Cubs merchandise or tickets for a future game. That might be the catalyst for a lifelong relationship with the club. The demographic of people who followed baseball was getting older, he said. Sports bettors "skew younger, they skew more diverse, they skew more engaged. They watch our games at home longer. If they're in the ballpark, they stay longer. So, literally, all the dynamics you're looking for, whether you're the Cubs or any team operator, of a deeper, more diversely engaged and broader audience." It all made sense—unless you had been following sports for longer than, say, the past five years.

If you had, the idea of a gambling parlor being constructed at one of the most iconic sports venues in America was nothing if not discordant. Almost exactly a century before, in the same city where Kenney was enthusiastically talking up the new partnership, the most damaging scandal in the history of American sports had been revealed to the public. It was a scandal instigated by gamblers who were betting large amounts of money on baseball, just as Kenney was trying to entice today's fans to do. The fallout prompted an aversion by sports leagues to anything affiliated with gambling that lasted almost a hundred years.

In 1921, eight members of the Chicago White Sox were banned from organized baseball for life for participating in, or at least knowing about, a plot to purposefully lose the World Series two years before. The origins of the plot involved weeks of negotiations between two Chicago players—pitcher Eddie Cicotte, and Chick Gandil, the team's first baseman—and a professional gambler named Sport Sullivan. The New York mobster Arnold Rothstein was also involved, along with other gamblers, including the former featherweight boxer Abe Attell. The precise details remain unclear. But the situation that motivated the players to throw the World Series was plain to everyone. Charles Comiskey, the owner of the White Sox, paid his players so little that they struggled to make a living. And it wasn't just Comiskey; he actually was less penurious than most owners. There was no baseball labor union at the time, and no open marketplace for players. The owners of the existing 16 clubs, eight in the American League and eight in the National, merely had to offer salaries that were slightly more enticing than the prospect of factory jobs or work in the mines. That led the players to reach out to Sullivan, who eventually offered $100,000 to be split among the participants.

The money, which would be the equivalent of some $1.7 million today, mitigated any sense the players might have had that purposefully losing games was morally wrong. Most of them needed it badly. "I had the wife and the kids," Cicotte, who signaled that the fix was in when he hit the first batter of the World Series with a pitch, told the grand jury.

The scandal horrified America. Illicit gambling was commonplace, and many individual games had seemed shady over the years. But this was different—it was the *World Series*. The eight transgressors (and eventually the rest of that 1919 White Sox team) became the Black Sox, for they had stained the national pastime. In response, baseball's owners made as public a show as possible of making certain that such a scandal could never happen again. They hired a US District Court judge, Kenesaw Landis of Illinois, to serve as baseball's first commissioner, then empowered him to do whatever he deemed to be in the sport's best interests. Soon enough, signs appeared in clubhouses warning players not to associate with gamblers. If they did, they were warned, they would be fined and suspended.

THE BLACK SOX SCANDAL was still fresh in the minds of Americans when Nevada opened the nation's first casinos in 1931. The state was on the verge of bankruptcy, a predicament that motivated it to defy the prevailing national sentiment against gambling. "Any state could have done it," said Anthony Cabot, who teaches gaming law at the University of Nevada, Las Vegas. "But no others did." In 1949, as pro football was starting to thrive, Nevada broadened its gambling laws to include sports betting.

Over the next half century, attitudes against gambling softened. Las Vegas emerged as a popular vacation destination where ordinary Americans could enjoy the thrill of a diversion that was illegal at home. Organized religion, which preached against the sin of gambling from its pulpits, played an increasingly diminished role in everyday life. With scant opposition in many cases, states legalized lotteries. In 1978, casinos opened in Atlantic City. A decade later, Congress passed a law permitting them on land owned by Native American nations. By 2003, a Gallup Poll revealed, nearly half of all Americans had played the lottery in the previous 12 months and almost a third had visited a casino. But just 10 percent had bet on a pro sports event, mostly because there were few legal ways to do it.

Despite the changing attitudes, the leagues had remained firmly opposed to gambling, or anything remotely connected with it. In 1963, the NFL suspended two of its brightest stars, the Packers halfback Paul Hornung and the Lions defensive tackle Alex Karras, for "associating with known hoodlums." ("The rule is posted in every clubhouse," NFL commissioner Pete Rozelle said impassively when he announced the one-year ban.) Baseball was even harsher. Pete Rose, who amassed more hits than any other player, admitted in 1989 that he had bet on several sports. Rose, who was managing the Cincinnati Reds at the time, was ruled permanently ineligible by commissioner Bart Giamatti. The ban extended to everything connected with organized baseball. It also eventually led the sport's most prolific hitter to be barred from the Hall of Fame.

By then, too, Las Vegas had grown into a metropolis of more than 1.5 million people, one that attracted some 36 million more annual visitors. It staged championship boxing matches, supported a Class AAA baseball team, and enjoyed big-time college basketball with UNLV's Runnin' Rebels, who even had won a national championship. Still, the major pro leagues avoided it as a den of iniquity. "The number one evil empire" is how Larry Brown, a Clark County commissioner and former professional pitcher, described the leagues' attitude toward the city. Gambling on sports was already happening all over the country, of course—at the corner bar, on illegal internet sites, in office pools. Somehow, that didn't make the idea of doing it legally any more palatable to commissioners and owners.

In one sense, that was easy to understand. Big-time sports were thriving. Each time a new television rights deal was announced, it seemed to set a record. The value of franchises had soared to dizzying heights. The only clouds on the horizon that anyone could see involved fans somehow losing confidence in the integrity of the competition through a scandal similar to the Black Sox. Accordingly, the leagues contorted themselves to avoid any association with gambling, known gamblers, and even places where gambling took place. It just didn't make sense to take the risk.

––––––––

NOBODY TRIED TO legalize betting on sports outside Nevada until 2010. By the time Chris Christie became New Jersey's governor that year, Atlantic City was in trouble. The novelty of its casinos had faded. Hotel bookings had plummeted, and tax-generating gambling revenues with them. Christie saw sports betting as a means to counter those losses. His first year in office, he pushed for a referendum that would allow it at any racetrack or casino in the state. The referendum passed, and Christie signed it into law.

There was only one problem. Through the Professional and Amateur Sports Protection Act of 1992—which, in a curious twist, had been sponsored by New Jersey's own Bill Bradley, the former NBA great who had become a US senator—the federal government had banned sports gambling throughout the country, beyond a few existing manifestations that were allowed to continue. Those included betting on bicycle racing in New Mexico and golf in Wyoming; several sports-based lotteries; horse racing; jai alai; and the bookmaking inside Nevada's casinos. In 2014, New Jersey's referendum was challenged by the NCAA. Christie refused to back down, calculating that the Supreme Court wouldn't uphold a law banning a recreational pursuit in 49 states that had been legal for decades in the 50th. He was right. The court, analysts noted, wanted to make a show of limiting federal jurisdiction. "They just happened to pick a gambling law to do so," Cabot said.

In May of 2018, in a case that been renamed as *Murphy v. NCAA* after Phil Murphy succeeded Christie as New Jersey's governor, the Supreme Court ruled that states did have the authority to allow betting on sports. The strangest thing about this was, the leagues themselves didn't object to the verdict. In fact, many franchise owners had been rooting for New Jersey to win the case *even though their leagues had joined the NCAA as plaintiffs*. All that queasiness about gambling that had kept the leagues out of Las Vegas and even discouraged its players from being seen at a blackjack table? It had seemingly vanished overnight.

How had that happened? Thanks to the proselytizing of a

few prescient owners, the leagues and their investors had come to understand how much they stood to gain if gambling were legalized. Foremost among those owners was Ted Leonsis, whose holdings included the NHL's Washington Capitals and the NBA's Washington Wizards. In the years leading up to the verdict, Leonsis had tirelessly explained to his colleagues how betting would provide vast new revenue streams for leagues and their clubs. He spread his gospel in owners' meetings, during private phone calls, and even while testifying before a Congressional committee. That gambling had been proven to be addictive, similar to drugs and alcohol in the way that it destroyed the health and well-being of those unable to moderate their exposure to it, was something that could be dealt with later. It was a truism in modern economics that billion-dollar businesses, which is what many sports franchises had become, needed to keep growing to maintain their momentum and continue to accrue value. That required more revenue. Gambling was an untapped source, vaster than anyone imagined.

Simultaneously, there were signs that America's love affair with pro sports was beginning to wane. The competition for attention, which had been minimal when the concept of sports leagues first began to coalesce in the late 1800s, had come to include basically every song, movie, or book ever created, available at the touch of a screen. Insidiously entertaining video games had been created for an emerging generation of digital consumers. Social media operated all day and all night, gobbling up hours at a time. It was no surprise that Nielsen ratings were sinking, or that the average age of those who said they followed sports closely was getting older by the year. Privately, team owners fretted that even their own children had little patience for watching entire games on television. By the time of the Supreme Court ruling, the fear that sports were losing relevance in American society had replaced the undermining of competitive integrity as its greatest existential threat. "The question is, 'Will sports as we know it even exist at all in 20 years?'" the chief executive of one of Europe's biggest soccer clubs said to me one afternoon while standing on the sidelines of an equally iconic venue. He gestured around us, at the grandstands packed with spectators. "Will anybody still bother to come do this?"

The *Murphy v. NCAA* verdict surprised the gambling industry. "You'd be amazed how many casino operators didn't see it coming," said Greg Carlin, the co-founder and chief executive of Rush Street Gaming, which owns casinos in Pennsylvania, New York, and Illinois. It didn't surprise Leonsis, though. He'd been planning on it for years.

―――――――――

TO TRY TO figure out what had happened, I went to see Leonsis in Washington that fall of 2018.

Leonsis, who held various executive positions at America Online from 1994 to 2007, said he didn't gamble—not on sports, or on anything else. Yet he had risked both his reputation and his capital on the future of sports wagering. He already owned a major stake in DraftKings. He had invested in Sportradar, which delivered, at high speed, information on games in progress to bookmaking websites, creating the sort of advantage enjoyed by Wall Street traders who, in Leonsis's words, "get a quarter of a second more to say, 'Buy that stock.'" He owned part of WinView, which holds numerous patents for various aspects of in-game gambling. He hoped to fill the schedule of the NBC Sports Washington cable channel, of which he owned a third, with chatter about point spreads and gambling opportunities. (He also envisioned simulcasts of every Wizards and Capitals game on an alternate channel, with a steady stream of betting information.)

Later that year, Sportradar's chief executive told me he expected
its $2.4 billion valuation to quintuple in three years with the open-
ing of the US market. That meant the same for Leonsis's stake.
And if franchise values continued to rise because of fans' increased
engagement in the sports they followed, Leonsis's NHL and NBA
teams could be his most profitable gambling plays of all.

Leonsis spoke exuberantly about gambling as an engine for
future growth. His conversation unfolded as logically as a business
plan. "We're going to create more jobs," he'd say. "We're going to
generate more taxes." He didn't worry about a 21st-century version
of the Black Sox. While big-league athletes were once paid poorly
enough to make the offers of payoffs enticing, he argued that the
vast majority are today far wealthier than anyone who might tempt
them. "I know this may be a naïve statement," he told me at one
point, "but I don't think an NBA player is susceptible to some hus-
tler saying, 'Shave the points, and here's $5,000 in $100 bills.'" Several years before the Supreme Court decision, Leonsis already had a
comeback whenever he heard a colleague express discomfort about
legalizing gambling. "What," he'd ask them, "are you so afraid of?"

At the time that we met, sports gambling had become legal in
New Jersey and several other states, but not in the District of Colum-
bia. Until it was, there would be no betting windows inside Capital
One Arena, where his NBA and NHL teams played. "But eventually,"
Leonsis told me, he would build a sports book where fans could "con-
gregate and watch games and bet on the games in whatever way they
want to," whether at the windows or on their own handheld devices.
He would outsource the bookmaking, because owning a team while
taking bets on its games would be perceived as a conflict of interest
(and probably be illegal). Instead, he would simply offer a site for eating,
drinking, and more gambling. "Except that I want to outlaw the word

gambling," he said. "Maybe call it 'interactive wagering.' When you hear 'gambling,' you think of Tony Soprano—'I'm with my bookie.'"

By 2021, Leonsis had implemented almost exactly that vision. A two-story, 20,000-foot William Hill sports book, not too different in scale from what the Cubs eventually decided on for Wrigley Field, opened that May. It had 100 television screens, 17 betting windows, and 12 more betting kiosks. By then, too, the annual betting handle in the 16 states that permitted online sports books was on pace to reach nearly $50 billion. Operators in New Jersey alone brought in $4.89 billion in wagers during the first six months of 2021. By that summer, Leonsis was fretting that he should have made his sports book larger.

———

LEONSIS DATED HIS personal revelation about gambling to November 2015, when he found himself visiting the remote southwest coast of Scotland. His daughter, who lived in London, had a serious boyfriend. Both families had flown in to spend Thanksgiving weekend at a manor house owned by the boyfriend's parents. On a clear day, Leonsis was told, you could see Ireland across the water. He never could confirm that because the weather was never clear. The basketball and hockey seasons were underway back home, but the house had no internet or satellite reception, so Leonsis couldn't follow his teams. It was foggy and cold. "There was nothing to do," he said.

The closest village of any size, Campbeltown, was 40 minutes away. One morning, they all drove in for lunch. Nobody seemed to be around. "The whole town is, like, two blocks long," Leonsis said. "And there's one restaurant and a pharmacy. And then we saw one place that had some life to it." Inside a storefront, a crowd was making noise. It was the betting parlor, Leonsis learned. The phrase didn't carry any connotation of disrepute, as it would in America. "It was just, 'This is where you go and watch a game and see your friends and hang out,'" he said. "It was the *Cheers* of Campbeltown."

From Scotland, Leonsis went to London. Driving through his daughter's neighborhood, he noticed one betting parlor after another. "Like in America, where you'd have a Starbucks," he said. He investigated and found that you could bet on sports at 8,500 outlets in the United Kingdom. As a comparison, he looked up Domino's pizza and saw that it had roughly 5,500 stores across the United States. "For me, that was the beginning of 'Hey, this is a true consumer phenomenon,'" he said. The parlors seemed inviting. They weren't seedy haunts for professional gamblers. "This is not Off Track Betting," Leonsis said. "This is Starbucks or Domino's. This is popularized and accepted in the most remote places and the most centrally located places. If you wanted to find a proxy of what could happen here, you just had to look at Campbeltown and London."

Adam Silver had been observing the same thing. From 1998 to 2006, the future NBA commissioner ran the league's video production and programming arm. On frequent business trips abroad, he couldn't help noticing how pervasive gambling had become. Stadiums had betting kiosks beside their snack bars. "There was this enormous legalized infrastructure in place," Silver said. Yet, somehow, leagues and teams hadn't been corrupted. In fact, they were thriving. Stern, the commissioner at the time, was a lawyer who had come to the sport during college basketball's betting scandals of the 1960s. Throughout his tenure, he remained opposed to gambling—he later changed his mind—and for years even refused to hold league meetings and other events in Las Vegas. "But the opportunity seemed fairly obvious to me," Silver said.

In 2014, the year that Silver succeeded Stern, he made an argument in a *New York Times* op-ed piece that didn't differ much from those advocating the legalization of marijuana. "Despite legal restrictions, sports betting is widespread," he wrote. "Because there are few legal options available, those who wish to bet resort to illicit bookmaking operations and shady offshore websites." Why not bring the action into the light, he proposed, where it could be regulated, and the movement of betting lines and the sums of money monitored?

Silver understood that nothing had the promise of generating more new revenue than legal gambling. It offered the advantage of not merely attracting new customers, as Kenney was hoping to do for the Cubs, but appealing to those the leagues already had. Part of the enticement of gambling was that it increased the amount of time viewers would spend on every game—if you had the Warriors giving 11½ points and they were up by 13 with a minute left, that wasn't garbage time to you, it was crunch time. "If we can take the roughly billion people globally who are already watching NBA games and convince them to watch 10 more minutes of each game," Silver said, "that's by far the most efficient way to grow our business."

A month before Silver's op-ed, the NBA had signed a record-setting, $24 billion television rights deal. At the league's board of governors meeting in New York, Leonsis, who was chairman of its media committee, presented the deal to the rest of the owners. Even as he celebrated the terms, he cautioned that such fees were unlikely to grow, though the cost of operating teams inevitably would. A smaller and smaller percentage of Americans were subscribing to cable television, which meant that viewership would inevitably fall. "The first thing someone used to ask when he moved into a new neighborhood was 'How do I get cable?'" Leonsis said. "That doesn't happen anymore." His point was that people got internet service for their phones and computers, but not the bundled television package. "It's not cord-cutting," he said. "They just never sign up at all. So, we have to find new pots of gold."

Leonsis believed he had found them. You can hold your nose all you want, he told his colleagues, but gambling offered a viable and wholly untapped source of revenue for professional sports leagues—the continued growth they all were looking for. He cited a study that $8 billion was going to be wagered in Nevada casinos on the coming Super Bowl, and $80 billion more in illegal, unregulated bets. "That means the guy who's going to a bookie, but it also means your grandmother who is in a pool," he said. Leonsis can be almost courtly in negotiations, and he was polite when he met with resistance. Privately, though, he shook his head. How could you ignore such an opportunity, ready to be taken advantage of the moment the law allowed? What are you so afraid of?

FOR DECADES, SPORTS gambling tended to be a static experience. You bet on a team and handed money to somebody, and maybe got a slip of paper in return. Then you waited to find out if you were right. That changed when three American options traders moved to Antigua in the mid-1990s to create an online gambling business they named World Sports Exchange. Instead of offering point spreads, World Sports Exchange operated like a commodities market. Before tip-off, options on the favored Lakers, for example, might cost $60 each. Options on the Knicks, the underdogs, might sell for $40. At the end of the game, the options on the losing team would become worthless, while the options on the winning team would each pay out $100.

But here was the novelty: you didn't have to wait until the game was over to cash in. If the Lakers scored the first eight points, the value of that $60 option might grow to, say, $72. You could sell it and pocket your $12 gain. You might then invest in the Knicks at a discount. Or, you might wait for the price to fall and buy another option on the Lakers. You could buy and sell options, on either team or both, throughout the game. Once you had started, it was hard to stop until the game ended. It was exhausting. It was also great fun. And even more than the other bookmakers operating beyond US borders, which were handling traditional bets, it seemed to threaten the monopoly on sports gambling that Nevada's casinos had long enjoyed.

I met one of those traders, Haden Ware, under a thatched roof in the Caribbean in early 2000. He was drinking beer and eating lobster salad. Steve Schillinger, a partner in World Sports Exchange, later confided to me that he and Ware were each making more than $1 million a year. Yet, as fugitives on the run, they were miserable. The Interstate Wire Act of 1961 had outlawed taking bets over telephone lines. In that era of dial-up internet access, that's exactly what World Sports Exchange was doing. Online gambling was "especially pernicious," in the words of Jon Kyl, who at the time was a US senator from Arizona. "You get up in the morning and log onto your computer and start to gamble. It plays to the addictive nature of many people, especially kids." Quoting an unnamed Harvard professor, Kyl called it "the crack cocaine of gambling." Kyl introduced specific legislation against internet gambling and vowed to indict expats taking bets online. In 1998, twenty-one US citizens were charged with Wire Act violations. Among them were Ware, Schillinger, and Jay Cohen, another partner.

Weary of living in exile, Cohen flew home. He was convicted and served 18 months in prison. Janet Reno, the US attorney general, backed Kyl's efforts. So did casinos, sports leagues, and gambling interest groups—just about everyone, in fact, except some Native American nations. Even the lobbyist being paid by World

Sports Exchange acknowledged that the opponents of digital gambling had a point: all that money they had invested in brick-and-mortar sports books should count for something. "The casinos worked a long time to establish legitimacy," he told me. Eventually, World Sports Exchange was overtaken by better-funded rivals. It ceased operations in 2013. That same day, Schillinger committed suicide. After serving his sentence, Cohen disappeared to Europe. But their insight that betting doesn't have to stop when play begins had revolutionized the industry.

At the same time that World Sports Exchange was fading into oblivion, DraftKings and its competitor FanDuel were founded on another innovative idea. They would curate a limitless number of fantasy leagues and let customers choose new players every day. The companies generated profits from participation fees, while the winners would be rewarded with cash prizes. For many fans, watching games became the equivalent of monitoring their investment portfolios, except that the investments were bets on individual players. Eric Schneiderman, New York's attorney general at the time, thought that sounded a lot like gambling. Games of skill are legal in every state; you can pay to participate in fishing or bowling competitions, for example, and recoup your money—and much more—if you do well. What you can't do is bet on who you think will win those competitions. The fantasy sites argued, somewhat tenuously, that constructing a winning team is more like fishing than knowing who is good at fishing. Schneiderman disagreed. In 2015, he shut down both sites and fined the companies. At that point, DraftKings and FanDuel began working to get bills passed in state legislatures that would certify fantasy sports as legal.

Soon after that, Leonsis bought part of DraftKings. He tends to characterize troubled companies in one of two ways—as either "falling angels," which eventually rise again, or as "falling knives," which don't. In DraftKings, he saw a falling angel. He anticipated that digital sports betting would soon become legal, and he agreed with Robins that the gaming industry giants everyone assumed would dominate the US market—the English bookmaker William Hill, or maybe the Bally's Corporation or Caesars Entertainment—were at a disadvantage compared with DraftKings. "We have a big database of customers that we know from research are already betting on sports, mostly with black-market websites," Robins said. "And we have a brand that is much more identified with winning money and betting on sports than any of them that we're competing with."

Leonsis also realized that, while betting windows in stadiums and arenas like the one he planned to build would be the most visible manifestation of legal gambling, digital betting would eventually be far more profitable. In the years following the demise of World Sports Exchange, handheld devices had proliferated. The prospect of gamblers placing legal bets on their phones, which could travel with them to bars and bleacher seats, was especially enticing to companies such as DraftKings, which didn't have to spend a dime on building actual betting parlors to do business. The real-time use of those phones enabled the sports books to offer modified versions of the same kinds of bets that World Sports Exchange had invented two decades before. You could get in and out, and back in again, every few moments, making or losing money with each transaction.

And because smartphones and tablets routinely capture the details of each transaction, proponents argued that games are actually better protected against manipulation when digital betting is legal. "If there was a huge bet placed against a team two hours before an announcement that its star player wouldn't be participating, that is something that should cause us to investigate," Silver said. "And it's something that, historically, we wouldn't have known." That idea, that the ability to monitor trends in digital bets to a greater extent than ever had been possible at a Las Vegas sports book would provide greater protection against manipulation, helped convince some previously reluctant team owners to support legalization. (It also helped that the accumulated data might even help sports books spot a potential gambling addiction, based on a customer's betting patterns and frequency, if they were inclined to look for them.)

As soon as the *Murphy v. NCAA* decision was handed down, DraftKings partnered with a casino, as New Jersey's law requires, and became the first company to take digital bets. Before long, its ads blanketed cable networks in New Jersey. "Get ready for thousands of ways to bet!" they shouted—and they weren't exaggerating. One DraftKings executive estimated that year that the company's app averaged 45,000 to 55,000 different propositions for gamblers to consider every day. Many of them had little to do with which team ended up winning the game.

By the end of the 2010s, announcers were telling us how hard baseballs were hit and how far they traveled, or how many miles a particularly active soccer player had run. Such information created new opportunities for betting, and more would continue to emerge. Hockey, for example, hadn't traditionally generated much in the way of metrics, but in order to learn which players were skating the fastest or shooting the hardest, the NHL had spent more than a year creating its own version of baseball's Statcast. It even put a chip inside the puck. "Leagues are building a fire hose of data around their product," Chris Grove, an analyst who consulted for gaming companies and investors, said at the time. "And the logical recipient of that data is the betting industry."

To Leonsis, perhaps the biggest benefit of gambling was that it allowed fans to become participants in their favorite sports. Rather than customers, he thinks of fans as an audience. "He understood that audiences want experiences," Peter Guber said. "This gives them a chance to walk away telling their own story—'I saw this opportunity, I recognized what this player would be able to accomplish.' When you have a tool that makes an audience more of a participant than a passenger, it's a very vital and vibrant element."

Perhaps nobody saw more dollar signs on the horizon than legislators. "I was talking to some economic development people from Alabama," Jack Evans, a member of the Washington, DC, city council, told me a few months after the court decision. "They were asking how they could raise money. I told them: 'Put in sports gambling and you can pay off all your debts on the Alabama–Auburn football game alone. One game, Alabama and Auburn. You'd make billions.'"

———

IN THE SUMMER of 2018, Silver announced that the NBA had granted the casino owner MGM Resorts the right to use league logos and data. The biggest market by far, though, was football. Greater than $30 billion was bet legally on football between 1992 and 2018, according to the Center for Gaming Research at the University of Nevada, Las Vegas. That's about 50 percent more than on basketball, and double the amount bet on baseball. (It's also a tiny fraction of the amount of money that was illegally bet on football during that time, from wagers at the golf club to offshore websites, to the parlays and scratch cards that circulate around offices and corner bars.) When we spoke at the time, Leonsis revealed his plans for the resurrected Arena Football League, in which he controlled two of the four franchises. His vision mandated a network partner that would market the game as the anti-NFL: informal, expressive, and gambling-friendly. It didn't matter that the league, which has since gone on indefinite hiatus, would have no history. Your favorite team would be the one you had money on at the moment.

In September 2021, New Jersey became the first state to handle $1 billion in legal sports bets in a single month. New York legalized face-to-face betting in 2019, but by the end of 2021 it still hadn't licensed online sports books. It had become a common sight to see bicyclists with betting apps on their phones pedaling across the George Washington Bridge on NFL Sundays to get money down. At that point, more than half the states in the country—a list that included the massive market of California—still didn't allow digital wagers. In other states, though, the annual tax revenue from sports gambling exceeded $50 million. Television analysts had started to frame their predictions in gambling terms. Gambling podcasts were flourishing. The additional engagement that betting had created during the pandemic, when fans had little to do for months at a time but watch games on their phones and laptops, was harder to quantify, but ultimately no less lucrative.

At the same time, the human cost of all of this, in terms of lives altered by financial losses and destroyed by gambling addictions, was impossible to know. As states passed laws legalizing sports betting, few set parameters on how it could be marketed. Companies such as DraftKings and FanDuel targeted potential new customers with seductive offers, such as putting up $1 to win $100 if Steph Curry made at least one three-pointer in a game that night, or if Philadelphia Eagles' quarterback Jalen Hurts completed one or more passes in that day's game. These were designed to give neophytes the endorphin kick of winning a bet, in the hope that they would strive to repeat it. Enough of them did that DraftKings' revenue jumped 57 percent in the summer of 2022 compared with the previous year, putting the company on track to earn more than $2 billion annually and validating the investment Leonsis had made in the company—and the sports leagues had made in the industry. Where all that money came from, ordinary fans placing bets on teams and losing them, was seldom discussed.

Legal gambling also opened the door to a new source of sponsorship income. In English soccer during the 2017–18 season, more than half of the 44 teams that competed in the sport's top two echelons wore uniforms that advertised bookmaking sites. As North America's leagues abruptly decided they were open to partnering with gambling facilitators, those same sites, and others, began bidding for similar sponsorships of US teams. Within a few months of the first legal bet placed in New Jersey, the NFL's Dallas Cowboys already had chosen an official casino partner, WinStar, even though sports betting was still illegal in Texas. In the fall of 2022, Leonsis's Washington Capitals became the first American team to put the logo of a gambling company, Caesars, on a uniform patch.

Across America, too, franchises struck deals like the one that the Cubs had done with DraftKings to create betting parlors that doubled as sports bars on the grounds of their arenas and stadiums. Leonsis had built North America's first one, but within a few years, the nearby Washington Nationals had their own, sponsored by MGM. So did baseball's Arizona Diamondbacks (Caesars) and basketball's Phoenix Suns (FanDuel). Chicago's United Center had a sportsbook on the way, and bills were under consideration that would make on-site gambling at sports facilities legal in several states, including New York. In July 2022, the Cincinnati Bengals went as far as to join DraftKings, FanDuel, and other companies by applying for one of the Type A online betting licenses—which would allow it to handle online wagers—that Ohio would be awarding at the end of the year. "What were once bright lines," sports columnist Tim Sullivan tweeted, "keep getting blurrier."

By 2022, sports gambling also had crossed the invisible barrier into what had become known as Web3. For the third time, one of the main protagonists was DraftKings. That June, it announced the creation of a fantasy football league based on the accumulation of non-fungible tokens, or NFTs, which would be bought at auction and used in a weekly game based on NFL performance. This new form of wagering on sports was the equivalent of a stock market derivative. It put another layer of distance between teams and the fans who followed them; you could invest in an NFT portfolio of players without even knowing who any of them were. The new fantasy league promised to bring a new generation of gamers, who had grown up watching other gamers play esports on Twitch, into the universe of sports gambling. Whether they would also become interested in the actual games, or develop any loyalty to the teams that were playing them, remained an open question.

But it couldn't be denied that gambling, the oldest, most popular, and most profitable form of analytics ever applied to sports, had already profoundly affected the way that fans perceived the games they watched. Leonsis, who remained a holder of a large block of DraftKings stock, was undeterred by potentially negative consequences to bettors. "If you're gambling too much," he told HBO's *Real Sports* in 2022, "there's an algorithm that says they'll shut you off." He felt the various iterations of legal sports gambling had arrived just in time, with that entire universe of entertainment beckoning from the phone in everyone's pocket. Gambling, he said, was the only way the leagues we'd grown up watching could continue to compete. "It has," he said, "kind of saved sports."

9

IT'S THE FUTURE!

ON OCTOBER 28, 2020, the day after the Rays' Kevin Cash pulled Blake Snell from Game Six of the World Series, Daryl Morey, who previously had been the general manager of the Houston Rockets, agreed to a five-year deal to run basketball operations for the Philadelphia 76ers. The two events appeared to have little in common. One occurred on baseball's biggest stage, with America watching. The other was a boardroom transaction by a basketball executive who was barely known outside the sport. But both illustrated the pitfalls, real or perceived, of the analytic approach. The Rays had constructed one of baseball's best teams essentially by being smarter than everyone else. Morey had done the same in Houston. Yet, a decade and a half on, neither had managed to win a championship.

For most MLB managers, using data to figure out how to play the odds had become the new orthodoxy. Often, the general managers to whom they reported, or the owners a level above that, insisted that they follow the analysts' guidance. To Cash, all those years of accumulated data sent a clear message: the chance of a player getting a hit in his third at-bat against *any* pitcher is far greater than in his first at-bat. "I value that," Cash said about the information that the analytic process had provided him. He valued it highly enough that he had based the most important decision of the history of the Rays' franchise on it. The move hadn't worked, but as Paul DePodesta had insisted when he ran the Dodgers all those years before, the decision was not a mistake. It merely produced the less-likely result.

Like the Rays' brain trust, Morey helped engineer his team's rise to the highest echelon. Along the way, he presided over the evolution of his sport. The club basketball he'd played at Northwestern in the 1980s had been based on working the ball inside for lay-ups and short jumpers. Morey loaded up his Rockets teams with excellent shooters and agile big men with passing skills who could spot an open man on the perimeter and get the ball to him with pace. By 2020, NBA teams routinely passed up even uncontested jump shots to whip the ball to the corner or the top of the key for three-pointers.

In the years since *Moneyball*, baseball's Astros and Red Sox and basketball's Warriors, among other teams, had disproved the classic critique of the analytic approach, which is that it doesn't work in the playoffs. However, it remained true that analytics has a *better* chance of adding value during the long sweep of a regular season. When you have the odds on your side, your chance of success increases with the growth of the sample size. (Cash maintained that if he removed Snell from that World Series game a hundred times, the strategy would have succeeded far more often than it would have failed.) It's not so different from the systematized play of the best professional gamblers, who might lose money on a given bet or even over an entire month, but invariably end each year in the black.

That's not the only reason why Morey, Billy Beane, and some

other analytically minded executives were still waiting to win their first championship. In each sport, the postseason was constructed differently than the regular schedule. In baseball's case, it consisted of series that were as short as a single game. (That was changed following the 2021 season.) And because nearly all the teams in the history of baseball that were good enough to make the playoffs won between 50 and 65 percent of their games, the outcome of any series between them wasn't too many deviations away from random.

Compared with the regular season, too, pitching played an outsized role in the playoffs. Without future games to consider, managers typically used their best pitchers more freely, sometimes running through their entire bullpens in a single night. That tended to help the wealthiest teams, who were able to stockpile elite relievers. Conversely, a particularly effective starter, such as the Dodgers' Clayton Kershaw or the Giants' Madison Bumgarner, would often remain in games longer that he might during a typical game because his season was nearing its end. That's what the analytics skeptics thought that Cash should have done with Snell: It was the last time he would pitch all year, no matter what happened in that game. He was clearly his team's best pitcher. Why not win or lose with your ace?

Cash's decision generated another topic of discussion over the months that followed, one that had little to do with the game's outcome. Optimizing his team's chances of winning, as Cash believed he was doing, deprived fans of the opportunity to learn whether Snell could complete a heroic pitching performance, one that might have rivaled the most storied in World Series history. For viewers without a rooting interest in either club, the possibility of seeing such a historically relevant game could have been a significant factor in their decision to continue watching. For some of them, experiencing such performances is the reason they follow sports.

But analytics has no place for heroism. It doesn't take into account entertainment value. And in the quarter century since Beane had taken control of the Oakland A's, the confluence of strategic factors brought about by analytics had created a version of baseball that featured far fewer of the exciting plays that most fans watch games to witness: doubles and triples, stolen bases, fielding gems. Instead, the average amount of elapsed time between balls in play—not between pitches, but the amount of time you have to spend watching a game on average before you'll see someone hit a ball between the foul lines—had jumped by 30 seconds over the course of the 21st century, to about four minutes. It is astonishing to learn that, over the last 26 minutes of that Dodgers–Rays game that ended the 2020 season, only *two* balls were hit into fair territory.

As recently as the 2016 season, MLB hitters combined for 3,200 more hits than strikeouts. Two years later, the number of total strikeouts in a season exceeded the number of hits for the first time in baseball history. In 2021, strikeouts exceeded hits by more than 5,000. Technological innovations such as Rapsodo and TrackMan had enabled scouts and coaches to calculate and hone the spin rates of pitches. Combined with a spike in the average velocity of big-league fastballs and sliders, too many pitches had become simply unhittable.

In the 2005 season, 50 major-league pitchers threw 200 innings or more. By 2021, there were only seven—and six of those seven didn't reach 210. One was Adam Wainwright of the Cardinals, whose career had started back in 2005. Wainwright threw 206 1/3 innings in 2021, a remarkable achievement for a 40-year-old in the context of modern baseball. Only two pitchers, Zack Wheeler and Walker Buehler, threw more than that. Had Wainwright thrown the same 206 1/3 innings in his rookie season, his workload would have ranked a paltry 39th among all major leaguers.

By 2021, starting pitchers were averaging around five innings and 80 pitches a start, the lowest totals in history. Knowing they were unlikely to see any hitters more than twice, they were empowered to throw their hardest from the first batter onward. They no longer hesitated to show a particularly dangerous hitter their best pitch the first time through the order, since they almost certainly wouldn't be around to face him with the game on the line.

Supplied with data on every one of each batter's previous big-league at-bats, fielders positioned themselves precisely where he was most likely to hit the ball. Sure, a hitter might be able to swing against the shift and dump a single to an unoccupied area of the infield, or even lay down a bunt and beat it out. But even with that, the odds of scoring a run with three singles in an inning were still less than having each hitter swing hard into the shift and hoping that one of them drove it over the wall. During the 2010s, the incidence of plate-appearance results that exist independent of fielding—the home runs, walks, and strikeouts dubbed the "Three True Outcomes" by baseball analyst Christina Kahrl—jumped from 18.5 percent to 23.4. That ratio declined slightly in 2021, perhaps because of baseball's mid-season decision to start vigorously enforcing laws against putting sticky substances on the ball to increase its spin. Still, even in 2021, when an MLB player came up to the plate, he walked, struck out, or homered nearly a quarter of the time. Intellectually, that's an interesting evolution of a sport that had been played under mostly the same rules for a century and a half. But it isn't much fun to watch.

Since the mid-2000s, no team had played more analytic baseball than the Rays. Starting in 2008, they had won 90 games seven times and won three division titles. They had participated in two World Series. But their annual attendance was either the worst in MLB or close to it. Sure, they had a lousy stadium and an indifferent fan base, but it was also true that the brand of baseball they were playing, though spectacularly successful, just wasn't very enjoyable. It was all strikeouts and walks, and a seemingly endless parade of new pitchers, game after game.

Analytics had helped the Rays' scouts identify and then develop young talent; its farm system was the consensus choice as baseball's best. But like Beane's A's, once those players became stars, the Rays couldn't afford to keep them. On December 29, 2020, Blake Snell, too, was traded—to the San Diego Padres, for yet another package of prospects. The executives who ran the Rays, beginning with general manager Andrew Friedman and manager Joe Maddon, and later those who replaced them, had provided the Tampa–St. Petersburg market with a decade of winning baseball. But it was a team that many fans were finding hard to like.

Analytics had optimized the Tampa Bay Rays. That much was certain. But for whom?

———————

THE SAME WAS happening in the NBA. In the 1980s, individual creativity transformed professional basketball from a dying sport into a global product. In the decades that followed, city playgrounds and suburban driveways were filled with the no-look passes and double-pump-fake lay-ups that the game's stars, Magic and Larry and Michael and Kobe and the rest, were showing off on *SportsCenter* night after night. That style of play turned out to be not the smartest approach in the three-point era. There wasn't any question that finding an open man on the perimeter to shoot a three-pointer made more sense than anything but the most wide-open dunk. But to many fans, it still wasn't as exciting to watch as a drive to the basket.

In September of 2021, I went to see Morey in Philadelphia. By then, he had been working there for nearly a year. He was at the center of a controversy regarding Ben Simmons, the team's best player. At least, Simmons had been the team's best player until the previous June, when he suddenly decided to stop taking shots, even those with a wide-open look at the basket. The reason was clear: he was afraid of getting fouled. Though he'd always been a reasonably accurate free-throw shooter, making 60 percent of his attempts or greater in three of his first four NBA seasons, at some point during the 2021 playoffs they became a psychological issue for him. Each one he missed made it harder to make the next. By the end of the playoffs, he was only making a sliver more than a third of his attempts, a record low. In the Eastern Conference championship series against the Atlanta Hawks, his percentage was even lower than that.

Needless to say, the Hawks noticed. As soon as Simmons attempted to put up a shot, one or another of the Hawks would foul him. Simmons would miss one of the free throws, or both of them. His parlous mental state would be exacerbated, and Atlanta would come away with the ball. Simmons decided to mitigate his embarrassment by making his own analytics decision, predicated on internal data: he wouldn't shoot at all. This led to a ridiculous situation in which five Hawks players were guarding four Sixers players while Simmons dribbled around, looking for a way to get rid of the ball. By the end of the playoffs, Simmons was getting criticized by nearly everyone outside the club, and several players and the head coach within it. Shortly before Morey and I met for lunch in a sidewalk booth that had been constructed for outdoor dining during the pandemic, Simmons announced that his time with the team was over, though he still had several years remaining on his contract.

The Hawks hadn't needed to make complex calculations to figure out that Simmons's unwillingness to shoot the ball could be used in their favor. His distress was clear. In the finely tuned NBA, the advantage that gave Atlanta was enough to diminish Philadelphia's chances of winning the series to practically zero. It also wasn't particularly enjoyable to experience, unless you were a Hawks fan or you simply wanted to revel in the weirdness of it.

I had no particular interest in Simmons's contract situation, but I did want to know how Morey felt about the iteration of basketball that he helped engineer. "We're an entertainment product," Morey acknowledged. "It turns out that 85 to 90 percent of the time, winning is the best entertainment. But that's not *always* the case." As the head of the basketball side of the Sixers, Morey's goal was to prioritize winning championships, which he calculated would provide the maximum entertainment value to the vast majority of the team's fans. That meant prioritizing wins, game after game. "But each of those steps aren't 100 percent congruent," Morey said. "You do have to remind yourself of that from time to time."

Morey, who also had a keen interest in baseball, proposed that the decision to remove Snell was one of those occasions when competitive success and entertainment were misaligned. That wasn't Cash's fault, or the fault of any of the Rays' decision-makers above him. They had been incentivized by winning, not creating a compelling narrative. "In an ideal world, the league offices need to set up the playing field such that, when you do optimize for wins, it's also entertaining," Morey said. "That's why the rules are very important, to be malleable and change."

Unlike baseball, Morey pointed out, basketball had a tradition of tweaking its rules as the athletic capabilities of its players evolved. The NBA added the three-point line to help unpack the mass of bodies beneath the basket. Later, the league decided to allow zone defenses when it became clear that modern players shot from the perimeter successfully enough to counteract it. Morey said he was the wrong person to ask about entertainment value; the extreme vested interest he had in the games rendered aesthetics irrelevant. But as someone who had thought quite a bit about how to stay ahead of the rest of the league, he was fascinated to see how Quin Snyder's Utah Jazz had taken what Morey's teams had been doing, then "gone 10 percent further. They designed their entire infrastructure to optimize getting open, and then catch-and-shoot threes." Did Utah fans want to watch that? They did, Morey said, if Utah won.

When Morey started working in Houston in 2007, he guessed that basketball was about a decade behind baseball in how widespread the acceptance of analytics was among executives of the sport. As of 2021, he figured basketball was still probably a decade behind. When he started in Houston, so many of the NBA's teams were still relying on conventional metrics, and the strategies built to optimize them, that Morey believed using data analysis could help generate an additional 10 to 12 wins for the Rockets over the NBA's 82-game season. That was the equivalent of adding $40 million to the team's salary cap. "Not quite a Kevin Durant," he says, "but maybe an Andre Iguodala." By the time we spoke, he believed the equivalent was down to between two and four wins. That's still hugely significant; imagine adding a player who will take you from a 48-win team to 52 wins, but without paying his salary or using a roster spot. "The best practices are still in flux," Morey said. "We're on a learning curve, and baseball is still quite a bit ahead of us. But we're trending toward the same place, where data is only going to be able to help in these tiny margins." In baseball, Morey estimated, teams are now looking for ways to create only a quarter to half a win over the length of the season.

In baseball's high-tech world of slow-motion video and biometrics, even flaws had become opportunities. Since *Moneyball*, smart teams had been searching for players who were undervalued because the things they did well weren't regarded as important enough to overcome their weaknesses. By around 2016, the attention of those teams had shifted to those with mediocre statistics who are elite at certain aspects of hitting or pitching, but below-average at others. If a team could identify those flaws, which had become far easier to do with the new technological tools, it could then help mitigate them, as the Dodgers had done with scrap-heap hitters Justin Turner and Chris Taylor, and the Rays and Astros seemed to do with several journeymen pitchers each season. Sometimes that meant figuring out what a player did better than almost anyone else and convincing him to do only that. " 'You have five pitches, but you should use only two of them,' " Morey explained.

After years of working to optimize his basketball teams' performances in the context of the rules of their sport, Morey had developed the ability to identify when a strategy wasn't constructed to work as productively as it should. Not long before our conversation, he'd sat down over lunch with Tom Fitzgerald, the general manager of the NHL's New Jersey Devils. The Devils are owned by the same two private equity investors who own the Sixers, Josh Harris and David Blitzer. But in terms of using data to question existing practices and exploit hidden opportunities, hockey is probably as far behind basketball as basketball is behind baseball.

Morey asked Fitzgerald why the best hockey players didn't spend more time actually playing in the game. Alone among major sports, each NHL team's players were active for shifts of 45 to 50 seconds.

Then they left the ice in favor of another group. Typically, each team had three or four rotating lines of offensive players and two or three defensive pairings. That meant that even the best players spent nearly two-thirds of the game on the bench, which is even more than in baseball or football. This is palpably bad in terms of entertainment value. But Morey wondered if there might also be a hidden opportunity to increase the team's performance.

"I'm completely ignorant," Morey told him. "But I can tell you that in many sports I've studied, a tired star is almost always better than a fully rested non-star."

"I don't think so," Fitzgerald said. "Our sport is different."

Morey deferred. What did he know? He'd grown up in Cleveland, which didn't have an NHL team. Then he'd spent much of his professional life in Houston, which also didn't have one. But after a moment, Fitzgerald conceded that the Pittsburgh Penguins' Mario Lemieux, one of the most productive players in the sport's history, would usually skate more than even the other top players. At 27 or 28 minutes, he'd be on the ice for almost half a game.

"How did that happen?" Morey asked.

"He was a big star and he just told the coach, 'I'm not coming off,'" Fitzgerald said.

Morey couldn't help thinking that he'd stumbled on something relevant. "I don't know anything about hockey, I don't even know your players," he told Fitzgerald. "But you'd be the only sport that's ever been studied where playing your best players more isn't a good thing."

ON MARCH 6 AND 7 of 2020, I attended Morey's MIT Sloan Sports Analytics Conference at the Boston Convention Center. Had it been scheduled for even a week later, it would not have happened. As it was, the first waves of concern about the novel coronavirus were rippling through the crowd of attendees. We were told to wash our hands frequently and not sit beside anyone in the seminar rooms if we could avoid it. At all but the least-attended events, that proved to be impossible.

I was there for the first time in years to figure out what the future of sports might look like in an increasingly data-driven world. But as the conference had gained in popularity, it had evolved. What had started with a roomful of quants now featured famous names whose comments were immediately dispensed over social media. The real advances in strategic thinking, I couldn't help but assume, were being made far offstage.

One of the seminars I attended was titled "Sports in 2040: Hindsight is 2020." The idea was that recent developments in sports would continue to accelerate over the next two decades, leading us somewhere new. It sounded like exactly what I was looking for. Thinking about the topic made me realize that, despite the emergence of analytics, the rules of most sports had hardly changed since 2000, which was as far away from 2020 as 2040 would be. In fact, they had hardly changed during my lifetime. But part of the point of holding the seminar was that we were living in a time of rapid evolution, one in which the ways that we had previously received information and entertainment seemed quaint when compared with the overwhelming array of options available in the digital era. The question was: How would the industry of sports adapt to the new opportunities, and increased competition, inherent in so many other forms of amusement?

Along with Morey and Jessica Gelman, the panel consisted of Bill James and Nate Silver. In the 1980s, James's annual *Baseball*

Abstract introduced the concept of using statistics to figure out what was actually happening on the field to a whole subculture of open-minded, slightly (or not-so-slightly) nerdy young enthusiasts. Silver was one of those enthusiasts. He made his name in the early 2000s by prognosticating the results of elections. Later, he was hired by ESPN to apply data analysis to sports and the world beyond. In a stroke of inspiration to keep the discussion from getting lost in the weeds, the panel was moderated by Katie Nolan, a quick-witted, irreverent sports media pop celebrity. (In the biography on the conference's website, Nolan boasted that she held the world record for stacking donuts while blindfolded.)

The panelists had the earnest intensity of enthusiasts who finally had a stage to discuss their pet ideas. Some of those ideas were benign, like Gelman's prediction that tickets would eventually be scanned at the same time a fan's car is parked. Others were bolder: The NBA should have a five-point line. Basketball games in overtime should be won by achieving a specific score, not by being ahead when the clock expired. (I liked that one.) Baseball games ought to last less than an hour. Soccer should have fewer players—only seven on a team instead of eleven. The sport should also ban heading the ball. Nolan, who appeared to be the only one on the stage who rather liked sports the way they were, moved the conversation along with a twinkle in her eye. "Why do basketball courts have to be rectangles?" she wondered at one point. "What if they were ovals?"

Throughout the weekend, I wandered a hallway where tech companies had set up display tables to show off their latest advancements. One of them, a company called Arise, was showing a video of what a game five years in the future would look like. In the video, everyone in the stands held up a smartphone and watched the action on its screen. The man across the table from me explained that fans at live events were becoming dissatisfied with the lack of available information. Why shouldn't they have access to as much of it as viewers did on their laptops? By holding up a phone to the action, a spectator could allow artificial intelligence to identify patterns in what was happening below. Measurements could be taken and statistics tallied. Together, they would provide a fully immersive, three-dimensional sports-watching experience.

"But to get that," I said, "you literally need to watch the game through your phone."

He misread my distaste for astonishment. "Yes! Yes!" he said. "It's not just a good idea. It's the future!"

———

AROUND THE HALLS and seminar rooms at MIT Sloan, nobody questioned that pro sports franchises were being run far more efficiently in 2020 than they were in 2000. From the food options at the park to the secondary ticket market, these had become high-performing businesses. "Really sexy businesses that attracted these really bright minds that we had ignored for 150 years," Beane had said at the same event a few years before. At that point, he called Major League Baseball one of the "smartest industries in the world."

Still, it had become clear that best practices, a concept lifted from consulting and strategic management, implied a certain amount of homogeneity. In any city, the experience of attending a game seemed uncannily familiar. The cadence of the announcer, the look of the video presentation, even the music on the sound system had probably been curated by the league office. All the quirkiness that separated one team from another, and a lot of the charm that came with it, had been deemed an inefficiency and removed. Along with it, one might argue, went some of the emotional attachment that drew us to sports in the first place.

And if that was the case, perhaps the practices that appeared best over the short term were actually eroding some of the value inherent in the equity. "If everything you do is financial or metrical, you're missing out on the biggest reason people want to support your club," Robert Elms, a London-based writer and broadcaster, told me. "You're creating customers rather than fans. And the minute you start treating them like customers, they become customers."

The problem with customers, Elms pointed out, was that when they have disappointing experiences, such as bad food or perfunctory service in a restaurant, they eventually stop returning. Now in his 60s, Elms has been following the Central London football club Queens Park Rangers since he was a toddler. A small club with only the fraction of the fans of Arsenal, Chelsea, or Tottenham Hotspur, all of which also played in London, QPR had spent only a few of the past 50 years in English football's top tier. More often, it played in a lower league. Elms's relationship with the club was the emotional one of a member, not the transactional one of a customer; it was no accident, he had told me once, that these were called *clubs*. His loyalty wasn't affected by whether his team happened to be up or down in any given season, or even if it won or lost. "If I was going to stop going because the football was rubbish," he says, "I would have stopped 25 years ago."

The quality of the football wasn't the point. Neither was the quality of the food (poor, I can attest) at QPR's stadium, which used to be called Loftus Road but had been renamed after the Kiyan Prince Foundation, or the comfort of the experience (hard wooden seats in cramped rows). Rather, it was the sense of community the club offered to its followers, many of whom, like Elms, had been attending matches since childhood. To them, an optimized experience meant something very different than it did to someone who had come to the sport recently, having chosen which club to follow because of its name, or the design of a uniform shirt, or a chance exposure on a video feed. It was precisely that dichotomy—those who enjoyed the experience of following a sport precisely for its quirks and oddities on one side, those seeking a 21st-century entertainment experience on the other—that created such a challenge for the businessmen who owned and ran the teams.

In September of 2021, the 36-year-old Cristiano Ronaldo returned to Manchester United. Between 2003 and 2009, he'd emerged there as one of the finest players in soccer. His first game back with his former club was a worldwide event. Viewers in 189 nations, including international pariahs North Korea and Afghanistan, saw him score twice in a 4–1 victory over Newcastle. But despite that vast global audience, the only people in England able to watch the game were those inside Old Trafford itself. That's because United–Newcastle kicked off simultaneously with five other games around the Premier League at the traditional time of 3 p.m. And 3 p.m games are not televised in England.

Saturday afternoon games in England have their roots in the Factory Act of 1850, which forbade manufacturers from keeping laborers on the job after 2 p.m. on weekends. It made sense to schedule games soon after that, at 3 p.m. And that's where most of them stayed long into the television era, even as one high-profile game each week was moved to Saturday evening and a few more to Sunday for the entire nation to watch together. Not only do games in the top-tier Premier League start at 3 p.m., but also those in the second-rung Championship, and League One and League

Two below that, and the layers of England's football pyramid down to the welders and waiters and store clerks who pull on uniforms and represent their villages across the country. Unlike Premier League clubs, which made millions of dollars from television rights and sponsorships and shirts they sell for $100 or more, those clubs in the lower levels relied on paying spectators to fund their continued operations. Given the opportunity to watch a telecast of Liverpool against Chelsea on a dreary Saturday afternoon in February, enough of the supporters of those smaller clubs might have decided to sit on their sofas rather than set out in the cold to pay 10 pounds to cheer on, say, Yeovil Town against Bromley. So, those in charge of English soccer decided years ago not to give them that choice.

The sociologist and sports historian David Goldblatt approved. In his book *The Game of Our Lives*, he wrote that "it is not just a question of efficiency and practicality, it is a question of meaning and values; fan surveys continue to highlight a hunger, nostalgic or not, for the 3:00 p.m. kick off, for a sense of temporal order, an acknowledgment of the ritual status of going to the game." Still, for clubs trying to compete in a global marketplace that provided an almost infinite number of entertainment options, the situation seemed absurd. Wasn't it counterproductive to play most of your games at precisely the time that fans around the country weren't allowed to watch them, no matter how much they might be willing to pay to do it? The debate over the blackout raged during the weekend of Ronaldo's return and over the weeks that followed. Emotion was high on both sides. Solutions were offered and then rejected. Everyone seemed to agree on only one point: that 3 p.m. is the perfect time to watch a football match. It's late enough that you could have a beer at the bar before walking to the stadium, someone said on one of the many podcasts that debated the issue, but early enough that you'd be home for dinner.

———————

A FEW MONTHS before, some of those same fans had spent a weekend protesting outside Premier League venues. A Manchester United game had to be postponed when the massed crowd wouldn't allow the bus carrying the visiting team, which happened to be Liverpool, to reach the stadium. The demonstrations had been provoked by an announcement on a Friday evening that 12 clubs from across Europe—including Manchester City, Manchester United, Chelsea, Arsenal, Liverpool, and Tottenham from England—were forming a pan-continental Super League.

The Super League was formulated as an insurance policy. It meant that clubs in the world's most competitive leagues could run up huge payrolls without the risk of missing out on the lucrative European games that provided the income to offset them. It was a closed circuit, an American-style competition that didn't require a team to do well in its domestic league to qualify. Oh, the 12 clubs would continue to compete in those domestic leagues, but they would no longer care if they finished in the top four places and reached the exalted Champions League; or the next two, which would put them in the consolation-prize Europa League; or even ended the season mid-table, earning nothing but a slot in the Premier League the following season. Their lucrative Super League matches against the biggest and wealthiest clubs in Europe would be a sure thing. As a result, other than who won the title in the Premier League and Spain's LaLiga and Italy's Serie A, where teams finished in those leagues would have very little meaning.

Across all categories, businesses strive for predictability. If you know in advance how much revenue you'll bring in each year, you can budget accordingly. The purpose of the Super League, the statement posted on Liverpool's website explained, was "improving the quality and intensity of existing European competitions throughout each season, and of creating a format for top clubs and players to compete on a regular basis." For a team such as Liverpool, which wasn't owned by the investment arm of a Gulf state or an oil magnate, the predictability of knowing that the next season's schedule would include games against Real Madrid, Barcelona, and Juventus, no matter how the team fared, was a major enticement. It meant that long-term plans could be put in place—to further expand the grounds at Anfield, say, or buy a feeder club in the Dutch or Belgian league—without the fear of the greatly diminished income that even a single season outside the Champions League would bring. That explained why John Henry was such a strong proponent of the concept; nobody among the Premier League owners who had been invited to participate, I was told by one participant on the Zoom calls, advocated harder for it than he did. "The whole aim of the Super League was optimization," Elms says now. "'We can optimize our budgets. We can optimize our revenues.'" Yet, rather than mollifying supporters, that aspect of the plan, especially, seemed to enrage them. "Their protests were driven by a deeper set of cultural values," Goldblatt said. "Even the most conservative of characters found that to be absolute anathema."

There was little doubt that the vast business that soccer had become had wreaked havoc on the sport's ecosystem. The Premier League, the first step in that process, was established for the 1992–93 season. It was a breakaway body from England's Football Association, but only in economic terms. As before, the top teams from the

old Second Division, which eventually was renamed the Championship, were promoted each season. Those at the bottom of the
Premier League were relegated downward. But the Premier League
was now able to detach its television rights and sell them around
the world for increasingly huge sums. That factor, and Champions
League success that brought added revenue and exposure, meant
that the teams at the top of the standings had a systemic advantage
over the others, an advantage that would grow ever larger as time
passed. Crucially, the Premier League, unlike the five major North
American sports leagues, put no limit on how much a club could
spend on salaries. It couldn't—not if it wanted its clubs to compete
successfully in Europe against teams that weren't constrained by
such restrictions.

Barring gross mismanagement, the wealthiest clubs quickly and
inexorably became the best. In the decade or so before the establishment of the Premier League, Birmingham's Aston Villa, Liverpool's
Everton, and Leeds United all won domestic titles in England. Ips-
wich Town, Southampton, and Watford finished second. Blackburn
Rovers managed to win the Champions League in 1994–95. None
of those clubs ever came close again. Instead, traditionally wealthy
and successful clubs such as Manchester United (13 Premier League
titles) and Arsenal (three titles) dominated. They were joined by
Chelsea and Manchester City (five titles each), the former of which
was funded by the billionaire Roman Abramovich and the latter by
the Abu Dhabi United Group for Development and Investment. In
late 2021, Saudi Arabia's royal family was allowed by the Premier
League to buy controlling interest in Newcastle United through
that country's national investment fund. The sale raised the issue of
sports being used to divert attention from the dictatorial cruelties of
a regime. It also risked upsetting the sport's competitive balance by

giving a club an almost limitless fund of money with which to buy players. But these problems were new only in terms of their degree.

Still, who could argue with success? After the establishment of the Premier League, English football became vastly more accessible around the world than ever before. And although it took several decades, the quality of its play eventually emerged as the best of any domestic league. Spain's Barcelona or Real Madrid might amass the most valuable roster in a given season, and Germany's Bayern Munich or Italy's Juventus might win the Champions League. But top to bottom, the Premier League was the richest league, and the vast majority of the best players gravitated there.

Because of the widely disparate situations of the clubs within the Premier League during any particular season, creating business strategies that appealed to all of them became increasingly difficult. A few weeks before the Super League was announced, I spoke with an executive who had run the business side of a Premier League club for years. Then he moved to a top club in another European country. The future of world football was bleak, he stressed. If the system was left unchanged, the rich would get richer and the poor would be left out. It was incumbent on the biggest clubs to create a different system, one that would be sustainable. But that wasn't ever going to happen in the Premier League because only about half a dozen clubs felt secure about their long-term prospects in the top tier. They weren't willing to allocate a chunk of the television revenue to create a general fund to help the league's smaller clubs because they didn't feel confident they would ever be in a position to collect from it. "The Big Six stay, and the rest of them rotate through," he said. "Half the teams aren't convinced they're going to be in that room next year."

He also felt that the world had become too small for the top

European teams to waste their time playing local and regional clubs in domestic competitions. The sport had grown around the world, helped in part by the FIFA video game and electronic fantasy leagues that captured the interest of an emerging generation of soccer enthusiasts. There were far more of those than there were legacy fans like Elms, who had supported their club for decades. Those new Chelsea or Arsenal or Manchester City fans might watch their team play against Burnley or Southampton, but they would be far more interested in a steady diet of games against Juventus, Barcelona, and Paris Saint-Germain. The old system had been created for a world in which travel and communications were limited by technology. These days, it was easier for a London or Manchester club to fly to Paris or Barcelona than it was to take a bus to Norwich. And with games available across the internet, football was now competing against all other kinds of entertainment for its audience. It needed to show compelling games—as many of them as possible.

For years, the idea of watching a game on a cold, rainy winter evening in an unromantic industrial town such as Stoke was seen as the Platonic Ideal of English football. It was the kind of game that stripped away glamour, style, and celebrity to focus on its bare essence, and on virtues such as perseverance, stoicism, and consistency that England held dear. But according to this executive, nobody but a few old men cared about those games anymore. "You get it and I get it," he said. "But look at any consumer research that has been done, and it all says the same thing. Some sort of way to get the biggest teams around Europe playing each other more often is inevitable."

When the Super League was rolled out soon after, I wasn't surprised to see that this executive's new club was included. Announced with fanfare by the chief executives of Real Madrid, Juventus, and others, it seemed an inevitability whose time had come to pass. The romantic notion of club- and domestic-based football was an anachronism, like playing major-league baseball only during the day. It didn't make sense set in the context of the instant gratification of the modern world.

But it wasn't inevitable, it turned out. And it didn't happen—at least, not in that form. The outcry among English fans, in particular, was so strong that by that Tuesday morning, some 72 hours after the announcement, the entire project had started to decompose. It had become clear to the executives who owned and ran these clubs—including John Henry, Stan Kroenke of Arsenal, and Manchester United's Glazers, all American interlopers who hadn't grown up watching those games in grimy settings on winter evenings— that each club's supporters were willing to take drastic measures to prevent the Super League from happening. "It was pretty extraordinary," said Goldblatt, who admitted he'd been surprised by the reaction. Manchester City, which had only joined the group at the last minute because it couldn't afford to have the Super League proceed without it, was the first to withdraw. By the end of that Tuesday, the rest of the Premier League clubs had followed. That made the Super League untenable.

It turned out that a critical mass of English fans believed that domestic games constituted the fabric of the sport. Those games were the centerpiece of the emotional relationship they had with their club in a way that the gloss of a steady stream of international games could never become. The fans not only understood that, but in a surprise to everyone involved, they were willing to disrupt the games of their favorite teams to try to prevent it from happening. It was not an economic protest, but a cultural and aesthetic one. There was no doubt that these clubs had become huge businesses, worth a billion dollars or more. But the point made by all the banners and the shouting was that they weren't only businesses but also community resources, a fact that everyone except the people who owned them seemed to understand.

In their 2018 book about Italian soccer, *What Happened to Serie A?* Steven G. Mandis, Thomas Lombardi, and Sarah Parsons Wolter wrote, "The players, the fans, the entire community need a mission, a greater purpose, than just winning." Most owners, they added, "don't appreciate that to be successful their entire strategy, both on and off the field, needs to be based on the 'why,' which essentially comes from the values and expectations of their fans and community." That's a compelling argument against pulling Blake Snell from Game Six of the World Series. And it's an argument, three years early, against Europe's Super League.

Protesting outside Chelsea's stadium, Stamford Bridge, on the night after the Super League was announced, one fan summed it up with a hand-lettered sign made from black tape and three colors of marker. It read, "We Want Our Cold Nights In Stoke."

10

WE'RE NOT ON A GOOD TRAJECTORY

WHEN THEO EPSTEIN sat down to play Scrabble with his 13-year-old son Jack one day in the fall of 2021, he discovered that the analytic revolution had reached his own living room. Jack had memorized all of Scrabble's legal two-letter words, more than 100 of them. He deployed them aggressively. When we talked a week later, Epstein described the game to me as "a horrible slog." It was a strategy, Epstein believed, that destroyed the entertainment value of the game. "Who wants to be blocked by a *jo* or a *qi* or a *ka*?" he said. "If I were the commissioner of Scrabble, I would institute a three-letter minimum and ban the two-letter word to make the game fun again."

At the time, Epstein was trying to do the equivalent with baseball. Teams had adopted as standard practice the baseball version of Scrabble's two-letter words—extreme infield shifts, starters throwing at top speed for four innings, hitters swinging for the fences rather than trying to direct an outside pitch to the opposite field. These strategies, all rooted in data analysis, were making baseball difficult to watch. "We're not on a good trajectory," Epstein lamented. "I iden-tify with traditionalists. I am a traditionalist. I love the traditions of baseball and the roots of baseball and the way it made me feel as a kid." But the widespread use of analytic thinking across the sport had sent it plummeting into what he termed an "existential crisis."

The previous November, Epstein had left his position as the president of baseball operations of the Chicago Cubs, where he'd gone after leaving Boston in 2011. In 2016, the team he'd con-structed in Chicago won that franchise's first World Series in 108 years. Now Epstein was working as an unpaid consultant to MLB commissioner Rob Manfred, hoping to redirect the sport. Epstein was dismayed by the standing around, the dearth of action. His goal was to move the game away from the Three True Outcomes and toward a version in which more balls were put in play. "There's never been a time in baseball history when we've had anything close to a 25 percent strikeout rate," he said in an interview that May. His goal was to restore the game "to its true self."

Ironically, Epstein was doing that by pushing for changes to some of the rules that had existed throughout baseball's history. Under discussion was altering the distance between the mound and home plate, limitations on where players could be positioned on the field, a time limit between the delivery of pitches, even the size of the bases themselves. All of those were attempted in experiments in various minor leagues during the 2021 season, and all but the first would ultimately be adopted in Major League Baseball for 2023. Already, the majors had undertaken an even more radical altera-tion. Every inning beyond the ninth in a regular-season game now began with a runner placed on second base, scrambling the precise bookkeeping that had been a feature of the sport for more than a century. (If a new pitcher started one of the extra innings, was he responsible if that runner scored? If not, who would be?)

To Epstein, that was a reasonable price to pay for creating a more entertaining product. "Would you rather have a game that appeals to romantic notions we had about it as a kid that becomes a fringe sport?" he asked. "Fighting off lacrosse and MMA for eyeballs?" Farther afield, Epstein talked about even more extreme changes, perhaps even to the composition of the batting order, so that the best players would be relevant when the game was on the line, as they were in other sports. "We need to be thoughtful about how the widespread use of analytics impacts the game on the field," he said. "It makes sense to put reasonable limits in place and protect the human element and the entertainment value."

Epstein had credibility within baseball because he straddled the line between innovation and continuity. Although many saw him as a symbol of the analytic movement, a Yale graduate who hadn't played beyond high school yet became MLB's youngest general manager, he didn't identify with it. "I never advocated for analytics on philosophical grounds," he insisted. "I was just trying to win. It wasn't personal to me, per se. It was just an effort to build better processes, make better decisions, and win."

But Epstein's success with analytics had helped spur the revolution he was trying to counteract. Each time a new collective bargaining agreement was negotiated between the players and owners, he would walk into the analytics room and drop a copy on a table. "Read through this and find us an edge," he'd say. Edges were the currency by which the analysts gauged their success. By 2022, all those edges they'd found through the years added up to create a markedly different game. At the same time, the franchises that packaged and sold this modern, analytically driven product had become almost unrecognizable from the midsize businesses Epstein first encountered in the 1990s.

Among the most evolved, and the most successful, were the

Houston Astros. Under the ownership of Jim Crane, who made his money in logistics and information services and then made more of it in natural gas, they won fewer than 60 games a season from 2011 through 2013. To many observers, they didn't even look like they were trying to win. But Crane, who had spent $680 million on the club, had a plan. With the high draft picks that those all-but-unwatchable seasons earned them, the Astros stockpiled talent. By 2015, they had qualified for the Wild Card Game. In every year from 2017 through 2022, with the exception of the COVID-shortened 2020 season, they won their division. In four of those seasons, they reached the World Series. They also were at the center of a sign-stealing scandal that resulted in the dismissal of several team executives, including their manager and general manager.

Inside the club's business offices, outfielders, analysts, third-base coaches, and everyone else were lumped together in the category of "assets." In *Future Value*, their book about baseball's scouting system, Eric Longenhagen and Kiley McDaniel wrote, "You don't have to wonder what the logical extreme of the McKinsey approach to baseball would be; we are seeing every aspect of it play out right now." They compared the Astros' strategy of firing all of the team's scouts and evaluating prospects purely through the use of video to "how McKinsey and Bain strip mine companies for parts and make big money in a short period of time."

———————

BY THE TIME that Epstein and his son sat down to play Scrabble, the analytics skeptics were fully in retreat. The philosophical battle had been won. Across all the major team sports, the analysis of data had become a crucial facet of almost every discipline touched by a big-league franchise. For MLB clubs, analytics had started with player evaluations—scouting, and the amateur draft. That was *Moneyball.* Then it extended to team strategies, and finally to individual performance. Despite having one of baseball's lowest payrolls, the analytics-heavy Rays won 100 games again in 2021. (And then, in what turned out to be the deciding game of a best-of-five Division Series against the Red Sox, Cash again pulled his starting pitcher— Collin McHugh—after two hitless innings and just 18 pitches. And lost again.)

In their 2019 book *The MVP Machine,* Ben Lindbergh and Travis Sawchik identified player development as the latest analytic frontier. They quoted Brian Bannister, the director of pitching for the San Francisco Giants, explaining that instead of looking for players who are already throwing or swinging close to optimally, teams were seeking out those who might only have had marginal success but were willing to work to improve their mechanics based on data assessments. The emergence of outside facilities such as Seattle's Driveline, the Texas Baseball Ranch, and the Florida Baseball ARMory helped to generate that data and accelerate the process. "How can we leverage the data and what we've learned from the data to get closer to that perfect pitch or perfect swing?" Bannister asked. He describes that open-ended search as "where the rabbit hole begins."

Across the major North American sports leagues, rooms of analysts spent much of their time deep in their own rabbit holes, digging through data like placer miners panning for gold—or bitcoin miners expending more and more energy to create a decreasing amount of currency. There were secrets hidden in the numbers, competitive advantages waiting to be exploited, if only they could be found. The process seemed remarkably similar across the various sports, which may have helped Paul DePodesta, the former Dodgers general manager who played football at Harvard, to engineer a remarkable turnaround by the NFL's Cleveland Browns. DePodesta had been working for baseball's New York Mets when he was hired in 2016 as the Browns' chief strategy officer. At the time, the Browns had played in only one playoff game since 1999, which is when they were reborn as an expansion team following the departure of the original Browns franchise for Baltimore. In DePodesta's first two seasons, they won one game and lost 31 while stockpiling talent from the draft. They were football's version of the Astros. In 2020, they were 11–5 and won a playoff game. DePodesta had gone quiet after expressing displeasure with the way he was portrayed in the *Moneyball* movie, but an ESPN report in 2021 found that no NFL team had more "staffers whose primary job is to perform data analysis or build football analytics tools" than the Browns did. The list of Browns employees in that category included DePodesta himself.

The NHL's most successful team, the Tampa Bay Lightning, won the Stanley Cup in 2020, won it again in 2021, and went to the finals in 2022. They were owned by Jeff Vinik, the former Fidelity fund manager and investor in the Red Sox, who bought the team in 2010. "I was very cognizant of the fact that many team owners and organizations were not that sophisticated at that time," he explained. "If you ran a team well, and like a business, you'd have a competitive edge." At the time that Vinik bought them, the Lightning weren't in nearly as bad shape as Tampa Bay's Rays; nevertheless, the NHL had no compelling reason to have a franchise on Florida's west coast. Twenty-five of the league's 30 teams did better at filling their arena every night. For the past three seasons, the Lightning hadn't even qualified for the 16-team playoffs. Vinik figured he had the answer. "I was 'Analytics—let's go, let's go, let's go.'" he says. "But the trick becomes time versus information. Typically, the last 5 percent of information you get takes you an incremental 100 percent of the time. So, where do you stop gathering information? It took us some time, but we figured out how to focus on just those aspects that had a high correlation with winning."

In basketball, tech billionaire Robert Pera of Ubiquiti Networks was just 34 when he bought the Memphis Grizzlies in 2012. In 2019, Pera hired Zachary Kleiman, a 31-year-old attorney (and a former public relations intern for the Lakers) as his general manager, in the Theo Epstein model. Kleiman then hired Taylor Jenkins, a University of Pennsylvania graduate who stopped playing basketball after high school, as the team's head coach. Among Jenkins's assistants were Sonia Raman, who played women's basketball at the Division III level and then spent 12 seasons as the head coach of the woman's team at MIT, where she included her players in analytics discussions. Run by the most unusual leadership team in league history, the Grizzlies had taken some of Golden State owner Joe Lacob's innovations in hiring and management structure to the logical extreme. In the 2022 playoffs, the Grizzlies extended their Western Conference semifinal with Golden State to six games. The Warriors then went on to win another championship.

Even English soccer, so resistant to change at the time of Liverpool's emergence just a few years before, had come to accept the doctrine of data analysis. Brentford was a small club from a West London neighborhood on the highway to Heathrow Airport. It had been languishing in soccer's lower reaches since World War II at the time that Matthew Benham, the professional gambler, bought it in 2012. Under Benham, who used data collection and analysis as the basis for all his personnel decisions, Brentford quickly advanced into the second-tier Championship.

Unlike most owners, who are wary of alienating fans, Benham bought and sold players without any regard to their popularity. His deals were based almost entirely on the difference between their actual and perceived value. After Brentford came within one victory of gaining promotion to the Premier League for the first time in its history in 2020, Benham off-loaded its two best offensive players, Ollie Watkins and Saïd Benrahma, on the theory that his return would never be higher. He had the same attitude toward them that Beane did about Jason Giambi and Miguel Tejada: the players he deployed were almost interchangeable; it was the system that mattered, and his manager's willingness to work within it. By buying low and selling high, a smart operator could keep a small team competitive. In May 2021, without Watkins and Benrahma, little Brentford won a playoff game against Swansea and moved up to the Premier League for the coming season. Against the likes of Manchester City and Liverpool and Chelsea, some of the top teams in the world, it performed well enough that it stayed up for 2022–23.

———————

TO SUPPORT AN industry full of analytically minded teams, a new class of analytics consultants had emerged. Ted Knutson, Brentford's former head of analytics, founded a company called StatsBomb that, by 2022, was supplying data to 140 soccer customers worldwide, ranging from Liverpool to Alianza Lima to the Italian national team. With his soccer data business thriving, he moved to Florida to try to do the same for the NFL. "We're going to change how football—American football—is coached at every level with the use of data," he said. "Within five years, nothing will be the same."

But Knutson wasn't alone. One NFL franchise had spun off its in-house analytics company so that it could build a business consulting for other sports franchises, and even companies in other industries. Across the street from Gillette Stadium in Foxboro, Massachusetts, where the NFL's New England Patriots and Major League Soccer's New England Revolution play, an outdoor shopping complex called Patriot Place rose from a sea of parking lots as if it had been dropped from the sky. Not far from the Rhode Island border, it was positioned in an ideal location south of Boston: close to the intersection of I-95 and I-495, two major interstate highways. At the time that the Kraft family, which owned the Patriots, built Patriot Place, in 2007, it was the largest real estate development any sports team had ever done. Robert Kraft described it as his legacy.

Halfway up a stairway leading to Patriot Place from the parking lot was a nondescript glass door. Open it, and you would find a bustling office. This was the Kraft Analytics Group, founded in 2016. What started more than a decade before that as a one-person analytics department—Jessica Gelman using her facility with numbers to help the Krafts with everything from managing inventory risk in their retail business to researching sponsorship opportunities— had grown into a company that led the industry. The Patriots had been the first team to use the NFL's salary cap to guide their team composition, the first to use data to grade the efficiency of their scouting staff, and the first to create a real estate development as ambitious as Patriot Place. Now they were outsourcing all that experience and expertise.

As of late 2021, dozens of teams across the five major North American leagues, even those with robust analytic departments of their own, were consulting with Gelman's company the way any billion-dollar company might use Bain or McKinsey. Even as Epstein and others were trying to mitigate the effect of pure analytics on the field, the Kraft Analytics Group was showing teams how to apply analytics more aggressively off of it. For the Krafts, too, the Analytics Group served as yet another revenue stream. Who could have predicted that an NFL team would own its own business consulting firm?

As of 2021, Gelman's group had 50 employees, Gelman told me, helping franchises use the data they were generating to improve their products and services. "We're doing a lot of all that for teams," Gelman said. "'How are you going to make all this work easy to consume, easy to apply, to move your business forward?' It's about taking lots of different pieces of information and stitching them together and then being able to say, 'This is where things are going.'" The more she talked, the less she referenced sports. Half an hour into our conversation, it occurred to me that she could have been consulting for textile companies or health-care providers. Which I guess was part of the point.

There is irony in the fact that an analytics company has spun off from an NFL team. On the field, football has been the slowest of the five major team sports to adopt analytic practices. In part, that's because the sport is ill-suited to analytic applications. Baseball has two easily quantifiable relationships that form the basis of the entire game: pitchers against hitters and fielders against batted balls. Football, by contrast, has dozens of relationships. Many of them are close to impossible to quantify. "There are too many variables," Daryl Morey explains. "It isn't nearly as clean as baseball or basketball."

Football also doesn't have the same culture of innovation that baseball and basketball—and, increasingly, hockey and soccer—have cultivated. As opposed to NBA owners such as Lacob, Ballmer, Ryan Smith, the 76ers' Josh Harris and David Blitzer, and the Bucks' Marc Lasry, all of whom had financed or run digital businesses, fully half the owners of NFL franchises as of 2021 had inherited the teams from other family members—husbands, parents, or siblings. They were steeped in the culture of football, but many of them had only a glancing familiarity with the worlds of tech and data.

That disparity helped create a business opportunity that the Kraft Analytics Group was positioned to exploit. When we met, Gelman mentioned two NFL teams that were underperforming off the field. "They have amazing brands," she said. "They should be getting more out of their brands. You can clearly tell that they aren't." Both of those teams were run by younger-generation family members who had grown up in the NFL and never worked in another industry. Until they started working with the Kraft group, they had barely changed the way the team operated from when the previous generation had owned it. "At least now they know that they need us," Gelman said.

———————

PERHAPS BECAUSE SOCCER is the world's game, it has the most room and motivation to adopt corporate practices. City Football Group was created in 2012 as the umbrella organization for the soccer holdings of the Abu Dhabi United Group, which had purchased the Premier League's Manchester City in 2008. By 2022, the group had affiliations or ownership with 12 other clubs around the world: in emerging commercial markets for soccer such as Japan, Australia, and India, but also in countries that were especially strong at nurturing and developing talent, such as Belgium, France, Spain, and Italy. Many of the clubs used the same sky-blue color scheme the owners had inherited when they bought Manchester City, and had the word *City* in their names. But those that already had built an established identity when the group bought them, such as Italy's Palermo and Spain's Girona, kept their own names and colors. The clubs didn't advertise their connection to each other, and they didn't sell Manchester City clothing or souvenirs at their team shops. Ferran Soriano, the chief executive of the group, compared their affiliation with each other to the idea of "Intel Inside," a marketing slogan used by an American technology firm that was discreetly displayed as a sticker on various models of laptops. "What we hope is that the fans understand that the team will have City inside, the way you have Intel inside your computer," he said. "We have no interest in City being a consumer brand."

Under Khaldoon Al Mubarak, a member of Abu Dhabi's ruling executive council who represented the Emirati ownership, Soriano ran the City Football Group as if it were an international corporation. He shifted employees from branch office to branch office as needed, while offering sponsors access points on five continents. That gave it an economy of scale that individual clubs, no matter how successful, couldn't match. "In other businesses, everybody understands how that works," Al Mubarak said to me one afternoon in Los Angeles, where he had rented a home for the summer. "In the business of football, nobody understands because it doesn't exist. Everybody is looking at it in one dimension."

When Al Mubarak took control of Manchester City in 2011, his only connection to soccer was as a fan. He'd been running energy companies and a commercial bank and supervising various investments for himself and the Emirati government. "Mature sectors with high-quality management systems," he says. He assumed that the world's biggest soccer clubs would be governed the same way. They weren't. "When you look at the revenue, when you look at the potential, you expected a higher quality level of CEO," he said. "It shocked me when I came in. There was a huge mismatch. It was far more underdeveloped than I thought it would be."

A year later, Al Mubarak hired Soriano to run Manchester City. Soriano had been the vice president and temporary chief executive of Barcelona. He also had served as chairman of Spanair, a Catalan airline, and founded a business consulting group. While at Barcelona, he had attempted to put a franchise owned by the club in Major League Soccer. That hadn't worked, mostly because Barcelona's board members considered the idea a needless diversion of money and energy. "There is only one club in the world called Barcelona," one of them told Soriano. "And it is in Barcelona."

During his interview with Al Mubarak, Soriano mentioned the idea of owning an MLS team. "And the conversation kept going," Al Mubarak says. " 'What if it's actually not just MLS? What if we look at ourselves as a group that owns clubs all around the world, in the big markets—China to the US to every continent? And the potential synergies and the commercial opportunities that could bring in?' We started thinking almost like venture capitalists about this concept."

Over the decade that followed, they put that concept into practice. As they did, the structure of City Football Group began to take the form of a multi-billion-dollar corporation. It had outposts around the globe, clubs operating autonomously, but with the support of each other as well as the central organization. "The basic business of a large, international organization," Roel de Vries, the chief operating officer, explained when I visited Manchester in 2022. De Vries had spent a decade running the marketing team at one of those large international organizations, Nissan Automotive, until 2020. He moved from Yokohama to Manchester and slotted seamlessly into his new position, barely noticing a difference beyond the weather. "You have talent management," he said. "You have standard processes and procedures. You have one entity learning from another entity. I think that's an enormous benefit that we have over stand-alone football clubs." Unlike Nissan, City's clubs were competing against opposition that was operating individually. That meant the "enormous benefit" was likely to show up not just on the profit statement, but also in the standings. During 2022, City Football Group clubs won championships in the Premier League, MLS, and India. Since the start of 2019, they also had won in Australia and Japan.

While in Manchester, I watched Marwood on a Zoom call with far-flung executives of the Manchester City scouting staff and the sporting director at Lommel, a small Belgian club owned by the company. As they discussed potential players to acquire, it struck me that the specific advantage that Lommel enjoyed was not wealth, the nearly unlimited resources of the Emirati ownership, but information. "There's no way that a team like Lommel would have a fraction of the access that it has right now to a global network of data, from Montevideo to Melbourne to Italy," Al Mubarak confirmed. "The value is in the data. The value is in the system that put it together and made it useful for everybody. It's taking *Moneyball* to a whole different dimension."

Several of the Lommel players were being groomed for a move— either to Troyes, in France's Ligue 1, or New York City FC in MLS. Eventually, one of them might find his way to the peak of the pyramid, Manchester City. But it wasn't only players who were able to be shifted from club to club. Executive moves were as commonplace as at any large international company. Beside me was a communications staffer who had been working in New York at NYCFC but had asked for European exposure after getting an offer from another

MLS team. Not long before, the head of charities at Manchester City had moved to Lommel as CEO.

Other MLS owners had ownership interests in continental clubs. Stan Kroenke of the Colorado Rapids owned Arsenal; Jason Levien of DC United owned Swansea, a Welsh team that played in England's Championship; the New York Red Bulls were owned by the same energy-drink magnate who had teams in Salzburg, Leipzig, Brazil, and Ghana; David Blitzer of Real Salt Lake had minority shares of England's Crystal Palace, Germany's Augsburg, and others. But only City Football Group could offer an umbrella organization and a systematic path from a subsidiary club to the flagship. It seemed far closer to what might be happening at the corporate headquarters of Nissan. And that, de Vries said when we spoke later, was intentional. "We can attract talent that other clubs can't attract because of what we are able to offer them," he said. "We have a great opportunity to become far more professional than any of our peers."

With the City Football Group, the professionalization of professional sports had reached an apotheosis. That success had come at a price. Manchester City had far more fans around the world than ever before, but if you supported a different Premier League team, Manchester City was probably the rival you liked the least. Part of that was simply a by-product of the club's success: four titles in five years in the most competitive league in the world. But by corporatizing the sport, many observers believed, City had pulled some of the romance out of it.

Among those were the supporters of the Dutch club NAC Breda. When City Football Group announced plans to buy Breda for $7.5 million early in 2022, it wasn't seen as a controversial transaction. The 110-year-old club had been aligned in a partnership with Manchester City since 2016. Several Breda players had been loaned out to City Football Group clubs around the world. And yet, when it came time for its club to be acquired, Breda's soccer community was so against the idea that it vowed not to let the sale happen. Its protests weren't limited to inside Holland; groups also traveled to Manchester to parade banners outside City's Etihad Stadium before a game. "If all of the soccer world is going to look like just a few networks of clubs, we won't let that happen without a fight," Leon Deckers, a member of one of the Breda fan groups, told a website affiliated with Arizona State's Global Sport Institute. "Your club gets stripped down and rebuilt. It loses all of its local flavor."

Faced with the process of an unfriendly takeover, City withdrew. But the Breda protests served notice that the outside world wasn't quite ready to embrace the idea of local clubs getting subsumed into corporate ownership. "It is ripping the soul out of what we're all about, a little bit," Peter Moore, who ran the business side of Liverpool FC from 2017 to 2020, told me after the Breda sale collapsed.

A former executive at Electronic Arts, Reebok, Sega, and Microsoft, Moore had grown up attending the games of his local club, Wrexham, "watching a game on crumbling terraces, typically in a mud pit." He was quick to say that he wasn't looking to revisit that kind of fan experience. Working under John Henry and Tom Werner, he had helped Liverpool expand into a thriving business, with one of the largest fan bases in the world. But he made a distinction between what Fenway Sports Group had done with a single club and the corporate approach of City Football Group. "They see themselves as a global conglomerate," he said. "And every conglomerate needs branch offices." By its nature, though, "football is tribal and local," Moore said. "So I don't quite see the advantage." The saving grace, he believed, was that no other ownership group would ever be ambitious enough to try to amass a similar soccer portfolio.

"It would cost millions and millions to go buy up clubs and then put the necessary structures in place," he said. "I just don't see that happening."

One thing was certain: Fenway wouldn't be the group to replicate City's success. In November 2022, the Athletic broke the story that Henry and his partners were open to selling a percentage of Liverpool FC to an outside investor. The motivation seemed to be to raise money to acquire other equities—perhaps Washington's NFL team, which Daniel Snyder was selling, or a future NBA expansion franchise in Las Vegas. Within a day, Billy Hogan, who had replaced Moore as Liverpool's CEO, acknowledged that, given the right offer, the entire club could be sold. The catalysts for the strategic shift were the $4 billion that American Todd Boehly had paid to take control of Chelsea FC some months before, which would appear to give Liverpool a similar valuation, and the collapse of the Super League concept that would have provided the predictable income stream that Henry craved. A week after Hogan's statement, Ian Graham announced that he would be leaving the club the following May.

In Liverpool and beyond, the developments were met with dismay. Fenway had been a successful steward of the club. Beyond that, though the idea of using data analysis as the foundation for making decisions remained distasteful to much of the English soccer establishment, it was clear that Liverpool had been run close to optimally for the better part of a decade, from its ticketing to its transfers to its commercial relationships. And if a club that had been at the forefront of most every innovation on and off the field during that time couldn't compete with the raw financial might of Manchester City domestically, and similar clubs abroad, what did that portend for the future of the sport?

AT THE END of the 2021–22 season, Girona won its playoff to move into Spain's top echelon. "That was a very important part of the plan, to get them into LaLiga," Al Mubarak said. The following month, Soriano completed the purchase of Palermo FC, which was what investment banks would call a "distressed equity." A once-proud club dating to 1900 that had finished fifth in Serie A as late as 2010, it had been penalized for financial misdeeds brought on by mounting losses. Then it was banned from organized soccer entirely in 2019 after it attempted to operate without an insurance policy. That fall, the club had been re-formed and slotted into Serie D. Now it was on its way back up the ladder, from Serie D to Serie C and then, for the 2022–23 season, to Serie B, just one level below the top. The club, which was Sicily's most important, had huge growth potential. And, crucially for City Football Group, there were no supporters groups likely to mobilize against an acquisition. They were all simply relieved that their club had found a savior.

With Girona joining Lommel and France's Troyes in the top leagues of their European nations, and Palermo projected to be back in Italy's Serie A within a year or two, Soriano disclosed that City Football Group was no longer looking for a Dutch acquisition to replace NAC Breda. There were only so many different levels for players to slot into, he told me, "and we have them covered."

Rather than a cautionary tale, it seemed that Breda would be nothing more than a blip in the company's march toward increased profitability and competitive success. "We don't need a team there," Soriano said.

EPILOGUE

THE AMERICAN LEAGUE'S wild card playoff race came down to the 2021 season's final weekend. All three of the teams involved played in the East Division. The Rays had clinched first place on September 25, but the teams directly behind them in the standings—the Yankees, Red Sox, and Blue Jays—were still competing for the opportunity to advance into the playoff bracket. Two of those three would make it.

On the season's final morning, the Yankees and Red Sox woke up tied. The Blue Jays were a game behind. The fact that three winning teams could be so closely bunched on the last day of the season, and that one of them would end up missing the playoffs based on what happened on that last afternoon, was a manifestation of baseball's uniquely compelling nature. If you were a fan of the Yankees, Red Sox, or Blue Jays, the MLB season had kept your interest over 161 games, from the first stirrings of spring into the chill of autumn, yet your team's fate still wasn't decided. No other sport was able to do that.

Unfortunately, it was clear enough to anyone who had been paying attention that further expansion of the postseason was coming, perhaps after a long and bitter lockout. In the future, the protagonists in the fight for survival at the end of that 162-game season wouldn't rank among the best teams in each league, as the Yankees, Red Sox, and Blue Jays had. All the elite teams would have qualified already. Rather, as in football and basketball and hockey, it would be the seventh-, eighth-, and ninth- or tenth-best teams fighting for survival during the season's final weekend, mediocrities that had little chance of winning a championship, and would hardly deserve to be called true champions if they did.

By 2021, even those of us who had defended the precepts of analytics for nearly two decades couldn't help noticing that baseball under their purview was becoming increasingly unpopular with everyone else. In an effort to address the problem, MLB had started tweaking its product. The rule that put a runner on second base to start the top and bottom of every inning after the ninth actually made sense during a pandemic; COVID had decimated pitching staffs across the majors, and pitchers had started that season without the slow-paced warm-up of a true spring training. The new rule drastically cut down on those extra-inning marathons that were thrilling to watch but took a heavy toll on the bullpens of both teams, to the point that pitching assignments were sometimes impacted for days afterward.

In March of 2021, though, Major League Baseball announced that the extra-inning rule would remain for the coming season. The length of an average game had crept so high that even one completed in nine innings was longer than in any other team sport. Casual fans who could watch a complete NFL game in three hours, and soccer or college basketball in two, were perhaps willing to keep the television tuned to baseball as a game entered its fourth hour, but the audience typically declined with each minute beyond that. And, even with COVID theoretically under control, managers cringed at the possibility of extending their pitching staffs beyond nine innings, since they'd often used half a dozen pitchers already. Theo Epstein was agnostic about the rule, but he made the point that at-bats typically become uglier in extra innings. Without that runner artificially placed in scoring position—"Manfred Ball," as purists had come to call it—too many hitters tried to send everyone home with one swing.

The last day of the 2021 season, October 3, provided a marvelous afternoon of baseball. The Red Sox and Yankees weren't playing each other, but they both entered the ninth inning of their games with the score tied. Watching one game and then the other, I was desperately rooting against extra innings in both of them. I knew that this might turn out to be the last great pennant race before playoffs were expanded (as, in fact, they were in the off-season that followed). I didn't want the fate of either team decided by the vicissitudes of Manfred Ball.

The Red Sox were in Washington, playing the Nationals. In the top of the ninth, Kyle Schwarber reached on an error. Then Rafael Devers homered to center field, Nick Pivetta retired the Nationals in the ninth, and the Red Sox were in. The one-game wild card elimination would be played at Fenway Park. The Yankee game was even more compelling. The Yankees were home against the division-winning Rays, who had no agenda but to finish the season so that the playoffs could begin. Through the first eight innings, neither team scored. Then the Rays went quietly in the top of the ninth. If Josh Fleming, the fifth Rays' pitcher of the afternoon, could keep his team's shutout alive, the scoreless game would advance into the 10th inning, and the new rule would kick in.

What happened instead transported me back to my own Golden

Age of the sport, the 1970s. The Yankees' Rougned Odor started the bottom of the ninth by lining a single to center. Tyler Wade then pinch-ran for him at first, and he tagged up and moved to second on a fly ball. Anthony Rizzo singled to right, advancing Wade to third. This was exactly the kind of baseball that the research done by MLB indicated fans wanted to see—fielders running after balls, runners sprinting around the bases. It didn't hurt that the game wasn't yet three hours old.

Kevin Cash came to the mound and replaced Fleming with Andrew Kittredge. The powerful Aaron Judge stepped to the plate. At six foot seven and 280 pounds, Judge may have been the most extreme version of a modern hitter playing in the major leagues. In 624 plate appearances to that point in the season, Judge had hit 39 home runs. He'd drawn 75 walks. He'd also struck out 158 times. Close to half the time that Judge came up, he hadn't put the ball in the field of play. If every hitter were like Aaron Judge in 2021, as opposed to the 2022 version that challenged for the batting title and broke the American League record for home runs, the sport of baseball never would have become the national pastime, and it certainly would have no chance of gaining a widespread audience today. How many people would want to spend three and a half hours watching a game if every second plate appearance resulted in a hitter trotting toward first base or trudging to the dugout while everyone else on the field did nothing?

But nobody is bigger than the game, as the crusty old baseball men used to say. Wonderfully enough, Judge didn't homer, walk, or strike out against Kitteridge. Instead, he slapped a ground ball to the right of the pitcher's mound. It two-hopped into the glove of the second baseman, who was on the edge of the grass. Sprinting home from third base, Wade arrived there at almost exactly the same time as the throw. By the time Mike Zunino, the catcher, could catch the ball, bring it toward the ground, and slap on a tag, Wade had slid across the plate.

I'm no Yankee fan, but I cheered out loud. Not for the outcome of the game, but for the triumph of the sport's glorious athleticism and improbable geometry over the business plans and mathematical equations that were attempting to optimize it—and, quite possibly, killing it in the process. I had no idea what would happen to baseball in coming years, or whether professional sports could continue to thrive in their current form or be forced to evolve into something else entirely. At that moment, I was just glad I was watching.

ACKNOWLEDGMENTS

LIKE SPORTS, EVERY book that gets published is a team effort. And like shortstops and shooting guards and defensive midfielders, my teammates in this project all played specific roles. With his deep appreciation for sports and business and the culture that surrounds each, Tom Mayer proved an ideal editor. His suggestions, both large-scale and small, greatly improved the book. The diplomatic skills and preternatural equanimity of my agent, Chris Clemans, were especially welcome given my occasional lack of each. The masterful Steve Attardo created a design for the book that is far prettier than any of my sentences. And I appreciate the relentless consistency of Lloyd Davis, the copy editor, who transposed everything in the manuscript into proper W. W. Norton form while leaving dozens of corrected typos, misspellings, errors, and redundancies in his wake.

The book has its origins in some of the journalism I've done over the past two decades about the ongoing professionalization of professional sports. Many of those pieces were commissioned and edited by Dean Robinson of the *New York Times Magazine*. Dean is a passionate advocate for stories in which he believes, and a remarkably skilled editor. Even when I'm writing a piece for someone else, his voice is in my head. Since Jake Silverstein took charge of the *Magazine* in 2014, it has become a far more interesting publication to be involved with (and, of course, to read). I appreciate his willingness to let me write about topics I care about, some of which are decidedly on the margins of mass interest.

I've also been contributing to the *Sports Business Journal* since the prototype for its first issue. Abe Madkour, who is both its editor and its publisher, has an innate understanding of the way sports franchises operate, and he has cultivated relationships with many of the people who own and run them. He continues to give me assignments to write about those people. The reporting I've been able to do on behalf of those stories has made this a far more appealing book.

My lifelong best friend, Scott Price, is the best reader any writer could have. Everything I write, I write with him in mind. My son, Teddy, also has developed into a keenly intelligent critical reader, and he too provided incisive feedback. My wife, Julie, reads everything I write, and she invariably contributes a crucial suggestion (or five) that never would have occurred to me. (Toby, you're next in line!)

Thanks to everyone who agreed to be interviewed, whether for one of the stories that provided the foundation for this book, or during the reporting for the book itself. Special thanks to Tim Zue, who endured many phone calls on a daunting range of topics involving the Fenway Sports Group; and to Daryl Morey and Jessica Gelman, not least because they were instrumental in fomenting the sports analytics subculture that informs much of this narrative. Among sources not quoted in the book, Mike Fitzgerald, Steve

Gans, Mike Gordon, and the late Nick Cafardo were especially helpful.

Finally, back to my family: Julie, Teddy, and Toby. Without their ongoing encouragement, and their willingness to let me be away from home far more than any husband or father reasonably should be, I could have done none of this. I love you all.

INDEX